libver 11

X

THE POETRY OF SEAMUS HEANEY

The Poetry of Seamus Heaney

All the Realms of Whisper

Elmer Andrews
Lecturer in Extra-Mural Department
University of Ulster

MACMILLAN
PRESS

First published 1988

Published by
THE MACMILLAN PRESS LTD
Houndmills, Basingstoke, Hampshire RG21 2XS
and London
Companies and representatives
throughout the world

Printed in Hong Kong

British Library Cataloguing in Publication Data
Andrews, Elmer
The poetry of Seamus Heaney: all the
realms of whisper.
1. Heaney, Seamus—Criticism and
interpretation
I. Title
821'.914   PR6058.E2Z/
ISBN 0–333–44160–5

For Jude, Jade and Neave

Acknowledgements

Of the many people who have helped, directly or indirectly, to shape my interest in modern literature, I should like to thank Seamus Heaney, who was my tutor at Queen's University, Belfast, and Michael Allen who supervised my research there. Neither of these is of course responsible for the shortcomings of my endeavours. For the more specific assistance of the late Jim Delaney-Reid and of Janne Delaney-Reid, and of my wife, Jude, in the production of this book, I am also grateful.

I should also like to thank the editors of *Twentieth Century Literature* and *Contemporary Review* who first published my work on Heaney; both of these pieces have been substantially rewritten and expanded here.

The author and publishers would like to thank the following for permission to reprint copyright material: Faber and Faber Ltd, for the extracts from *Death of a Naturalist*, *Door into the Dark*, *Wintering Out* and *North* by Seamus Heaney; Farrar, Straus & Giroux, Inc., for the extracts from *Poems 1965–1975* by Seamus Heaney: Copyright © 1966, 1969, 1972, 1975, 1980 by Seamus Heaney; Faber and Faber Ltd and Farrar, Straus and Giroux, Inc., for the extracts from *Field Work* by Seamus Heaney: Copyright © 1976, 1979 by Seamus Heaney, *Sweeney Astray* by Seamus Heaney: Copyright © 1983 by Seamus Heaney, *Station Island* by Seamus Heaney: Copyright © 1985 by Seamus Heaney, and *Preoccupations: Selected Prose 1968–1978* by Seamus Heaney: Copyright © 1980 by Seamus Heaney.

Contents

and I would stand,
Beneath some rock, listening to sounds that are
The ghostly language of the ancient earth,
Or make their dim abode in distant winds.
Thence did I drink the visionary power.

Wordsworth, *The Prelude*, Book 2, 326–30

1
The Gift and the Craft

In a 1981 interview with John Haffenden, Heaney remarked 'It's possible to exacerbate . . . I believe that what poetry does to me is comforting . . . I think that art does appease, assuage.'[1] In *Field Work* the poet, newly 'landed in the hedge-school of Glanmore', renews his commitment 'to raise/A voice caught back off slug-horn and slow chanter/ That might continue, hold, dispel, appease'. 'The Harvest Bow', one of the best poems in this volume, ends by quoting Coventry Patmore, 'The end of art is peace.' Heaney expresses a view of poetry as secret and natural even though it must operate in a world that is public and brutal. He has found himself caught in the sectarian crossfire with fellow Catholics pressing him to write political verse and liberal critics congratulating him on not taking sides.

For Heaney the great question is:

> How with this rage shall beauty hold a plea
> Whose action is no stronger than a flower?

His answer is also from Shakespeare – lines from *Timon of Athens* which have become, he says, 'a touchstone' for him:

> Our poesy is as a gum which oozes
> From whence 'tis nourished.[2]

The concept of nourishment becomes a central preoccupation. The first part of his *Preoccupations: Selected Prose 1968–1978* discusses the things which have nourished his poetry and contributed to the development of a poetic voice which, like Wordsworth's, emerged out of a music overheard in nature and in childhood.

Preoccupations begins with the word 'Omphalos', the Greek word for a navel, or a central point. Significantly, it is the sound of the word which first recommends it to his attention: he immediately relates it to the sound of water gushing from the pump in the yard of the farm where he was brought up. The source of his imaginative power, we are to understand, lies in his rural childhood experience that is centred and staked in the image of the pump. The pump, like his poetry, taps hidden springs to conduct what is sustaining and life-giving. The centre of the poet's imaginative world is also the centre of family and community life: the women of five households came with their big enamel buckets to draw water from that pump. Its rhythms are the elemental rhythms of nature itself, that continue undisturbed by the American bombers returning to their base nearby, indifferent to the great historical events of the 1940s. The pump is a symbol of the nourishment which comes from knowing and belonging to a certain place and a certain mode of life.

For Heaney, a sense of self depends, among other things, on a sense of place and a sense of history, something which is typical of the Irish writer and derives to some extent from the Irish writer's desire to protect and preserve what is threatened and diminished. Possession of the land, like possession of different languages, is a matter of particular urgency in Ireland. The Revival of the late nineteenth century marked a re-discovery of confidence in the writer's own place, his own history and his own speech, English and Irish. After Yeats, and the exhaustion of the heroic–romantic myth of Ireland, new directions were called for. What was required was a readjustment of social and poetic strategies which would allow the writer to express his own most authentic experience. With Patrick Kavanagh, an alternative to the esoteric, mythological systems of the writers of the Revival was affirmed. Kavanagh's demonstration of the poetic validity of the parish, as opposed to the nation viewed as a spiritual entity, his interest in the local and ordinary, had a decisive influence on Heaney. And, from the other side of the cultural and religious divide there was the Ulster regionalist experiment of John Hewitt, whose 'lifelong concern to question and document the relationship between art and locality has provided all subsequent Northern writers with a hinterland of reference should they require a tradition more intimate than the broad perspectives of the English literary achievement'.[3]

That larger tradition had, of course, its own useful models to offer, most conspicuously Wordsworth, being 'perhaps the first man to articulate the nurture that becomes available to the feelings through dwelling in one dear perpetual place' (*P.*, p. 145). Wordsworth wrote out of a tradition which, as Kavanagh admiringly explained, divorced English literature from England the nation, leaving the writer free to 'go on quietly unconcerned, undeceived by the latest reports on anything'.[4] free to evolve his own individual myths, his own sustaining structures to nourish his inner life and help him to express it. Kavanagh yearned for a myth and failed to find it (an artistic dilemma which he states explicitly in his poem 'A Personal Problem'). Heaney's career becomes a strenuous effort to reconcile the vital abundance of Kavanagh with an explanatory or consoling myth-making faculty: he wants to be a celebrant of instinct and mystery and, at the same time, through the ritual of art, to aspire to the intelligence and mastery of a Yeats or a Hopkins, whose austere genius he considers with warm and sympathetic understanding in 'The Makings of a Music', 'The Fire i' the Flint' and 'Yeats an Example?' in *Preoccupations*.

Heaney's poetic career, however, begins with modest ambitions, by his delving into his own childhood past. But gradually he extends his excavation of self to place it in relation to a communal past. He likes to think of his poems as 'soundings' that probe the landscape for a shared and diminished culture. He attempts to define and interpret the present by bringing it into significant relationship with the past. Dominated by a sense of nature's powers, he sees history, language and myth as bound up with nature, with territory and landscape. The landscape is sacramental. He is peculiarly responsive to the emblematic character of natural objects and processes. They evoke in him a deep sense of the numinous. He is open to intuitions that relate human female psychology and sexuality to the landscape. Landscape becomes a memory, a continuity, a piety, a feared and fecund mother, an insatiable lover.

This sacral vision of place has its origins in his childhood apprehension of nature on and around the family farm, which he recalls in the first part of *Preoccupations*. Lost among the pea-drills, he finds himself in a 'sunlit lair':

> . . . a green web, a caul of veined light, a tangle of rods and pods, stalks and tendrils, full of assuaging earth and leaf-smell.
>
> (*P.*, p. 17)

The experience of another 'secret nest' in the hollow of a birch tree introduces the image of the wood-lover and tree-hugger which underlies the Heaney/Sweeney identification of recent work:

> Above your head, the living tree flourished and breathed, you shouldered the slightly vibrant bole, and if you put your forehead

to the rough pith you felt the whole lithe and whispering crown of willows moving in the sky above you.

                                                              (*P.*, p. 18)

He remembers bathing naked in a moss-hole:

. . . treading the thick-liver mud, unsettling a smoky muck off the bottom and coming out smeared and weedy and darkened.

                                                              (*P.*, p. 19)

This incident is recalled as a 'betrothal' and an 'initiation', the ritual intensity of Heaney's language indicating an involvement with nature through which his religious and sexual impulses also find expression.

Beyond the security of the farmyard lay 'forbidden grounds', the 'realm of bogeys' (*P.*, p. 19), the haunt of recluses and mystery men who lived on the fringes of the bog. As childhood perspectives widen, the physical landscape assumes a social and historical dimension as well. He comes to recognize division as well as community. Mossbawn, the name of the family farm, lay between Castledawson and Toome, between English influence (Castle-dawson) and native experience (Toome), the demesne and the bog. The demesne was Moyola Park, an estate occupied by Lord Moyola, formerly Major James Chichester-Clark, the ex-Unionist Prime Minister of Northern Ireland. The bog was where hoards of flints and other relics had been found, reminders that this was one of the oldest inhabited places in the country. Mossbawn itself is a name made up of two words: 'Moss', a Scots word brought to Ireland by the Planters; and 'bawn', the name the English colonists gave to their fortified farmhouses. Mossbawn – the Planter's house on the bog. Heaney comments, however, that the preferred pronunciation was Moss bann, that *bán* is the Gaelic word for white, and that the name may therefore mean the moss of bog-cotton: 'In the syllables of my home I see a metaphor of the split culture of Ulster' (*P.*, p. 35). Mossbawn is bordered by the townlands of Broagh and Anahorish, 'forgotten Gaelic music that leads back to the ancient civilization that was destroyed by soldiers and administrators like Spenser and Davies (*P.*, p. 36). At the same time, Heaney acknowledges that his own perceptions have been conditioned significantly by the English tradition. The countryside of Grove Hill and Back Park which also bordered the family farm is recognized as 'a version of pastoral', and while 'Grove and Park . . . do not reach me as a fibre from a tap-root', they are part of 'the intricate and various foliage of history and culture that I grew up beneath' (*P.*, p. 36).

From an early age there was another love in Heaney's life as well as that of nature: 'I was in love with words themselves (*P.*, p. 45). Words as verbal music is another source of assuagement, and it is the poet's delight in words which more than anything else nourishes his poetry. 'The secret of being a poet, Irish or otherwise', Heaney says, 'lies in the summoning of the energies of words' (*P.*, p. 36).

In *Preoccupations* he traces his love of words back to childhood as he does his love of nature. He recalls his first experience of how words as bearers of history and mystery began to invite him: listening to his mother recite lists of affixes and suffixes, Latin roots with English meanings, rhymes that had been part of her schooling. Then there was the 'exotic listing' (*P.*, p. 45) of Stuttgart, Leipzig, Oslo, Hilversum, on the wireless dial; the 'beautiful sprung rhythms' (*P.*, p. 45) of the old BBC weather forecast: Dogger, Rockall, Malin, Shetland, Faroes, Finisterre; 'the gorgeous and inane phraseology' (*P.*, p. 45) of the Catechism; the litany of the Blessed Virgin. At school there was his introduction to the classic canon of English poetry, the 'roadside rhymes' (*P.*, p. 26) chants that were scurrilous and sectarian, and the reading of Irish myths and legends. Later came the conscious savouring of the music of an English education: Keats, Webster, Anglo-Saxon verse, Wordsworth and Hopkins, who receives a special mention because of the similarity between his energetic, hard-edged, consonantal music and Heaney's own Ulster dialect.

All this he mentions as contributing to the process of finding a poetic voice. That voice, he explains, is composed of two elements. There is that part of the poetry which takes its structure and beat, its play of metre and rhythms, its diction and allusiveness, from the literary tradition. And there are also those 'intonations and appeasements' (*P.*, p. 62) offered by a poet's music which are instinctual, unconscious and pre-verbal, made up of the kinds of noise which assuage him, pleasure or repel him, drawn from the world around him. They are the inklings and echoes which reach him from 'all the realms of whisper'.[5] Heaney speaks of the private and cultural 'depth-charges' (*P.*, p. 150) latent in certain words and sounds and rhythms and kinds of rhyme. There is a 'binding secret' between words, 'which delights not just the ear but the whole backward abysm of mind and body' (*P.*, p. 150). One is reminded of Eliot's 'auditory imagination':

> The feeling for the syllable and rhythm, penetrating far below the conscious levels of thought and feeling, invigorating every word; sinking to the most primitive and forgotten, returning to the origin and bringing something back.[6]

The personal and Irish pieties Heaney thinks of as vowels, and the literary awareness nourished on English as consonants. His poems, he hopes, will be 'vocables' (*P.*, p. 37) adequate to his whole experience.

One way in which Heaney describes the process of turning feeling into words is as an 'oozing' that starts with the 'gazing heart', the 'listening ear', a 'wise passivity'. Poems come up out of the dark, organically oozing up into consciousness:

> I have always listened for poems, they come sometimes like bodies come out of a bog, almost complete, seeming to have been laid down a long time ago, surfacing with a touch of mystery. They certainly involve craft and determination, but chance and instinct have a role in the thing too.
>
> (*P.*, p. 34)

The voice in Heaney's poetry is the voice that is found to express what Eliot termed 'a dark embryo'. It originates in a primary generating surrender to the poet's *données*. Discussing the difference between 'technique' and 'craft', Heaney says:

> The crucial action is pre-verbal, to be able to allow the first alertness or come-hither, sensed in a blurred or incomplete way, to dilate and approach as a thought or a theme or a phrase. . . . That first emergence involves the divining, vatic, oracular function.
>
> (*P.*, p. 49)

This is technique. Technique is what allows the first stirring of the mind around a word, a rhythm, an image or a memory to grow towards articulation, articulation not necessarily in terms of argument or explication, but in terms of 'its own potential for harmonious self-reproduction' (*P.*, p. 48).

The second activity is 'the making function' that depends on 'craft' – the 'thought' finding the words. Sometimes, Heaney admits, it is not easy to distinguish between feeling getting into words, and words turning into feeling. His title, *Door into the Dark*, he says, was a gesture towards the idea of words themselves being doors.

Wordsworth is Heaney's primary model of the poet as diviner. Wordsworth is attentive to the invitations of 'the mind's internal echo', and sets out to discover the verbal means which will amplify his original visionary excitement into 'a redundant energy/ Vexing its own creation'. Heaney begins a discussion of his own poetry in 'Feeling into Words' by quoting from *The Prelude*:

> The hiding places of my power
> Seem open; I approach, and then they close;
> I see by glimpses now; when age comes on,
> May scarcely see at all, and I would give,
> While yet we may, as for as words can give,
> A substance and a life to what I feel:
> I would enshrine the spirit of the past
> For future generations.

Heaney embraces these lines as a statement of his own view of what poetry means to him:

> Implicit in those lines is a view of poetry which I think is implicit in the few poems I have written that give me any right to speak: poetry as divination, poetry as revelation of the self to the self, as restoration of the culture to itself; poems as elements of continuity, with the aura and authenticity of archaeological finds, where the buried shard has an importance that is not diminished by the importance of the buried city; poetry as a dig, a dig for finds that end up being plants.
>
> (*P.*, p. 41)

The Wordsworthian method of composition is contrasted with the Yeatsian view of poetry:

> When he talked about poetry, Yeats never talked about the "ooze" or "nurture." He always talked about the "labour" and the "making" and the "fascination of what's difficult."[7]

Heaney develops this contrast between 'receiving' and 'making' into a view of poetic creation as either a 'feminine' or 'masculine' activity:

From Shakespeare's ooze to Eliot's dark embryo, we have a vision of poetic creation as a feminine action, almost parthenogenetic, where it is the ovum and its potential rather than the sperm and its penetration that underlies their accounts of poetic origins. And out of this vision of feminine action comes a language for poetry that tends to brood and breed, crop and cluster, with a texture of echo and implication, trawling the pool of the ear with a net of associations.

(*P.*, p. 83)

Poetry to Keats, says Heaney, has a physical equivalent in a mother's birth pangs. But Hopkins brings to his craft a "siring instinct":

Keats has the life of a swarm, fluent and merged; Hopkins has the design of a honeycomb, definite and loaded. In Keats the rhythm is narcotic, in Hopkins it is a stimulant to the mind. Keats woos us to receive, Hopkins alerts us to perceive.

(*P.*, p. 85)

Hopkins strikes his fire from flint and, unlike the organic 'oozy marshlight' of symbolism, Hopkins' poetry is fretted rather than fecund, maintaining a design rather than releasing a flow, exuding a masculine brilliance and revealing the presence of 'powerful and active thought' (*P.*, p. 86) that disciplines the music and takes charge of the language and emotion. It is possible for the two opposing spirits of poetry to be reconciled: Yeats is said to prove 'that deliberation can be so intensified that it becomes synonymous with inspiration' (*P.*, p. 110).

Everywhere in his writings Heaney is acutely sensitive to the opposition between masculine will and intelligence on the one hand, and, on the other, feminine instinct and emotion; between architectonic masculinity and natural female feeling for mystery and divination. It is the opposition between the arena of public affairs and the intimate, secret stations of 'the realms of whisper'. He uses it to describe the tension between English influence and Irish experience ('The feminine element for me involves the matter of

Ireland and the masculine strain is drawn from involvement with English literature' (*P.*, p. 132)). It underlies two different responses to landscape, one that is 'lived, illiterate and unconscious', and one that is 'learned, literate and conscious' (*P.*, p. 131). Early poems like 'Digging' and 'Follower' establish his troubling self-consciousness about the relationship between 'roots and reading', the lived and the learned. In attempting to resolve these contrarieties, the example of Patrick Kavanagh was invaluable. Kavanagh, the son of a country shoemaker in Inishkeen, Co. Monaghan, made the move from his native parish to London in 1937, and then in 1939 to Dublin, where he spent most of the rest of his life. Kavanagh's career seemed to Heaney to parallel much in his own, especially the conflict between 'the illiterate self that was tied to the little hills and earthed in the stoney grey soil and the literate self that pined for "the City of Kings/ Where art, music and letters were the real things"' (*P.*, p. 137). 'The Great Hunger' was of special interest because of the balance Kavanagh achieved between 'intimacy with actual clay' (*P.*, p. 122) and 'the penalty of consciousness' (*P.*, p. 118). The poem was a model of the poet's imaginative self-sufficiency within his own parish. Kavanagh's assertion that 'parochialism is universal, it deals with fundamentals'[8] gave Heaney confidence in the poetic validity of his own preoccupation with his County Derry childhood. From Kavanagh's most successful work he could learn from a poet whose management of ironic points-of-vantage on his material promoted the expression of more subtle, complex feelings about the relationship between poet and place.

The pervasiveness of the masculine/feminine opposition in Heaney's writings about himself and other poets originates in a deep-seated sense of his own divided feelings and experience. His poetry reflects the attempt to reconcile the tension. The poem, Heaney says, should be a 'completely successful love act between the craft and the gift'.[9] But it is the gift, the initial incubatory action, he keeps reminding us, which is for him the crucial stage in the creative process. A poem, he believes, can survive stylistic blemishes that are due to inadequate craftsmanship, but 'it cannot survive a still-birth' (*P.*, p. 49). Poetry is essentially a mystery, a corpse from the bog, a whispering from the dark, a gift from the goddess. The poet is passive receiver before he is an active maker.

There are times, however, when Heaney has felt guilty or exasperated with this essentially passive role and has wanted poetry to do something; when he wished to be a man of action making direct political statements rather than an equivocator, a parablist, a supplicant or withdrawn aesthete. From the beginning, from that opening image in the first poem in his first volume, 'Digging', the shadow of a gunman is present, as if to convince us that the pen can be as mighty as the gun. He compensates for his failure to follow men of action by making promises: he'll dig with his pen he says. The theme does not become prominent until *North*, where art and the role of the artist come under his tormented scrutiny. By then Ulster was in a state of war.

Despite the lapse of confidence in art which *North* evinces – and the intensity of the anguish it occasioned should not be underestimated, as the last poem in *North*, 'Exposure', would testify – the great bulk of Heaney's prose statements, comments to interviewers and reviews of other writers are made from the point of view of a poet. When he turns to fellow poets, he tends to focus on their use of language, their verbal music, before theme or meaning. He never comments from the point of view of a politically committed spokesman, rarely even from a strictly academic viewpoint. He registers his appreciation of poetry as 'self-delighting buds on the old bough of tradition' (*P.*, p. 174). He takes the politically committed artist to task, in this case the Marxist, for attempting 'to sweep the poetic enterprises clean of those somewhat hedonistic impulses towards the satisfactions of aural and formal play out of which poems arise, whether they aspire to delineate or to obfuscate "things as they are"' (*P.*, p. 174). Typically, Paul Muldoon qualifies as 'one of the very best' for 'the opulence of the music, the overspill of creative joy', for his exploitation of 'the language's potential for generating new meanings out of itself . . . this sense of buoyancy, this delight in the trickery and lechery that words are capable of' (*P.*, p. 213).

'During the last few years', Heaney stated in 1975, 'there has been considerable expectation that poets from Northern Ireland should "say" something about "the situation"'. Heaney's comment on this demand was that 'in the end they (poets) will only be worth listening to if they are saying something about and to themselves'.[10] Poetry for Heaney is its own special action, has its own mode of reality. In his review of the Russian poet, Osip Mandelstam, who had found it impossible to make an accommodation with Soviet realities under Stalin, Heaney writes:

> We live here in critical times ourselves, when the idea of poetry as an art is in danger of being overshadowed by a quest for poetry as

a diagram of political attitudes. Some commentators have all the fussy literalism of an official from the ministry of truth.

(*P.*, p. 219)

What Heaney's review asserts is the urgent need to fight for the very life of poetry in a world which seems increasingly to discount it. He elevates the artist's work above the moralist's. The principle of the autonomy of art frees the artist from tendentiousness, vulgar moralizing and political propagandizing. A cut below the surface, however, are the whole world's concerns which, by virtue of the poet's 'aesthetic distance', can be treated with a kind of passionate detachment, a concerned disinterestedness. Heaney speaks as an apologist of the 'religion of art'. The Mandelstam review begins with this impassioned pronouncement:

> "Art for Art's Sake" has become a gibe because of an inadequate notion of what art can encompass, and is usually bandied by people who are philistines anyhow. Art has a religious, a binding force, for the artist. Language is the poet's faith and the faith of his fathers and in order to go his own way and do his proper work in an agnostic time, he has to bring that faith to the point of arrogance and triumphalism.
>
> (*P.*, p. 217)

Inevitably, however, politics come into communication with the poetical function. But only legitimately so when the political situation has first been emotionally experienced and reduced to subordinate status in an aesthetically created universe of symbols. If Heaney's poetry automatically encompasses politics, he is careful that it should not serve them. In this respect the Yeatsian aesthetic is exemplary. There is a passage from Yeats's essay, 'Samhain: 1905', part of which Heaney quotes at the beginning of *Preoccupations*:

> One cannot be less than certain that the poet, though it may well be for him to have right opinions, above all if his country be at death's door, must keep all opinion that he holds to merely because he thinks it right, out of poetry, if it is to be poetry at all. At the enquiry which preceded the granting of a patent to the Abbey Theatre I was asked if *Cathleen ni Houlihan* was not written to affect opinion. Certainly it was not. I had a dream one night which gave me a story, and I had certain emotions about this country, and I gave those emotions expression for my own

pleasure. If I had written to convince others I would have asked myself, not "Is that exactly what I think and feel?" But "How would that strike so-and-so? How will they think and feel when they have read it?" And all would be oratorical and insincere. If we understand our own minds, and the things that are striving to utter themselves through our minds, we move others, not because we have understood our thought about those others, but because all life has the same root. Coventry Patmore has said, "The end of art is peace," and the following of art is little different from the following of religion in the intense preoccupation it demands.[11]

Like Yeats, Heaney writes political poetry; but, also like Yeats, he is not political in any doctrinaire sense. As a man like any other man, politics are part of his life: being a poet does not separate him from the concerns of common humanity. What being a poet means is that his concern cannot simply be with abstract ideas, but with ideas suffused and shaped by emotion, and absorbed at the deepest levels of consciousness. The Yeatsian declaration that poetry is 'expression for my own pleasure' is echoed by Joyce's shade in 'Station Island', when he advises the poet, 'The main thing is to write/ for the joy of it.' Art and politics may come from different imaginative 'levels' of the personality if the art is good, original, deep, authentic enough: if the latter is the case (that is, in the case of good writers) the artistic insight is prophetic, 'true', at a deeper level, and for a longer time, than any political idea can be.

In an interview with Seamus Deane, Heaney sought to explain the political nature of his poetry:

Poetry is born out of the watermarks and colourings of the self. But that self in some ways takes its spiritual pulse from the inward spiritual structuring of the community to which it belongs; and the community to which I belong is Catholic and Nationalist. I believe that the poet's force now, and hopefully in the future, is to maintain the efficacy of his own "mythos", his own cultural and political colourings, rather than to serve any particular momentary strategy that his political leaders, his para-military organization or his own liberal self might want him to serve. I think that poetry and politics are, in different ways, an articulation, an ordering, a giving form to inchoate pieties, prejudices, worldviews, or whatever. And I think that my own poetry is a kind of slow, obstinate, papish burn, emanating from the ground I was brought up on.[12]

Heaney will not renounce tribal prejudice as the rational humanist would urge, but write out of it in such a way as to clarify his own feelings, not to encourage – or discourage – prejudice in others. That would be propaganda – the didactic achieved at the expense of the poetic. 'We make out of the quarrel with others rhetoric', Yeats has said, 'but out of the quarrel with ourselves, poetry.' Clearly, Yeats, like Heaney, was preoccupied with the opposition between the divided selves of the poet, between the poet as poet and the poet as a human being like other human beings. 'In most poets', writes C. Day Lewis, 'there is an intermittent conflict between the poetic self and the rest of the man; and it is by reconciling the two, not by eliminating the one, that they can reach their full stature.'[13] Heaney strives for such a reconciliation – a reconciliation between primitive piety and rational humanism, between illiterate fidelity to origins and a sense of objective reality, between the feminine and the masculine impulses.

Long years of debating this synthesis for and in his own poetry have promoted some large and luminous insights into the work of other poets. Heaney is remarkably acute to the way the making of a music by other writers betrays their concern either to flee external pressures on creativity, or to find an ideology in which to lodge their own casual, vagrant impulses. In his essay, 'Envies and Identifications: Dante and the Modern Poet', he begins with the idea that all poets turn to the great masters of the past to re-create them in their own image. Eliot, he says, discovered the political Dante, the poet with a 'universal language', the artist as seer and repository of tradition, one who was prepared to submit his intelligence and sensibility to the disciplines of 'philosophia' and religious ortho-doxy: 'Eliot's ultimate attraction is to the way Dante could turn values and judgements into poetry, the way the figure of the poet as thinker and teacher merged into the figure of the poet as expresser of a universal myth that could unify the abundance of the inner world and the confusion of the outer.'[14] This was the 'stern and didactic'[15] image of Dante which Eliot discovered in the struggle to embrace a religious faith.

Mandelstam, on the other hand, in the effort to free himself from the pressures of Stalinist orthodoxy, discovers a different Dante: 'Dante is not perceived as the mouthpiece of an orthodoxy but rather as the apotheosis of free, natural, biological process, as a hive of bees, a process of crystallization, a hurry of pigeon flights, a focus for all the impulsive, instinctive, non-utilitarian elements in the creative life.[16]

For Heaney's own part, Dante is the great model for the Irish poet who would explore the 'typical strains' the consciousness labours under in that troubled land: 'The main tension is between two often contradictory commands: to be faithful to the collective historical experience and to be true to the recognitions of the emerging self.'[17] He responds to the Dante who 'could place himself in a historical world yet submit that world to scrutiny from a perspective beyond history', who 'could accommodate the political and the transcendent'.[18]

Heaney's own poetic preoccupations as revealed in his interpretative approach to Dante may, finally, be pursued with the help of psychoanalytic vocabulary, especially as it has been developed in the light of structuralist and post-structuralist theories of discourse. Separation from the Edenic past, from the organic society, from home and heritage, from origins, from the female matrix of being, from the 'life-force', is enforced by having to come to terms with the masculine realities of the wider, public world. Heaney's struggle for a 'bi-sexual' form of writing sets up a play of unconscious drives, of deep symbols and rhythms, of silences and absences, a 'ghost-life' issuing from 'all the realms of whisper'; and these irruptions of unruly energy counterpoint and colour received social meaning and value. The fluid and diffuse, evocative, vowel-based, eroticized element in his poetry offers a resistance to the male metaphysical world of abstraction, division and fixed essence. Modern society is what the post-structuralist would call both 'phallocentric' and 'logocentric' (to use the terms expounded by the French philosopher Jacques Derrida): 'phallocentric' because it is a male world, and the phallus is the symbol of certain, self-present meaning; and 'logocentric' because it believes that its discourses can give us total and immediate access to the essence and presence of things. Heaney's poetry includes a force within society which disrupts and opposes it – a force embodied by, for example, the figure of Sweeney or Antaeus. There is in his poetry a kind of pleasureable excess over precise meaning, a libidinal gratification within the systematizing or mythologizing structures which transgresses or interrogates their limits. This feminine mode of discourse is both 'inside' and 'outside' the masculine 'symbolic order'[19] of linguistic, social and sexual power: in a similar way, the indigenous Gaelic reality is represented within a colonial framework, fixed by the sign, image and meaning of another culture, yet because it is also the 'other' or 'negative' of that social order always possesses something which eludes representation.

In dismantling the unified subject, in fracturing and throwing it into contradiction, Heaney poses some radical questions to existing society, but this does not lead to the proposal of a new kind of politically activated subject nor to a wholesale scepticism which acknowledges only the infinite play of textual inscription. His feminine mode of being and discourse is not an alternative to the male, authoritarian 'symbolic order' (not that that in itself would constitute a politically revolutionary gesture), but an internal limit of its conventional, privileged value. The perennial image is that of the mutual embrace. In the early 'Lovers on Aran', the poet wonders whether it is the fluid, timeless, female sea which 'possesses' the land or the hard, male arms of rock thrust out by the land which force the sea's submission:

> Did sea define the land or land the sea?
> Each drew new meaning from the waves' collision.
> Sea broke on land to full identity.[20]

Poetry is such an act of love. In its embrace the intractable raw materials of experience are brought into relationship with each other in a way which promotes 'new meaning' and 'full identity'. Implied here is a notion of poetry which is empiricist, humanist and organicist. Empiricist in that knowledge is seen as the product of experience, personal and historical (as opposed to the modern structuralist emphasis on the arbitrary and conventional nature of language which leads to the view that knowledge is not at all the product of experience): Heaney insists on the referential function of poetry, on being 'faithful to' and 'true to' experience. Humanist in that his belief in art's relevance to life confers upon poetry a role once ascribed to religion or philosophy: it can help us cope with the problems of everyday existence. Poetry achieves this status because it both includes reality within itself and at the same time, by virtue of its organic form, resolves the conflicts of mind and history, creating in us a state of equilibrium rarely afforded by other kinds of experience. It is not something to galvanize us into action because it remains an essentially contemplative mode; it is not the vehicle of an irredeemable alienation because it recreates what is found to be lacking in the world. Heaney's project is the achievement of that momentary peace – that sunlit space, that 'home' or 'haven' – in which all oppositions are harmonized in the self-contained, transcendent poetic symbol. For a sceptical, defensive, displaced poet, torn by conflicting dogma and troubled by the nightmare of history, constantly threatened with the dissolution of the self yet deeply suspicious of the more obvious forms of ideological control, the Romantic symbol with its offer of totalization and timelessness exerted a profound attraction.

The morality of Heaney's symbol is not something to be grasped as a formulated code or explicit ethical system: it is rather a sensitive preoccupation with the whole quality of life, which encourages us to reverence the world for what it is, to respect the sensuous integrity, the rich variousness of its manifold objects and processes. It is rooted in the 'concrete' life and its 'immanent' meanings, which he comes to know with experiential, intuitive or, as Leavis would say, 'irresistible' certainty. Poetry is a re-discovery of the 'life-force'. On this last point, Heaney seems happy (as Leavis was) to celebrate intuitively what he takes to be a vibrant, universal presence, but what in reality is a vague, Romantic idealist fiction championed before him by writers such as D. H. Lawrence and Martin Heidegger who used it to justify rampant sexism, racism and authoritarianism. This only serves to highlight the way that Heaney's poem, like the Romantic symbol, is imbued with a transcendent mystical authority that is not to be challenged. His poem is the product of a thoroughgoing irrationalism closely linked with the religious impulse. Heaney's organicism, reflected in his ubiquitous invocation of natural analogues for poetry, and in his notions of the poem's autonomy and teleological unity, is fundamentally theological: the poet imitates the generative activity of nature or the 'life-force', if not the creative act of God.

2
Death of a Naturalist and *Door into the Dark*

From the very beginning of his career the conflict between the impulse to use poetry as a response to social demands and a notion of poetry as divination and revelation has been present in Heaney's work. Interviewed by Seamus Deane in 1977 about the relationship of Ulster poets to 'the Northern crisis', Heaney said:

> . . . the root of the troubles may have something in common with the root of the poetry. The very first poems I wrote, 'Docker' and one about Carrickfergus castle for instance, reveal the common root. The latter had William of Orange, English tourists and myself in it. A very inept sort of poem but my first attempts to speak, to make verse, faced with the Northern sectarian problem. Then this went underground and I became very influenced by Hughes and one part of my temperament took over: the private County Derry childhood part of myself rather than the slightly aggravated young Catholic male part.[1]

'Docker' deals with the 'Northern sectarian problem' in terms of a typological portrait of a Protestant labourer. The poem is an attempt by the young Heaney to deal with the ugliness of bigotry. He yields instead to mere ridicule of the docker – his family life, his job, his appearance – and disregards the matter of prejudice almost entirely. There is a metaphorical ingenuity and directness of expression, but the poem lacks the complexity and subtlety of his later treatment of the Protestant farmer in 'The Other Side'.

There are only a few poems included in the first two collections where the poet turns to the oppression of the native Irish, and in none of them does he attempt the kind of direct confrontation of 'Docker'. He steps back and tries a new, less hysterical approach. Instead of confronting the troubles of Ireland's present, he deals with the troubles of Ireland's past. 'For the Commander of the "Eliza"' adopts a persona – that of a British naval officer during the

Famine whose sympathy for the plight of the starving comes into
conflict with his orders to withold food from some men dying in a
rowing-boat. This poem relies on its controlling ironic mode to
contain the indignation of the aggravated young Catholic poet, and
this prevents the poem from bleeding off into tendentious polemic:

> Sir James, I understand, urged free relief
> For famine victims in the Westport sector
> And earned tart reprimand from good Whitehall.
> Let natives prosper by their own exertions;
> Who could not swim might go ahead and sink.
> 'The Coast Guard with their zeal and activity
> Are too lavish' were the words, I think.

'At A Potato Digging' begins with sharp visual description of
labourers in a field gathering potatoes. Description of the potatoes
as 'live skulls, blind-eyed' is repeated at the beginning of Section III,
which turns to the human misery occasioned by the Famine.
Heaney is trying to associate past and present and give historical
suffering and dispossession ('A people hungering from birth') a
contemporary application. But the metamorphosis of 'blind skulls'
is forced and awkward. His fusion of present rural experience and
the larger national history is part of a mythologizing procedure that
deliberately excludes any political or economic consideration. Since
the myth assumes the existence of an indifferent deity, the relevance
of human blame or indignation is ruled out and feeling is channelled
into acceptance and supplication. The poem is an early experiment
with the timeless perspective of myth and ritual that is more subtly
and tellingly handled in later poems about 'the matter of Ireland'.
Contemplating the 'ragged ranks' of the potato gatherers in the
field, he sees them as devotees of a pagan Earth cult:

> Heads bow, trunks bend, hands fumble towards the black
> Mother. Processional stooping through the turf
> Recurs mindlessly as autumn. Centuries
> Of fear and homage to the famine god
> Toughen the muscles behind their humbled knees,
> Make a seasonal altar of the sod.

At the end they are seen propitiating the spirit of the 'bitch earth' by
spilling 'libations of cold tea'.

Underlying the social and political world are elemental, religious forces which are the real springs of action. This is what distinguishes Heaney's poem from Kavanagh's 'The Great Hunger', which in some places 'At A Potato Digging' echoes. Kavanagh's poem is rooted in the here and now. There is no sense of the present being suffused with the past. As Heaney said: 'At the bottom of Kavanagh's imagination there is no pagan queen, no mystique of the national, the mythic or the tribal.'[2] What Kavanagh offered in his long anti-pastoral was an anguished denunciation of the spiritual starvation of country life on the hillsides of County Monaghan, uncomplicated by any cultural or national purpose. But Heaney explores a hidden Ulster. His poem is redolent not just of his personal life and observation but of the history of his people, disinherited and dispossessed. He probes the psychic roots of his community to discover an identity bound to immolation and propitiation.

'Requiem for the Croppies' reveals a similar sensibility at work. Though there is no explicit attempt to relate past and present, the political turn of events in Ulster in the late 1960s was to confirm the poem's prophetic force. When he wrote the poem, Heaney says, he had no idea 'that the original, heraldic murderous encounter between Protestant yeoman and Catholic rebel was to be initiated again in the summer of 1969, in Belfast'.[3] That phrase 'original heraldic murderous encounter' indicates the consciously ritualizing impulse of Heaney's imagination. The poem was, in fact, written in 1966 to commemorate the 1916 Rising, and to do so Heaney turns to the 1798 rebellion of the legendary 'croppy boys', assisting in the transformation of historical facts into myth. The poem begins with a reference to the barley corn which the 'croppies' had in their pockets to eat while on the march, and ends by describing how it sprouted from their common graves. As Heaney explains: 'The oblique implication was that the seeds of violent resistance sown in the Year of Liberty had flowered in what Yeats called 'the right rose tree' of 1916.'[4] Revolutionary republican idealism and national feeling are dignified by being linked to the elemental life force. Political struggle is understood in terms of a pattern of ineluctable, archetypal recurrance. The heroic peasantry for whom 'the hillside blushed' with blood and shame are fertility gods whose deaths ensure renewal and continuance. Heaney speaks as one of that 'fatal conclave' but is careful to avoid controversy: the Rising of 1916 is commemorated, not by an allusion to the contemporary situation, but by reverting to events of more than a hundred years earlier, and even then taking care not to name the croppies' enemy, who are referred to simply as 'they'.

In all these poems Heaney is looking for poetic strategies to contain the aggravation of the young Catholic male, and to understand the historic deprivation of his people in more fundamental terms than those offered by the particular momentary strategies of politics. It is this desire to discover and tap the unconscious sources of power, the elemental rhythms, that at least partly explains his return to childhood experience. Heaney's preoccupation with his own childhood is indicative of a pietism which looks for an inviolate origin, a pure source. In childhood the poet may recognize the secret movements of his deepest self. The responses of the child are the primary movements of the imagination by which the individual discovers and furthers his humanity, and finds and enlarges his freedom. Where the child's view differs from the adult's apprehension is in his acceptance of an amazing universe, a universe which astounds him but of which the child never despairs. Preoccupation with the child's imaginative perception implies a desire to escape from the jurisdiction of doubt, and embracement of a disposition untainted by conventional valuation or routine expectation. Aware, as the title *Death of a Naturalist* suggests, that he is on the brink of outgrowing the bucolic world of childhood, Heaney declares in 'Poem' that he will 'perfect' his rural childhood experience before proceeding to order his adult life.

Re-entering the life of a child, he concentrates on the natural world, the 'calendar customs',[5] the 'customary rhythms'[6] and rituals of rural life. These intimate a tough force of survival into which those who work the land are tied, and which has had most to do with the intimate shaping of his own personality. They are a crucial source of the nourishment on which his imagination has lived. So it is that the main thrust of his early work takes him beneath the tribal and historical to the primal world of instinct and sensation. In taking this direction the influence of Ted Hughes was decisive:

I remember the day I opened Ted Hughes' *Lupercal* in the Belfast Public Library. (There was) a poem called "View of a Pig" and in my childhood we'd killed pigs on the farm, and I'd seen pigs shaved, hung up, and so on. . . . Suddenly, the matter of contemporary poetry was the material of my own life. I had had some notion that modern poetry was far beyond the likes of me –

there was Eliot and so on – so I got this thrill out of trusting my own background, and I started a year later, I think.[7]

What Heaney responded to in Hughes was the English poet's urgent, unsentimental intimacy with the hidden country, his attraction to the archetypal and pagan, the interlacing of natural life with mythic life. In Hughes, Heaney saw the heath-dweller, the *pagus* whose England was a primeval landscape, a racial memory, which inhabited the mind with religious force.

What is it that the natural world meant to the young Heaney? His father ploughing and digging, butter being churned, his own collection of frogspawn, picking blackberries, hanging around the barn and river-bank, looking down wells – all these memories Heaney makes vivid through his gift for recreating the physical actuality of the external world. The remembered world is undisputably there, its objects, its animals and its processes. Much-loved, much-anthologized poems such as 'Blackberry Picking', 'Churning Day' and 'Death of a Naturalist' display a brilliancy of description. They convey a sense of the occasion at once, with clarity and accuracy. They are a triumph of evocation. The poems are serious, unpretentious attempts to re-create, and so clarify, unfalsified, and in the strongest terms possible, a powerful complex of emotions, sensations and impressions. There is a primitive trust in the force of onomatopaeic recreation and simple visual imagery to convey an experience or render the thick, heavy textures of the physical world. Eschewing affectation, abstraction and intellectualism, the poetry has the virtue of accessibility. It offers the attractions of sensuous and aural gratification. The spade 'sinks into gravelly ground', the bubbles of a flax-dam 'gargled delicately', the churning staff 'slugged and thumped', splashing the churners with 'flabby milk', a rat 'slapped' across the water in a well. Words create sound, movement, texture. But there is more than the unpursuing satisfaction of contemplating a triumph of evocation, more than an insulated enjoyment of the poem's own mimetic magic. It is the poet's attitudes, lacking subtlety and refinement though they do, which make these early poems something more than faithful accounts of the past, often with a nod to Estyn Evans' *Irish Folk Ways* (1957). He isn't able to follow his father's plough ('Follower'), or dig, like his father and grandfather ('Digging'); every year the blackberries stank and rotted ('Blackberry Picking'); kittens are drowned ('The Early Purges'); he is terrorized by rats ('The Barn') and frogs

('Death of a Naturalist'); his feelings about his ancestral photographs are equivocal ('Ancestral Photograph'). A pen resembles a gun ('Digging'), the urns that will hold the butter are 'pottery bombs' ('Churning Day'), a trout is like a 'fat gun barrel' and it 'darts like a tracer bullet' ('Trout'); frogs are 'poised like mud grenades' ('Death of a Naturalist'), the dawn comes up, 'a bright grenade' ('In Small Townlands'), a waterfall goes over 'like villains dropped screaming to justice' ('Waterfall'). Sensation and perception are indivisible. The hallmark of Heaney's poetry is already discernible in the way the mind's most piercing perception is always grounded in sensory particulars. His aim is to realize the completeness of a deeply felt event of his own life. What in the event may be called an 'idea' or an 'attitude' remains wholly engaged in the particular instances in which it was experienced. It is only when we attend to the details of Heaney's recreation of the rural world that we find implications of a larger social and moral order, an inheritance for which the poet feels incapacitated by his own sensibility. There is a notion of discontinuity, a feeling of loss, a sense of guilt, an apprehension of violence as well as of beauty and mystery, lying deep in things. These feelings constitute in germinal form the basic postures and dynamics underlying Heaney's entire poetic oeuvre.

The centre of the early poetry is not nature *per se*, but the shaping of the natural world in imagination. The transforming power of the creative imagination is continually being foregrounded. An imaginative process is, of course, involved in any creative work, but what is distinctive about Heaney is the explicit emphasis it receives as absolute theme and necessity of his art. In 'The Peninsula', the exhausted or dispirited poet sets out to seek stimulation in the sensuous variety of the phenomenal world. But directly observed reality appears boundless and featureless. Only after it has been distanced in time and space and recreated in the dark of the imagination, does it assume preternatural form and clarity. 'Poem' expresses the paradox of transforming life's failures and disappointments into 'perfection' through the magical power of art. As such, the poem evinces a faith in poetry, in fictions, in transcendence, in the absolute validity of the design and autonomy of art, untroubled by any of the niggling metaphysical implications of such a proposed aesthetic: How can the product of the ritualizing, aestheticizing mind claim to be other than self-deception, escapism or enchantment? What is the relationship between the imperfect reality of experience and the perfection of pure vision? These are matters which come to preoccupy Heaney later, but here there are no ambiguous feelings about the transforming imagination. For the moment Heaney contents himself with expressing confidence in poetry as an act of retrieval with healing and redeeming powers, as a striving for value, for significant form, against the resistant drag of the merely habitual, the transitory and the imperfect. 'Poem's' emphasis is complacently personal and private, not metaphysical. Bearing a dedication to the poet's wife, Marie, it is a love-offering, its aesthetic ultimately sacramental:

> Love, you shall perfect for me this child
> Whose small imperfect limits would keep breaking.
> Within new limits now, arrange the world
> Within our walls, within our golden ring.

In 'The Barn' and 'Death of a Naturalist' imagination works, not to contain or conquer what is chaotic or frightening, but to exacerbate such experiences. The natural world fills the child with dread and loathing, not because of its intrinsic qualities, but because of what the child's imagination makes of it. In 'Death of a Naturalist' Miss Walls' natural world is tamed, domesticated, made harmless and useful. But this is not at all the reality so vividly and directly perceived by the child. Like Hughes, Heaney opposes the idealised, genteel picture of nature by emphasizing its predatory, terrifying aspect (motivated here by the child's guilt at having stolen frog-spawn). The frogs become monstrous, legendary creatures, authority figures from an obscene fairy-tale, dimly suggestive of the sexual obsessions of puberty. Their habitat is the flax-dam festering in the heart of the countryside, a dark and frightening recess of unknown horror and uncontrollable fecundity.

We begin to see the significance of Heaney's title, 'Death of a Naturalist'. This poem is not the product of a naturalist who is content with looking and describing. Being a poet is being concerned with other things. Heaney's starting point is a Darwinian notion of huge process and slow evolution, but for the poet what counts are the negotiations with nature of the imaginative mind as receptor and sensor. His title thus refers to that process of moving beyond a mechanical, scientific, descriptive view of nature to undertake poetic 'soundings'. 'Death of a Naturalist' is involved with the relationships between man and nature, which extend into his relationships with land, society, nation, self. Heaney's continual preoccupation with language indicates the desire to discover the means to sound out these relationships and give them expression in the poem's verbal organization.

The same note of what Wordsworth called 'troubled pleasure' sounds in 'The Barn'. The opening stanzas acclimatize us to a highly figurative perception of the barn. The exotic mingles with the mundane and the sinister: corn lies piled 'like grit of ivory/ Or solid as cement'; the dark 'hoarded an armoury'; the floor was 'mouse-grey'; the zinc roof 'burned like an oven'. Perception is creative: 'Slowly bright objects formed when you went in.' The dark, womb-like interior which the poet explores is psychic as well as physical. In the black depths the 'two-lugged sacks' turn into 'great blind rats' advancing on the boy. Nauseated by his alien, bestial vision in 'Death of a Naturalist', he 'turned and ran'; in 'The Barn' he lies 'face-down' to avoid the encroaching terror.

The effect of Wordsworthian fear is not restrictive or paralyzing, but enlarging and provocative of growth; it stimulates, says Words-worth, a sense of the 'Wisdom and Spirit of the Universe'.[8] Fear was the agency which released from 'familiar shapes of hourly objects' 'huge and mighty forms that do not live like living man'.[9] It generates a 'dim and undetermin'd sense/ Of unknown modes of being'.[10] In the presence of fear he is released from the conventional rigidities of rational thought and enters a state of being conversant with infinity. It is then he feels 'the sentiment of Being spread/ O'er all . . . lost beyond the reach of thought/ And human knowledge, to the human eye/ Invisible, yet liveth to the heart'.[11]

Without wishing to make too large a claim for early poems such as 'The Barn' or 'Death of a Naturalist' – neither possesses the same mystical force as Wordsworth's famous episodes of snaring, boating and skating in Book 1 of *The Prelude* – it is still possible to see in them an effort to affirm a 'visonary power', to register awareness of an order of perception beyond normal seeing and hearing. Like Wordsworth's, Heaney's fear turns out to be more than a simply destructive element. In the dark, fear is aroused because the ordinary conceptual structure of the world is deranged and different orders of being flow in on one another. The constancy and separateness of received forms of existence dissolve, boundaries are upset. This liquefaction of set limits occasioned by fear was, for Wordsworth, what engendered his sense of the mysterious unity of Being. No such large, numinous apprehension of experience is part of the vision of 'The Barn' or 'Death of a Naturalist' but these poems contain in germinal form – before the solitary state of fear that is both positive and intense, grows into wonder – Heaney's early intuition of the world's mystery. Ultimately, it is in response to the dark that he finds his poetic career. It is in fear and darkness that the growth of the poet's mind begins.

In 'Personal Helicon' a 'scaresome' childhood experience of dark depths is presented as an analogue of the sources of poetic inspiration. He peers into the depths of the well, not with the self-admiring intention of Narcissus, but to discover self, to give life and form to the engulfing darkness:

> Now, to pry into roots, to finger slime,
> To stare, big-eyed Narcissus, into some spring
> Is beneath all adult dignity. I rhyme
> To see myself, to set the darkness echoing.

Poetry turns out to be the main theme of the poem. The poem seems to proclaim the sovereignty of language: the poet who used to receive an image of himself when he looked into the well now does so only when he 'rhymes'. There is no simple specular relation between subject and object. Heaney has gone beyond what psychoanalysts have identified as the pre-linguistic, narcissistic 'mirror stage', the domain of the Imaginary, and takes account of the 'symbolic order', the order of language and self-knowledge in which wholeness, presence and representation are lost, and meaning is no longer governed by any reliable relation to reality.[12] Language, it has been shown, disrupts the self-sufficient visual presence of object to subject in the 'mirror stage'. It is no longer the obedient vehicle of some referent, intention or idea that lies outside it. It is primary and meaning, far from preceding language, is an effect produced by language. This is the kind of argument psychoanalysis uses to prove that the self is not an inviolate entity or simple origin. But for Heaney, 'rhyming' is not a purely formal strategy: it is also a medium of lived and felt experience, dependent on such moral imperatives as 'maturity'. The poem ultimately subscribes to a mystification deriving from ancient notions of divine inspiration. Acknowledgement of the poem's rhetorical status co-operates with and is subsumed in faith in a knowledge anterior and superior to human reason. The allusion to the Greek fount of inspiration instals the poet as diviner, as an instrument of something separate from him which governs him from without. Poetry is a divinely ordained occurrence with the poet as mediator.

'Personal Helicon' starts off by asking us to take it in a specific, precise and homely way. The strong sounds and images give the experiential world irrefutable, palpable presence. Heaney describes a response to something grounded in or represented by nature, but ultimately it is felt as something of great depth and mystery. The force of nature as Muse is neatly registered in the reflection of 'slime' in 'rhyme' and of 'spring' in 'echoing'. Like Wordsworth who spoke of 'The Bible of the Universe' as a store of 'types and analogies of the infinite', Heaney found in nature a system of symbols and a machinery of realization. For both Wordsworth and Heaney, nature fulfilled a similar function as 'magic' did for Yeats, with the difference that Wordsworth's and Heaney's natural symbols enjoyed a public, constant quality that is missing from Yeat's private, arbitrary ones.

In 'Personal Helicon' Heaney is no longer running from the dark, from self, from the mystery of the 'universal earth', but willing to enter into communion with it. The title of his second collection, *Door into the Dark*, emphasizes this resolve. The title is a phrase from 'The Forge' – another dark, mysterious interior. Inside nothing can be clearly discerned. There are only intimations of what might be. Nothing exists save what can be asserted through the force of imaginative recreation. Significantly, the poet feels it must be the anvil, tool and symbol of the blacksmith's craft, which occupies the central position. Its presence is indisputable, immutable; it belongs to the fabulous realm of legend, ritual and religion:

> The anvil must be somewhere in the centre,
> Horned as a unicorn, at one end square,
> Set there immoveable: an altar
> Where he expends himself in shape and music.

Creativity is linked with the dark. It involves intense and violent labour. The smith, a surrogate figure of the artist, represents the kind of artist Heaney admires – one whose quiet, sturdy integrity and traditional craftsmanship are opposed to the brash modernity of the world outside.

Another model of the poet's magical powers is found in 'The Thatcher'. The first word of the poem, 'Bespoke', is an archaism that immediately places the thatcher's craft in a bygone era. Though 'bespoke', he is his own man, and turns up unexpectedly. Metaphorically speaking, 'Bespoke' also introduces the poem's key image of the thatcher/poet as source and controller – as the hub – of his created world. In patiently 'pinning down his world', the thatcher achieves heraldic and heroic status – he is 'couchant for days'. He displays 'a Midas touch' that can manipulate and transform the raw materials of hazel and willow into a work of art, turning 'a stubble patch' into a 'kingdom'. The slow ritual of his craft leaves his onlookers gaping in wonderment.

As magician, the artist is dedicated to both mystery and craft. Where 'The Thatcher' and 'The Forge' emphasize the 'making' function of craft, 'The Diviner' emphasizes the mystery of 'technique' as Heaney defines it in his essays. 'The Diviner', he comments, 'is remarkable, not for its own technique but for the image of technique which it contains.' For Heaney, the water-diviner represents 'pure technique': 'You can't learn the craft of dowsing or divining – it is a gift for being in touch with what is there, hidden and real, a gift for mediating between the latent source and the community that wants it current and released.'[13]

> The bystanders would ask to have a try.
> He handed them the rod without a word.
> It lay dead in their grasp till nonchalantly
> He gripped expectant wrists. The hazel stirred.

Technique being 'what allows that first stirring of the mind round a word or an image or a memory to grow towards articulation', Heaney comments on the felicitous rhyming of 'word' and 'stirred' that 'brings the two functions of *vates* into the one sound'.[14]

The poet's preoccupation with digging, ploughing, fishing, peering down wells, probing secret recesses and dark interiors – at first a childish fascination fraught with fear, eventually a desire to enter into communion with mystery – is expressive of his notion of art as divination and revelation. The smith in 'The Forge' is a master of the powers of darkness. The dark is close to the centre of religious faith. 'In Gallarus Oratory' describes how the monks of old, who 'sought themselves in the eye of their King', found renewal by submitting themselves to the dark. The poem is based on a personal experience, 'a moment that was a kind of small epiphany', when Heaney visited Gallarus Oratory, an early Christian dry-stone oratory in County Kerry:

Inside, in the dark of the stone, it feels as if you are sustaining a great pressure, bowing under like the generations of monks who must have bowed down in meditation and reparation on that floor. I felt the weight of Christianity in all its rebuking aspects, its calls to self-denial and self-abnegation, its humbling of the proud flesh and insolent spirit. But coming out of the cold heart of the stone into the sunlight and the dazzle of grass and sea, I felt a lift in my heart, a surge towards happiness that must have been experienced over and over again by those monks as they crossed the same threshold centuries ago.[15]

Light and darkness, the earthly and the spiritual are part of a total vision. In 'The Peninsula', it is only when 'you're in the dark again' that revelation becomes available. Similarily, in 'In Gallarus Oratory', submission to the dark is the prerequisite of illumination – 'This surge towards praise, this sudden apprehension of the world as light, as illumination.'[16]

In 'The Given Note' and 'The Plantation' the serious artist is the solitary adventurer who must go bravely into strange, deserted places if he is to discover the secret forces of creativity. 'The Given Note', as the title indicates, refurbishes the Romantic view of art as a gift that is given. But the gift is available only to the free, unconsenting spirit which, abandoning all the claims of current ideological or social systems, takes its inspiration 'from nowhere'. The poem asserts the priority of the mystery of nature, the spirit of place, of instinct and emotion, over all civilized systems of thought and over the demands of society. Poetry is found in the domain of paganism: 'loud weather', 'the wind off mid-Atlantic', 'spirit music'. At the centre of the poem is the traditional idea that the gifted fiddler can hear the music from the other world. This music is redolent of the past. It comes off the bow 'gravely' – seriously, but from the graves too. This ghostly sense of the past coming off the air, rephrasing itself, then disappearing again is, of course, an expression of our own experience of the Gaelic past.

In 'The Plantation' the poet is represented by another traveller who penetrates beyond the picnickers' belt into the chaotic, uncharted interior where solidity and definition elude him. Entering the 'hush and the mush/ Of its whispering treadmill' beyond the comforting sounds of the traffic, he finds himself in a realm of primal silence, a mythic, fairy-tale world with stumps and toadstools 'Always repeating themselves'. The symbol of this mysterious zone of being where there are no certainties, no direction and no limit is the circle. The poem presents an image of that mental state the operations of which no longer base themselves on some external point of reference. Purpose, meaning, structure are not given or objectively 'there'. In this realm, knowledge is a product of the mind, which can only interpret the world, never fully possess it.

The plantation is where poetic inspiration is found. In his negotiations with the plantation, the poet has to surrender to the irrational and at the same time remain controller of the situation:

> You had to come back
> To learn how to lose yourself,
> To be pilot and stray – witch,
> Hansel and Gretel in one.

The poem works by setting up oppositions – oppositions between pilot and stray, order and disorder, outside and inside, sound and silence, light and dark, conscious and unconscious, reason and imagination. These contraries operate in a particular system of meaning, a specialized, hierarchical realm of structuration and figurative licence that itself defies rational commentary (every bit as much as the experience of the plantation which is one of the elements it embraces) and is at the command of the God-like poet. Through deploying a rhetoric of irreducibly aesthetic figure and paradox which lies outside the practice of pure logic, the poem can be closed off within its own formal limits. The conceptual status of structure, which is denied by the experience of the plantation, is assumed in the poem's teleological formal strategies. The poem derives from a binary habit of thought in which the terms of the oppositions remain discrete conceptual units and are not seen to inhere in each other in the endless play of difference which characterizes the plantation, and which we recognize as the post-structuralist enterprise. Since the poem's antitheses are ultimately resolvable into a closed, transcendent unity, they never really threaten our need for coherence.

Within the poem's solid structures lie rich possibilities of meaning. The poem is a living product of the imagination relying for its meaning on conditions and parameters, a structure of concerns – the codes – which have already been 'planted' in and by prior texts. The title, for example, may evoke for us an elaborate prior discourse to do with the Romantic, organicist view of the poem as a plant. The tendency for any plant to defy the cultivator's control has its analogue in Heaney's wayward, vital, female energies which threaten to escape the defining, 'piloting' activity of masculine will and reason. Or, again, 'The Plantation' may be seen to participate in the discursive space of a specifically Irish culture: the question of intertextuality moves into a political realm. The word 'Plantation' has strong historical and political overtones in Ulster, so that a political reading of the poem might see it as referring to the imposition of English rule and culture on the 'wild' indigenous Gael.

Heaney constantly returns to the theme of dark hidden forces of instinct and unreason which are the seat of a disturbing vitality, an atavism that lies beyond conscious mind or civilized control. *Door into the Dark* opens with an oblique and resonant image of nightmarish animality: the 'Dull pounding' and 'uneasy whinny' in the dark of the stable in 'Night-Piece'. In 'The Outlaw' the poet registers his fascination with an unlicenced bull used for the illicit servicing of a Friesian cow. The nervousness of the first part of the poem is suddenly dissipated by a brutal, consonantal hammering. The language summons a sense of absolute immediacy: 'The door, unbolted, whacked back against the wall'; sound co-operates with image: 'Unhurried as an old steam engine shunting,' the bull 'slammed life home, impassive as a tank.' The blunt force of the rhyming couplets is counterpointed by the sinuous drive that carries the syntactic unit across the typographical division separating one couplet from the next. These are all positive aesthetic tools which enact the bull's untamed, instinctive power, the nonchalant 'ease' of this 'business-like conception'. After the brute rite is accomplished, the bull 'in his own time, resumed the dark, the straw'.

'Gone' suggests the deadness and coldness that result when such passionate, intuitive energy is missing. In the darkness the poet has access to a dream-reality and the attempt to deal with it directly promotes stylistic experimentation. 'Dream', like 'Night-Piece', employs a formal organization that is more fluid, individual and unpredictable than allowed by the pre-established expectations of conventional verse rhythm. The tenuity and slightness of rhythm is an appropriate medium for the fugitive nature of the poem's experience. The poet is hacking a thick stalk with a billhook when, suddenly:

> The next stroke
> Found a man's head under the hook.

Before I woke
I heard the steel stop
In the bone of the brow.

The sickening impact of the vision, the feeling of stunned horror which accompanies the poet's murderous act, are made palpable in the verbal organization. The phrasing is broken and monosyllabic, producing an unusual and dramatic starkness and clarity. The strong break in the phrase at the end of the first line reproduces the guilt and terror of anticipation, the much longer second line blurting out the awful finding. There is a congruence between the climactic act of violence and the moment of waking, emphasized by the full-rhyme of 'stroke' and 'woke', but the poem does not end with a sense of release. Instead, it forces attention on the moment of violence itself through a complicated pattern of repetition: the metallic harshness of the *st* sound in 'stroke' is echoed in 'steal' and 'stop'; there is the long, deepening assonantal moan of the vowel in 'stroke', 'before', 'woke', and 'bone'; the turmoil of jarring, irregularly disposed para-rhyme in 'stroke' – 'hook' – 'woke', 'head' – 'heard', 'found' – 'brow'; and finally the dull thud of the alliteration in the last line. The structural principle is designed to protract the dire moment, to freeze it, to present it nakedly, stripped of all that would insulate its terror, and to make it resonate. And this suggests the intensity of the poet's feeling on recognizing his own frightening, destructive potential. From the dark of the unconscious an image emerges of an uncontrollable, guilt-ridden, primal urge, with sexual implications.

Rooted in the same elemental source are more benign energies. In celebrating the natural world, Heaney is sensitive to the primeval mystery which is proclaimed by the visible realities. This is the foundation for a marvellous or magical view of the world. Nature is sacramental, and Heaney approaches it in a spirit of reverence for life and a feeling for the miraculous of its common operations. In the vibrant bloom of the whin he sees an emblem of nature's vitality, and in its resistance to fire a stubborn force of continuance and durability ('Whinlands'); death and defeat cannot obliterate the spirit of renewal and natural process ('Requiem for the Croppies'). A mutual dependence characterizes the affairs of man and active nature: more particularly, nature exemplifies the principle of female sexuality. When the pump is thawed out in spring ('Rite of Spring') or a farmer unblocks his drain ('Undine') so that the life-giving water can run freely again, there is a marvellous sense of primal release and a revelation of the great bond of love that exists between man and nature.

Heaney wants to make us aware of the latent power in things that continually pulls them – and us – toward the centre. In 'A Lough Neagh Sequence' he describes how the life of both fishermen and fish belongs to the same timeless, instinctual pattern. This sequence of seven poems is an ambitious experiment, embracing a whole vision of life and employing a wide range of poetic styles and effects. The first poem, 'Up the Shore' tells of how, despite the advantages of new technology, the fishermen still observe the old hardened and limited forms of tradition. They still regard their work as a ritual activity, a game with nature, governed by certain unspoken rules of fair play: only going for one fish at a time, sailing far out, never learning to swim. Only the fishermen know the hidden dangers, but they refuse to abandon the old ways and accept the risks stoically: ' "We'll be the quicker going down" they say.' What they enjoy is the nourishment engendered by intimacy with their place, which is hallowed for them through the history, legend and folk-wisdom that surround it. The poem ends as it began with a statement of fatalistic resignation: 'The lough will claim a victim every year.' These are the men who, in the fourth poem, 'Setting', are 'Not sensible of any *kyrie*', who simply accept their lives as destiny. Assisting at their ritual are the 'responsive acolytes', the 'umbrella' of gulls which swoop down to 'encompass' the left-over worms when they are thrown into the water. In 'Bait', both worms and fishermen are enclosed by circles. The activity of the men is defined by the 'compass' of their lamps' beams; the worms, 'whorling their mud coronas', make 'the globe' a perfect fit. Even when fixed to the hook, the worms become 'a garland' – elements in another ritual cycle.

'Setting' opens with the fishermen/poet probing subconscious depths, participating in a proliferating, timeless mystery where action assumes a ritualistic, mesmeric quality:

> The oars in their locks go round and round
> The eel describes his arcs without a sound.

The combination of hieratic eloquence ('Not sensible of any *Kyrie*', 'responsive acolytes', 'mud coronas', 'describes his arcs') and commonplace ('follow their noses in the grass', 'out of sight and out of mind', 'go round and round') dramatizes the poems' double perspective of learned and literate divination on one hand, and lived illiterate instinct on the other.

'Beyond Sargasso' is a fine poem whose flowing structure beautifully expresses the sinuous potency of the eel. Variously described as a gland, a scale of water, a muscled icicle, a sleek root, the eel is governed by an invisible cosmic influence as it drifts across the Atlantic. 'The Return' describes the female eel which, gifted with the same uncanny homing instinct, makes her way through new trenches, sunk pipes, swamps, streams, the lough, to the river. To complete the cycle is to re-commence it: 'Where she's lost once she lays/ ten thousand feet down in/ her origins.'

Once lifted into the boat, the eel surrenders identity, becoming part of an undifferentiated mass with no beginning and no end:

> . . . a knot of back and pewter belly

> That stays continuously one
> For each catch they fling in
> Is sucked home like lubrication.

A similar pattern is created by the wakes of the boats: they become so 'enwound' that it is impossible to tell which boat is which. And to the question of when this all began the fishermen's robustly practical reply, 'Once the season's in', does not attempt to address the absolutes. Everything about eel fishing is described as part of a mysterious cycle. The fishermen, whose work is performed with blind, ritualistic absorption, share the elemental rhythm of the fish themselves. There is a correspondence between the disturbing, irrational aspect of nature and the atavisms of the human mind. This is demonstrated in 'Vision', the last poem of the sequence. Like 'Death of a Naturalist' or 'The Barn', it describes a young boy's nightmarish experience of the natural world. Watching the eels at night move through the grass 'like hatched fears', it's as if the field, 'a jellied road', was flowing past him. Instead of dissipating, the vision is 'confirmed' by Time. The brute world of the eels is part physical, part state of mind. The sharp, visual impression of their slimy, muscular physicality enhances their symbolic value. The description registers a sense of the miraculousness and wondrousness of being, but also evokes, as in a dream, a nexus of fear and sensation associated with pubescent sexual turmoil and dread of annihilation. The child feels threatened by a mysterious 'horrid' power which yet defines his whole world of experience: 'To watch the eels crossing land/ Re-wound his world's live girdle.'

As well as the universal, elemental mystery, nature and landscape proclaim the spirit of place. In the last three poems in *Door into the Dark* Heaney opens up new ground, probing the numen in locale. 'Shoreline' is about the power of landscape – its sights and sounds – to evoke the past, To the poet, a history of invasion is implied by the Moher basalt which 'stands to', the strands which 'take hissing submissions', the tide which is 'rummaging in/ At the foot of the fields'. In the different sounds of the many-mooded sea, he hears the predatory Danes with their 'black hawk bent on the sail', the 'chinking Normans' and the Celts in their 'curraghs hopping high/ On to the sand'. What used to be great strongholds – Strangford, Arklow, Carrickfergus – are now only forgotten monuments to the past.

Another image of what is now only a vestigial reality is the alluvium which 'holds and gluts' in 'Bann Clay'. But what becomes a favourite image for Heaney to represent his ideas – one with greater necessity than the shoreline and greater complexity than Bann clay – is that of the bog. The bog as the memory of the landscape. Akin to, but more retentive than the 'slime kingdoms' of flax-dam and quagmire, the bog is a fathomless subconscious memory sucking seasons and civilizations into itself. There is a congruence between bogland viewed as a repository of the past and the internal world of the poet's preserving, shaping imagination and, beyond that, the national consciousness. Heaney proposes the bog as a significant Irish myth, an equivalent to the frontier and the West in American consciousness. Heaney's poetic realm as he identifies it in 'Bogland', is not the wide-ranging, expansive prairie: it is vertical rather than horizontal, lying in the depths of personal and communal experience.

The inspiration for 'Bogland', Heaney tells us, came from recollection of the way older people used to warn children in the area away from the pools of the old workings by telling them that there was no bottom in the bog. The substance of the poem, that is, was itself a buried memory that only surfaced into consciousness some time after the poem was written.

'Bogland' is earthed in the actual. A commonplace landscape is literally presented, but contemplated with such intensity and susceptibility that it becomes a 'prospect of the mind', and the image and expression of a culture. As Heaney remarked of Kavanagh's poetry, it is only when 'the ethereal literary voice incarnates itself in the imagery of the actual world that its messages of transcendence become credible'.[17] This is what happens in 'Bogland', where the mythical and the mystical spring naturally out of the mundane and the colloquial:

> Melting and opening underfoot,
> Missing its last definition
> By millions of years.
> They'll never dig coal here . . .
>
> The bogholes might be Atlantic seepage,
> The wet centre is bottomless.

Normally, millions of years would help a country to achieve and define itself. Not so in Ireland. There is, in Heaney's poetry, a sense of Ireland as an old dark culture, the longest part of which – Gaelic culture – in a language which is now dark to most of us. In submitting to the attractions of the dark, the secret depths, the cultural past, the pioneer in search of origins runs the risk of getting lost in mists and swamps – 'the wet centre is bottomless'. Beneath the very floor of memory, beyond all possibility of retrieval, lies the formless, primeval level of history and consciousness – the mysterious source of life.

The primal intuitions of Heaney's poetry are sensuous. The soft textures of organic decay exert a powerful fascination:

> We hoarded the fresh berries in the byre.
> But when the bath was filled we found a fur,
> A rat-grey fungus, glutting on our cache.
> The juice was stinking too
>
> ("Blackberry Picking").

> All year the flax-dam festered in the heart
> Of the townland; green and heavy headed
> Flax had rotted there, weighted down by huge sods.
> Daily it sweltered in the punishing sun.
> Bubbles gargled delicately, bluebottles
> Wove a strong gauze of sound around the smell
>
> ("Death of a Naturalist").

He remembers as a child 'puddling through muck', splashing in 'the sucking clabber', visiting 'the slime kingdoms' to collect the 'warm thick slobber' of frogspawn; he would 'pry into roots . . . finger slime'. These activities, as 'Personal Helicon' makes explicit, are essentially poetic. The sensuous intensity is an integral part of the deeper meanings of his poems.

Blake Morrison has isolated the mediation between speech and silence as a major theme in Heaney's work.[18] Heaney, Morrison explains, grew up with a farmer's distrust of words. Taciturnity is a mark of proficiency amongst his ploughmen, fishermen, thatchers, water-diviners and blacksmiths. For a Catholic boy in Ulster there were practical reasons for keeping quiet: 'Whatever you say, say nothing', was the folk-wisdom Heaney's mother passed on to him, and was to form the title of one of his later poems. This silent ancestry, Morrison points out, shaped Heaney's view of his art. But what strikes a reader far more forcibly about Heaney's poems, especially the early ones, is not so much the mediation between speech and silence as the mediation between speech and the sensuous textures of things. In later poems he aspires to 'the rough porous/ language of touch' (in 'Bone Dreams' in *North*), a poetry of 'words entering almost the sense of touch' (in Glanmore Sonnet II in *Field-Work*). His preoccupation with nature's rich, palpable, organic processes, with the feel of ooze and ripe fullness leads him through a door into the dark – into the hidden, pre-verbal recesses of being. We can see why the bog emerges as his central symbol.

At this stage in his career Heaney might well have compared his ideal of a poem to 'mud'. Continuing the Shakespearian notion of 'poesy' as 'a gum which oozes from whence 'tis nourished', Heaney wants his poetry to insinuate a sense of natural release, of words coming fluently towards us out of the alluvial depths of self. Poetry is like the water which runs free in 'Undine', making its own little channels and currents, once the man has cleared the drain. Few of the early poems, however, actually behave like that, for the thickly-textured language of mud has a tendency to clump and clog.

In terms of Heaney's own definition of 'technique', the poetry of the first two volumes works only intermittently; it is the masculine, making function that tends to strike us first. We see him more centrally involved with finding words than with that crucial, pre-verbal, feminine activity – that 'primary generating surrender' wherein '"the lump in the throat" finds "the thought"'.[19] Words have a tendency to count more for themselves that for the concise and coherent development of a thought. Poems, instead of existing through images, exist for them. They tend to be an art of words through which the young poet impresses us with his virtuosity, rather than an art of which words are the transparent medium, and through which the self – the poet's own reality – is distilled, and his stance defined.

It is not surprising, of course, that a young poet should begin with craft, with aspirations chiefly concerned with making. 'Craft is what you can learn from other verse',[20] Heaney has said. And it is not hard to trace the influences in his own early work. A poetic antecedent in the development of his expression of animal spirits and animal sensitivity is the heavily-stressed, extravagant, consonantal voice of Hughes. That combines with the verbal energy of Hopkins, though rarely in quite such a heavy-handed manner as in an early uncollected piece, 'October Thought':

> Minute movement millionfold whispers twilight
> Under heaven-hue plum-blue and gorse pricked with gold,
> And through the knuckle-gnarl of branches, poking the night
> Comes the trickling tinkle of bells, well in the fold.[21]

Alliteration so reminiscent of Hopkins can be lacking in subtlety, so much so that it sounds like parody.

For Heaney, the making function was centrally concerned with concrete realization, the virtues of which he said he learnt from MacLeish and Verlaine, Eliot's 'objective correlative' and the whole modernist experiment with imagist exactitude. This is the subject of another early, uncollected poem, 'Lines to Myself':

> In poetry I wish you would
> Avoid the lilting platitude.
> Give us poems humped and strong,
> Laced tight with thongs of song,
> Poems that explode in silence
> Without forcing, without violence.
> Whose music is strong and clear and good
> Like a saw zooming in seasoned wood.
> You should attempt concrete expression,
> Half-guessing, half-expression.[22]

In the first two books, Heaney the craftsman is adept at keeping up a capable verbal display and a rhythm, but the effect is ultimately often rhetorical. In 'Docker' there is the anomalous comparison between a Protestant Belfast docker and a Celtic cross. 'Turkeys Observed' has some acutely observed details, but the apprentice poet yields to conceits that are more contrived than helpful:

> I find him ranged with his cold squadrons:
> The fuselage is bare, the proud wings snapped,
> The tail-fin stripped down to a shameful rudder.

Our attention fixes on the ingenuity of the word rather than the significance of the world it is supposed to illuminate:

> Blue-breasted in their indifferent mortuary,
> Beached bare on the cold marble slabs
> In immodest underwear, frills of feather.

Love of words themselves can displace a firm sense of the poem as a whole structure. 'Trout' begins dramatically with inversion and a collapsed syntax that is squeezed together telegraphically in the effort to convey the latent power of the fish as it waits, silent and motionless: 'Hangs, a fat gun-barrel,/ Deep under the arched bridges.' The constraints of the set quatrain also work to intensify the sense of pent-up power waiting for release. The rest of the poem extends the gun image, inviting us to consider the trout as torpedo, dart, tracer-bullet, volley and ramrod. Before long we find ourselves becoming too conscious of the poem's insistence. The language, instead of promoting the impression of speed and power, inclines toward mere word-play. The dramatic potential is circumscribed, the poem's kinetic energy dissipated.

'Digging', the first poem in the first volume, Heaney regarded as a breakthrough. It was the first poem, he felt, in which 'technique' had a part to play: ' "Digging", in fact, was the name of the first poem I wrote where I thought my feelings had got into words, or to put it more accurately, where I thought my *feel* had got into words. . . . This was the first place where I felt I had done more than make an arrangement of words: I felt I had let down a shaft into real life.'[23] At the back of the poem lies a sense of guilt at having departed from family tradition to take up the pen rather than the spade. Heaney celebrates the diggers' intimacy with the land, and the skill with which they carry on old family traditions. As a poet, Heaney still wants to feel a part of all this. Just as the diggers extract new produce from the ancient soil, he reasons, so the poet delves into his experience to produce poems. It is the natural, easy movement, the precise rhythmic control of his father and grandfather that he particularly wishes to embrace:

> The coarse boot nestled in the lug, the shaft
> Against the inside knee was levered firmly.
> He rooted out tall tops, buried the bright edge deep . . .
>
> Nicking and slicing neatly, heaving sods
> Over his shoulder, going down and down
> For the good turf. Digging.

Here the stanza is bound together by the internal echoes of the participial endings (which emphasize a notion of protracted activity) and the repetition of the forceful *d's* and *g's* and straining *n's*. The deft and delicate skill of the short-vowelled 'nicking and slicing' contrasts with the strain in the long-vowelled, assonantal emphasis of 'neatly, heaving'. A sense of tense, rhythmic action is reinforced by the way the syntactic unit ('heaving sods over his shoulder') is broken, held momentarily in suspension by the line division, so that we must wait for the heavily-stressed first syllable of the second line to complete the effort, which then expends itself, like breath exhaled, in the fall-off, unstressed second syllable. A regular rhythm re-establishes itself, the repetition of 'down' deepening penetration into the ground, creating a self-retarding movement that is accentuated by the line break in the middle of another syntactic unit. The sudden curt simplicity of the single-word sentence that rounds off the stanza distances us from the strenuous labour. The entranced close-up dissolves.

The poem attempts a direct transcription of particular moments like this dug out of memory. But the poem as a total structure evinces less of the natural fluency which the poet celebrates in the skill of the diggers. It gives the impression of being a 'made' thing, of parts impressive and memorable in themselves which are cobbled together rather than emerging as an organic burgeoning of feeling and image. Thoughts and images do not ooze out and into one another, they are hammered into unity. This localized quality of the poem's effects is reflected in the irregularity of line, stanza and structure. Rhymes are sporadic, in no regular pattern, sometimes occurring internally, relying especially on the echo of assonantal and consonantal repetition. Sound and accent are disposed to reinforce specific descriptive effects.

We can see why Heaney himself should say that the 'rhythms and noises' in 'Digging' 'still please me', but that it is 'a big coarse-grained navvy of a poem'.[24] There is something rather too conscious, voluntary and assiduous in its composition. The image he gives us of the poet at the beginning reinforce these feelings:

> Between my finger and my thumb
> The squat pen rests; snug as a gun.

The word 'squat', the comparison of pen to gun, the sturdy, deliberate thump of heavily-stressed, monosyllabic words, the compacted power in the half-rhymes of 'thumb', 'snug' and 'gun', all contribute to an impression of brute force and carefully maintained poise. The lines, Heaney has said, 'have more of the theatricality of the gun-slinger than the self-absorption of the digger'.[25] The poet is not seen as an attentive, flexible mediator, but a ruthless force ready to hammer form out of intractable material. Unlike 'Follower', 'Digging' ends in affirmation. By the end the gun has gone, replaced we may assume by the heroic strength, the self-absorption and deft craftsmanship of the digger.

'Follower' comes at us from deeper down in the poet's psyche. Within its tamed stanzas there is a more flexible, less emphatic style, that is capable of unburdening and amplifying the poet's original feeling and binding the poem's constituent elements of image, cadence and sound into active unity. It begins with celebratory recollection. The poet recalls his father's expertise as a ploughman, his almost mystical oneness with the natural world. It's as if he was embracing all of life:

> His shoulders globed like a full sail strung
> Between the shafts and the furrow.

The pride and admiration the poet has for his father is tinged with an exoticism that associates the ploughman with Atlas and the heroic adventurer-seamen of old. The father assumes legendary, larger-than-life proportions. In the last stanza, rhythmic control disintegrates and the feeling of the poem is suddenly complicated:

I was a nuisance, tripping, falling,
Yapping always. But today
It is my father who keeps stumbling
Behind me, and will not go away.

The word 'stumbling' had been used earlier to describe the child,
but it is then that his father picked him up and, carrying him on his
back, resumed his work with the same steady rhythm. The last
stanza conveys the poet's sense of failure at ever being able to repeat
his father's skill and nurture. Heaney feels he cannot redeem the
father's 'stumbling' with his own kind of rhythmic order. The
movement of the poem enacts its own insights. Its texture of
implication and echo expresses the pain and sadness which the poet
feels as he explores his relationship with his father who becomes a
shadowy presence, a past, memory, conscience.

It is not surprising that a young poet should begin with craft
rather than technique: neither is it surprising that he should begin
with childhood. Poems like 'Blackberry Picking', 'Churning Day'
and 'Death of a Naturalist' are composed out of a rudimentary
language of instinct and sensation and they are so successful
because they are principally intended to be simply evocation. In
Heaney's early work, the feelings and experience which seek
expression are, for the most part, those of childhood, substantially
and understandably constituted by the basic, comparatively uncom-
plicated emotions of wonderment, fear, guilt, and the pain of loss.
He is able to give full rein to his remarkable gift for realizing, freshly
and vigorously, the physical world: it is, after all, the focus of his life
as a child. What he has still to learn is how to retain his sensuous
particularity while making his poetry less dense, less emphatic,
more resonant, more flexible. He has still to develop out of rhetoric
an internal language for the utterance of the deep rhythms of the
adult personality. He must discover ways to venture further beyond
the normal cognitive bounds and 'raid the inarticulate', to get at
more of life, to find the means to invoke more complex conditions of
mind and spiritual states. This development of 'technique' involves
more than a dynamic alertness that mediates between speech and
touch or speech and silence: it involves, through a sensitization of
the auditory imagination, a mediation between speech and sound.
It is the whole creative effort of the mind's and body's resources to
bring, in Heaney's own words, 'all the realms of whisper' within the
jurisdiction of form. For these realms represent a dimension of

memory and experience which is the source of certain feelings that are the chief impulses of individual life, and at the same time exemplars of deep, cosmic rhythms.

More ambitious 'technique' requires more refined 'craft'. To be able to let the feeling or the idea crystallize out of the detail, the numen to shine through an extraordinary strong sense of the concrete particular, requires of the poet a rare integrity of intelligence. It asks for subtlety in selecting and restraint in not exaggerating or over-accumulating the sensuous detail. If it takes the percipience of 'technique' to receive and to seize, it takes the temperance of 'craft' not to expose unduly or abruptly the 'meaning' of experience. These virtues of intellectual continence and moral sensibility are what promotes the 'wise passiveness' of which Wordsworth spoke. They enable the poet to accept the totality of his experience without forcing it, and to record it without distorting it.

Heaney's first two volumes contain evidence of such a widening of sensibility. He has documented for us the way in which a complex accrual of feeling and private association found its way into words, in 'Undine'. His account of the poem's composition illustrates the operation of 'technique', the way 'the first gleam attains its proper effulgence'.[26] It was a poem, he says, that arose out of 'the almost unnameable energies' that, for him, hovered over the sound of the words: 'It was the dark pool of the sound of the word that first took me: if our auditory imaginations were sufficiently attuned to plumb and sound a vowel, to unite the most primitive and civilized associations, the word 'undine' would probably suffice as a poem in itself. *Unda*, a wave, *undine*, a water-woman – a litany of undines would have ebb and flow, water and woman, wave and tide, fulfilment and exhaustion in its very rhythms.' Then he recalled a more precise dictionary definition of the word. An undine is a water-sprite who has to marry a human being and have a child by him before she can become human. 'With that definition, the lump in the throat, or rather the thump in the ear, *undine*, became a thought, a field of force that called up other images.' One of these was a childhood memory of seeing a man unblock a drain and watching the water run free. This image, he says, 'was gathered into a more conscious reading of the myth as being about the liberating, humanizing effect of sexual encounter'. Out of this nexus, the poem uttered itself, as the poet's seminal excitement escaped from 'incoherence into the voice of the undine herself'.[27] Its great strength lies in the way the sexual imagery arises naturally from the situation:

the mingling of sensuality and reverence is in keeping with the spirit of the myth where Undine gains a soul through the experience of physical love.

Another poem of sexual encounter, 'The Wife's Tale', also demonstrates the poet's developing skill in using language as both medium and meaning. Here, the poem's energy finds its 'objective correlative' in the form of a monologue. By adopting the wife's persona, Heaney heightens the dramatic potential of the situation, and the language, instead of calling attention to itself as in the self-conscious poetry of bucolic heaviness, is so deployed to specify exactly the nature of that point of intersection of inward, geological feeling and the detached, external particulars of a life. The poem's staid measures are an entirely appropriate medium of the wife's robust acceptance, her traditionalism, which combine with a poignant awareness that is free of resentment. Right away she presents herself in the role of one who tends and serves as she lays out the cloth and calls the men. She is an outsider to the men's world, and perceives their world in terms of a noisy, monstrous power:

> The hum and gulp of the thresher ran down
> And the big belt slewed to a standstill, straw
> Hanging undelivered in the jaws.

Onomatopaeia and alliteration register more than a sensuous delight in observable phenomena. They are the dramatic expression of an attitude, elements of a kind of psychic code, a way of working into the texture of the poem the wife's essential patterns of perception, feeling and thought.

Ever attentive, she butters her husband's bread the way he likes it, noting at the same time his self-possession and self-satisfaction in the posture he adopts on the grass waiting to be served. She recalls his praise for her clean white cloth and how quickly, how easily and how thoughtlessly, it is dispelled in his next remark about labouring men having no time for such niceties. Once again the fact is borne home that a woman's efforts can only be incidental to the important business of the men. The square of cloth, symbol of the woman's realm of influence, is a genteel miniature of the rough square of field the men work. Her isolation is reinforced by the wink she notices passing between the men.

There is an unceremonious invitation for her to enter the men's world momentarily, when the husband tells her to go and look at

how good the seed is. The man's gesture, however, only highlights
the gap between them. She has no more understanding or apprecia-
tion of the men's work than the husband has of her civilizing ritual
of laying out the cloth. But obediently she goes, unwilling to risk
offence. Running her hand through the bags of cool, hard seed, her
gratification is as secret as it is unexpected. And this secret
marginalized life, the sensuous intensity, the whispering intelli-
gence that we hear behind the authoritarian (male) structures of
linguistic, sexual and social power, imply a whole (female) order of
being that we recognize as an essential part of Heaney's own most
authentic experience.

Standing amid the stubble, the men's world registers itself ever
more strongly in terms of a gross, brutal power with phallic
undertones:

> The bags gaped
> Where the chutes ran back to the stilled drum
> And forks were stuck at angles in the ground
> As javelins might mark lost battlefields.

For a short time there is silent respite from the 'battle' as the men
draw round the wife's bright square of domestic order. But she is
aware of their essential difference and separation, of the ritual
nature of their contact:

> And that was it. I'd come and he had shown me
> So I belonged no further to the work.
> I gathered cups and folded up the cloth
> And went.

Heaney's probing of the relationship between the sexes discloses
in intimate detail the way the woman's life is determined by the
man; and the revelation of her sensitive awareness co-existing with
acceptance of her condition, without protest, without rancour, is no
small triumph of intuition and finesse. The poem is reminiscent of
one of Frost's dramatic idylls such as 'Home Burial'. Both poets use
properties that are everyday ones, and never exotic; their language –
cautious, dry, reticent, slow, countrified – is the depth of their roots
in their own countryside; allusiveness and economy the means of
their psychological penetration.

The love poems in the first two volumes also show an increasing maturity of style and deepening of insight. Poems like 'Lovers on Aran', 'Valediction', 'Twice Shy', 'Scaffolding' and 'Honeymoon Flight' in *Death of a Naturalist* are the work of a competent craftsman, but they are unambitious in form and without much complexity of feeling. In comparison, 'Night Drive' and 'At Ardboe Point' in *Door into the Dark* attempt a good deal more. In 'Night Drive' the speaker is motoring through France to rejoin the woman he addresses. Alone in the darkness, he perceives with a heightened sensual awareness 'the smells of ordinariness' – the rain, hay, woods and air. The journey seems to enact, over and over again, his ache of want:

> Signposts whitened relentlessly.
> Montreuil. Abbeville, Beauvais
> Were promised, promised, came and went
> Each place granting its name's fulfilment.

The earth itself shares his sexual longing: 'I thought of you continuously/ A thousand miles south where Italy/ Laid its loin to France on the darkened sphere.' The poet's unease is reflected in his resistance to the consistent deployment of full-rhyme: there are times when he prefers the incomplete chiming of the half-rhyme with its intimation, rather than satisfying realisation, of coincidence. His longing for 'fulfilment' is set against a background in which a combine is 'groaning' its way homeward and seeds 'bled' across its work-light; a forest fire is 'smouldering out' and the cafes are shutting up one by one. These images intensify and drive through the dark, their intimations of mortality serving to heighten and validate love. Painful reminders of death, defeat and separation are the very things which 'renew' ordinariness.

In 'At Ardboe Point' the two lovers are enveloped by 'a smoke of flies', 'a hail of fine chaff', an 'invisible veil', 'a rash', a 'green pollen'. The poem's sound and movement enact the 'smattering' swirl of mosquitoes opening and closing. Reference to their 'just audible siren' and their 'infiltration' of clothing heightens the feeling of unease associated with the mosquitoes. Traditional symbols of death and destruction, the flies are linked with the plague of locusts visited on Pharaoh. But by the end of the poem Heaney rejects the harmful connotations that have been attached to them through hear-say and legend, and which have been reinforced by scientific observation. His own impressionistic response takes the form of a definitive statement, for it springs from his own imaginative need:

> For these are our innocent, shuttling
>
> Choirs, dying through
> Their own live empyrean, troublesome only
> As the last veil on a dancer.

Their swarming energy cannot be divorced from their 'million collisions', just as the intensity of human love cannot be separated from awareness of mortality. The flies are troublesome only because they increase desire.

Heaney's early work collected in his first two volumes is, then, uneven, displaying the limitations of a poetic tyro finding his voice, but also pointing the way ahead to what makes the mature poetry so exciting: a kind of creative exploration in which form is so deployed as to become meaning. Moreover, as 'Night Drive' and 'At Ardboe Point' demonstrate, there is the opportunity for despair and passivity, but the poetic disposition which makes Heaney so magnificently a helpful influence, so redemptive a poet, is the enduring sense, strong and sane, of the marvels of existence. These poems combine suggestions of depth and mystery with what Keats called 'thoughtful and quiet power'.[28] Their attitude is one of respect for, and love of, life. They represent a stage in the refinement of sensibility, wherein intensity of feeling is submitted ever more severely to the play of intelligence, and intelligence continually renews intimacy with feeling. Language is the medium of this process. Through language feeling is clarified by thought and thought is charged with feeling. The sharpening of the intellect, when it is kindled by the imagination, has a moral as well as aesthetic virtue, and the resulting comprehensiveness of mind is what gives us the mature poetry. What we can expect to find there is the poet's feeling for the numinous in nature, his attunement to 'all the realms of whisper', extending itself and making itself intelligible; and also the converse – intellect animated and made nervous by feeling, dignified by the Wordsworthian 'most watchful power of love',[29] by a concern for value and, resisting the modern annihilating suspicion of the word, inextricably involved with the inmost quality of language, its generative, unimaginably variable capacity for surprise, potency and revelation. The dialect of the tribe is purified not only to express what is active and contemporary but increasingly to contain deeper and more ancient tones, the sounds of the early Irish nature poets, the voice of the Anglo-Saxon Wanderer and Seafarer, the inflections of Dante. Local accent with all its tang and verve preserves traditional parochial continuities: by subtle modulations it can attune itself to all that is most deeply civilized in the wider world, and to all that constitutes the most private experimental events of the intimate world of mind.

3
Wintering Out

The title of Heaney's third volume, *Wintering Out*, indicates a move away from the bucolic world of childhood and engagement with the harsher adult world. It highlights the notions of survival, continuance and durability amid the severities of 'winter'. We anticipate some account of the conditions that give rise to this exacerbated feeling, and some indication of the sustaining and assuaging resources that make continuance possible.

Most of the poems in *Wintering Out* were written between 1969 and 1973, a time when the political situation in Northern Ireland had become suddenly volatile and violent: 'There was an energy and excitement and righteousness in the air at that time, by people like myself who hadn't always been political',[1] said Heaney. Up to then Heaney had made a reputation as a poet of the parish pump, providing local interest and colour, employing a regional voice that tended to be regarded by his English audience as essentially diversionary, harmless and rustic. He wrote of folksy-crafty things like butter-making and thatchers. '*Door into the Dark* will consolidate him', Christopher Ricks believed, 'as the poet of muddy-booted blackberry picking.'[2] But with the resurgence of the Troubles in the late 1960s, Heaney's notions about what poetry should be changed: 'From that moment the problems of poetry moved from being simply a matter of achieving the satisfactory verbal icon to being a search for images and symbols adequate to our predicament.'[3] the prefatory poem, part of a sequence entitled 'Whatever You Say, Say Nothing', which originally appeared in *The Listener*, presents a series of nightmarish images of Ulster's Troubles: the internment camp, a bomb crater, machine-gun posts which 'defined a real stockade'. To complete the feeling of unreality, a white mist enshrouds the horrifying scene:

> and it was déjà-vu, some film made
> of Stalag 17, a bad dream with no sound.

The last stanza questions the quality of life that is possible amid such conditions. The rest of the poems in the book have to be read in the

48

context of this numbed despair. In Part I, 'our predicament' is treated in cultural and political terms, but in Part II he presents a series of more personalized dramatic images – often from the point of view of women – in which human loss, hurt, derangement and alienation are absorbed within a timeless, archetypal and cosmic perspective.

'Fodder', the first poem in *Wintering Out*, suggests the poet's vulnerability and need, and introduces 'the backward look' as a source of assuagement. He yearns for the prelapsarian, childhood world where nature's providence (imaged in the hay-rick) offered the possibility of 'comfort'. Another source of assuagement for the poet is knowing who you are, and where you come from. There is nurture in belonging to and knowing imtimately a certain place and people and life-style. In his first two books Heaney concentrated on natural cycles, the rituals of rural life, the carrying on of family traditions: this emphasis on durability is extended into a preoccupation with his and his people's cultural history. He is looking for roots that go deeper than the purely personal ones of childhood. The title, *Wintering Out*, comes from 'Servant Boy', where the suggestion of continuity in the use of the present tense ('He is wintering out') and the emblematic power conferred upon this first line through its appropriation as title for the volume, emphasize identity between poet and servant boy: 'how/ you draw me into/ your trail', writes Heaney. Despite dispossession and hardship, the servant boy, 'old work-whore, slave-/ blood', is associated with the life-force, as the croppies had been. He comes 'first-footing' to the Big Houses carrying the 'warm eggs', symbols of regeneration, survival and warmth, even in winter. 'Resentful/ and impenitent', the servant boy is neither unaware of his condition nor broken by it. Not far beneath the surface of the poem is 'the slightly aggravated young Catholic male'.

In 'Bog Oak' the poet takes another 'backward look' into the past to affirm his ancestry amongst 'the moustached/dead, the creel-fillers'. They are also the pathetic dispossessed, wild men of the woods, nosing among the primitive facts: 'geniuses who creep/ "out of every corner/ of the woodes and glennes"/ toward watercress and carrion'. These ancient figures survive as shadowy spirits of place, possessors of 'hopeless wisdom', poised between life and death. The privileged, aristocratic values of imperialist power, represented by Sir Edmund Spenser 'dreaming sunlight', have little relevance to the dark indigenous reality. In a *Guardian* article Heaney explained:

From his castle in Cork, he (Spenser) watched the effects of a campaign designed to settle the Irish question. "Out of every corner of the woods and glens they came creeping forth upon their hands, for their legs could not carry them; they looked like anatomies of death . . ." At that point I feel closer to the natives, the geniuses of the place.[4]

Another shadowy genius is 'The Last Mummer' for whose demise the poem is a lament. A sense of loss pervades the poem, achieving repeated and cumulative emphasis from the way each section ends with an image of the mummer's withdrawal and disappearance. Heaney cannot claim the travelling player as a specifically Irish phenomenon (as Hardy's mummers in *The Return of the Native* would serve to remind us), but the mummer's intimacy with his people, his reliance on a sense of community and tradition, and his skill in portraying the mores and manners of the folk, give him a special place in the poet's esteem. A pagan, poetic spirit, he had led the imagination out of the miasma of blood and feuding into the realms of myth and magic:

> The moon's host elevated
>
> in a monstrance of holly trees,
> he makes dark tracks, who had
>
> untousled a first dewy path
> into the summer grazing.

Now, his popularity has been supplanted by the new magic of television. The lack of attention and appreciation he now receives breeds frustration and anger. The traditional values he had embodied with such tact and skill are perverted into violence, as he beats the bars of the gate and throws the stone onto the roof.

All three of these poems dispense with the comforting echo of regular rhyme. This highlights the facility of Heaney's choice of words, sentence structure and individually imposed principles of organization. 'Servant Boy' and 'Bog Oak' use a short, four-lined stanza form, 'The Last Mummer', the couplet, but despite this kind of punctuation imposed by the line arrangement, the general run of these poems is more like that of blank verse rather than the couplet or any stanza form (even though there are a few sporadic rhymes and a few lines are shorter than the others). This looser, more fluid, fainter and more tenuous kind of versification gives the poems a more immediate psychological spontaneity than rigidly traditional forms would permit. Freedom is attained not by breaking down the form but reshaping it. It is a poetic idiom related to a concern with the living speech of the day and the place, but as well as that it marks a continuing development of technique. The poems are in essence meditative and reminiscent, a half-shy, uncertain snatching at a fleeting vision. Heaney's fondness for the run-on line gives them an insinuating quality, the syntactical movement always tending to diverge from the rhythmical movement provided by the ideal metrical norm. This is why there is an exploratory and tentative feel about the rhythm, for it is out of the play of sense and sound that the penumbra of the past is conjured into time present, with the associative and emotional logic of a dream or day-dream. In 'Bog Oak' it is out of the 'smoke' and 'mizzling rain' which 'blurs the far end/ of the cart track', that the poet dimly discerns his ghostly ancestors. The servant boy is 'a jobber among shadows', the last mummer a dream-figure who 'moves out of the fog'.

This lack of definition is typical of many of the poems in *Wintering Out*. The heavy, thickly-textured idiom which Heaney used to evoke the visible world in his first two books is severely tempered. In *Death of a Naturalist* and *Door into the Dark* there was a sense of the poem's completeness and self-containment because each poem had its own 'action' – Ned Kelly's bull servicing a Friesian cow, a thatcher at work, butter churning, gathering blackberries, digging bait, lifting the catch into the boat – which depended on the concrete particularity of the language for its precise and vivid evocation. By contrast, poems like 'Servant Boy', 'Bog Oak' and 'The Last Mummer' emerge as extensions of the poet's mind, as the products of dream. They are gestures toward something that remains imprecise and, accordingly, their hold on the physical world relaxes. The external world is still there, but not so emphatically, for Heaney is now setting out to pursue ideas rather than simply recreate objects and processes. Sensory impression is organized and constructed within a probing intellectual purpose. As a result, the poems often strike us as reveries or musings. Sometimes much is left to the reader, if he is to discover from the poem's pulse of feeling, its fractional connections and private images, the implicit order amongst the array of particulars. This is particularly true of the

series of poems entitled 'A Northern Hoard' at the centre of the
book, and, to a slightly lesser extent, of 'Gifts of Rain'.

In 'Gifts of Rain' Heaney is once again the water diviner. The
Moyola's flood-water is the music of the place, the place giving
tongue, uttering its secrets like the hidden source in 'The Diviner'
'suddenly broadcasting through a green aerial its secret stations'.
The water cleanses, re-vitalizes, satisfies thirst, creeps into the
earth's secret recesses and leaves behind the 'word-hoard' of its
singing in the alluvium of language and history. Heaney burrows in
that 'word-hoard' to re-create that music. The poem is a version of
composition as 'soundings', as a listening, a wise passiveness. The
Moyola, like Wordsworth's Derwent, acts as tutor of his poetic ear,
and the strength and originality of the poem lie first in the poet's
trusting the validity of his intuitions once the normal inhibitions of
consciousness are relaxed; then in discovering through the opera-
tion of his auditory imagination the sounds and rhythms proper to
his sense. He dispenses with the facile continuity of pursuing a train
of thought, opting instead for a variety of angles of approach, a
restlessness of poetic style, and a somewhat strained metaphysical
ingenuity and use of words with double or multiple meanings – all
suggestive of a desire to devour a wide range of experience and
ensure that the poem is neither attenuated by customary perception
or conventional expectation, nor idealized away into a thin and
misty abstraction.

It begins by directing our attention outwards, into the country-
side, with two strongly visual images – of the animal in the mud,
and a farmer wading lost fields – both suggesting the primal bond
between inanimate nature and all living things. Animal and flood
are one:

> A nimble snout of flood
> licks over stepping stones
> and goes uprooting.

This mysterious unity of being is further emphasized in the image of
the farmer's quasi-sexual relationship with the land:

> and sky and ground
>
> are running naturally among his arms
> that grope the cropping land.

The mud water which he disturbs swirls up and mingles with his reflection. The man

> breaks the pane of flood:
>
> a flower of mud-
> water blooms up to his reflection
> like a cut swaying
> its spoors through a basin.

These complicated conceits, so exquisitely and so economically organized, again emphasize the continuity between man and nature. The life-giving water, when it is disturbed, 'blooms up' like a flower, and flows over and into the man. It merges with human life as the homonym of 'pane' suggests; the mud-water becomes human blood, then both are linked with animal life through the reference to the tracks of a hunted animal.

After this, the poem flows inward. The river-water streams hypnotically in the background, gathering, slabbering, brimming, whispering, spelling itself, chanting, breathing, as it gradually 'deals out its being' (to use Hopkins' phrase) to the poet. He is a still consciousness, a finely attuned instinct, attentively sounding like the 'still mammal' in part I. And, like the farmer in part II, he is involved in a quasi-sexual communion with nature, alert to the 'shared calling of blood', the 'mating call' of sound which rises to pleasure him. In the sound of the rain he can hear ancestral voices calling to him, whispering of the famine and nature's destructive power. 'Waterfall' was an early version of the same thing: in its 'slabber and spill', the poet heard 'the cries of villains dropped screaming to justice'. In 'Gifts of Rain' the flood-voices have a distinctly tribal or racial timbre, as the double-meaning implies in the reference to 'the race/ slabbering past the gable'. Language itself seems to be conditioned by landscape: the name Moyola strikes the poet as an onomatopaeic re-creation of the river-water itself. The landscape 'breathing its mists/ through vowels and history' represents a continuity that is inextricably connected with language and history.

All these perceptions depend on the intimacy and precision of the correspondence which exist between the external landscape as a system of signs and the poet's internal landscape as a system of thinking and feeling. He is 'Dives/ hoarder of common ground', and the flood-voices 'arrive' to meet his 'need/ for antediluvian lore'. The word 'need' is telling. It points to a concern with establishing relationships – relationships with nature, landscape, history, community. From the beginning of his career – in 'Digging' – Heaney is troubled by a sense of exclusion, a feeling which continues into much later poems, such as the tormented 'Exposure' with which his next collection ends. There, he is still a marginal figure whose chosen stance is one of indirection. It is within this framework that we must see his preoccupation with relationships. There is the vital connection between man and nature in the parable of the diviner, the binding force of communal ritual which is motivated by a feeling for the land in 'At a Potato Digging', the ancestry the poet seeks in 'Servant Boy' and 'Bog Oak', the 'soundings' he makes in 'Gifts of Rain'. These are the product of an outsider desperately seeking to assuage his alienation and establish a direction for himself through embracing a communal consciousness and a sense of the mysterious unity of being that breathes through river mists, through vowels and history.

'In Ireland our sense of the past, our sense of the land and even our sense of identity are inextricably interwoven',[5] Heaney has said. When he asks himself who he is he is compelled to make a connection with a history, a landscape, a heritage. The sense of place, the feeling for a place, assuages and steadies him and gives him a point of view. Landscape is hallowed by associations that come from growing up and thinking himself into a place. Anahorish, Moyola, Broagh, Toome, Derrygarve, are names of what is known and loved, cherished because of their tribal, etymological implications. Heaney thinks of himself as a survivor, a repository, a keeper: he is 'Dives/ hoarder of common ground'. Names and placenames are precious because they are bearers of history and ancestry, resonant clues to a shared and diminished culture. Unlike Kavanagh, and more like John Montague, Heaney's imagination is historic and mythopaeic. And at the bottom of it is the 'life-force' itself. The 'soft blastings' pronouncing the word 'Toome' are like explosions opening up a valuable find – 'loam, flints, musket-balls/ fragmented ware/ torcs and fish-bones'. From the 'loam' of the recent past to the neckware of the ancient Irish to the 'alluvial mud' and 'bog-water', the poet traces through a 'hundred centuries' to the primeval source of self and race.

In comparing Heaney with the older, Protestant poet, John Hewitt, we can see how Heaney is bound to his place in a way

Hewitt is not. For Hewitt the Glens of Antrim constitute 'the world my pulses take for true',[6] but he is always aware that he cannot share 'the enchantments of the old "tree magic"'.[7] In 'The Colony' he asserts attachment and identity by argument and formulated proof, whereas Heaney works on the level of implication, in terms of something that is naturally and automatically received, and can therefore be understated. Heaney is bound to his place though a lineage which he traces back to origins in 'alluvial mud' and through the figure of a mythological goddess. Hewitt's attachment on the other hand, as Heaney has pointed out, originates in rights conferred by Act of Parliament. Hewitt's primeval symbols, as Heaney further remarks, are 'bifocal',[8] including the Rollright Stones of Oxfordshire as well as Ossian's Grave. Hewitt's is the urbane, rational voice of a civilized man, Heaney's the voice of instinct probing the soft mulches of feeling and sensation, articulating 'realms of whisper'.

'Anahorish' – 'soft gradient/ of consonant, vowel-meadow' – rehearses in sound the landscape it names. In Heaney's place-name poems language is pushed towards a magical relationship with the things it is speaking about. The word 'Anahorish' means 'place of clear water', and the poem begins with an image of pristine beauty cast in the past tense:

> My 'place of clear water',
> the first hill in the world
> where springs washed into
> the shiny grass

This modulates into a darker picture of winter-time, past merges with present, and the feeling of loss and hardship intensifies. At the end the well-water no longer runs freely and cleanly and the 'mound-dwellers', though still in touch with the life-force, are now lost in dreamlike mists.

'Broagh' is another place-name which seems to Heaney to echo the sound of the rain, 'its low tattoo/ among the windy boortrees/ and rhubarb-blades.' The name (meaning 'riverbank') contains residual sounds of the native Irish language: 'that last/ gh the strangers found/ difficult to manage'. 'Broagh' is a highly formalised poem, intent and concentrated, each word asking for scrutiny as to how good it is making these 'soundings'. Exploring the relationship between landscape, language and people, it ends by alerting us to the nationalistic implications of all this.

What the place-name poems proved to Heaney was that, while using English, he could still express a sensibility conditioned by belonging to a particular place, an ancestry, a history, a culture, that was not English:

> I had a great sense of release as they (the place-name poems) were being written, a joy and devil-may-careness, and that convinced me that one could be faithful to the nature of the English language – for in some senses these poems are erotic mouth-music by and out of the Anglo-Saxon tongue – and, at the same time be faithful to one's own non-English origin, for me that is County Derry.[9]

Ultimately, it is not even relevant that he should use English for it is a language of nature he aims for. 'Oracle' gives us the image of a child – the incipient poet – hiding in the hollow trunk of a willow tree, taking in and re-producing the sounds of nature:

> small mouth and ear
> in a woody cleft,
> lobe and larynx
> of the mossy places.

'The Backward Look' recognizes that the Irish language is a thing of the past. Heaney describes its faltering career in terms of the flight of the snipe, the irregular, short-lined stanza-form reinforcing the sense of uncertain, fugitive movement. The snipe flees its nesting ground, just as the language fled its origins into dialects and variants. The etymologist transliterates Irish and English: the snipe's tail-feathers drum an elegy for the language and culture as the bird follows in the slipstream of the vanished wild goose and bittern. By the end of the poem, snipe and language disappear among 'gleanings and leavings/ in the combs/ of a fieldworker's archive'. The sense of loss is imbued with a vaguely elegiac, romantic feeling, as Heaney follows the snipe 'over twilit earthworks/ and wall-steads'. In 'Traditions' and 'A New Song' it is more difficult to deduce his attitude.

'Traditions' begins with an image of violation, a brutal sexual metaphor to describe the displacement of the feminine Gaelic vowel by the hard consonantal language of English:

> Our guttural muse
> was bulled long ago
> by the alliterative tradition

The Irish 'are to be proud' of their Elizabethan inheritance, the notion of enforced submission in this phrase leading to ironic self-congratulation at having mastered the colonist's language. There is resentment against the pride of the planter in re-modelling the Ulster dialect, and against the English who do not take the Irish seriously. The third part of the poem begins with a reference to Macmorris in *Henry V*, the first stage Irishman, 'gallivanting' about the Globe, 'whingeing' about his national identity: '"What ish my nation?"' Despite dispossession, despoliation and caricature, the poem resolves itself 'sensibly', in resignation and bathos, with the words of Joyce's Wandering Jew, Leopold Bloom, who answers Macmorris: '"Ireland . . ./ I was born here. Ireland."'

'A New Song', like 'Anahorish', opens with a nostalgic, soothing vision of an Edenic past. The recreation of the poet's colourful Arcadian childhood in Derrygarve implies acceptance of irrecoverable loss. But that abruptly changes:

> But now our river tongues must rise
> From licking deep in native haunts
> To flood, with vowelling embrace,
> Demesnes staked out in consonants.
>
> And Castledawson we'll enlist
> And Upperlands, each planted bawn –
> Like bleaching-greens resumed by grass –
> A vocable, as rath and bullaun.

He contemplates the possibility of retrieval and advance, but is unsure whether this will be effected through natural evolution or by force, an uncertainty conveyed in the ambiguity of 'must rise'. 'Embrace' suggests an act of love, the military metaphors ('staked out', 'enlist', 'bawn', 'rath') something more ominous. Castledawson and Upperlands are 'planted bawns' – 'bawn' being the word, adapted from the Irish *Bábhun* (bulwark, rampart; a fold, enclosure for cattle), which the planters used to refer to their fortified farmhouses. Curiously, it is these he wishes to 'enlist'. The neutral word 'resumed' in the penultimate line does not help to clarify his attitude as it could refer equally to the forceful repossession of the 'bleaching-greens' of the planters' disappearing linen industry by the native Irish, or a peaceable return to origins in which both communities will participate. The linguistic token of the new dispensation is the 'vocable' (the crossing of Irish vowels with English consonants) displayed in survivals like 'rath' (a rath being a prehistoric hill-fort or fairy building) and 'bullaun' (a bullaun being basin stones some of which may have been the bases of small crosses). The poem moves from past tense to future tense, the 'backward look' giving way to a tentatively optimistic, but some-what confused, forward look.

Other poems like 'The Wool Trade', 'Midnight' and 'Linen Town' are imbued with a sense of cultural loss that culminates by appropriating an intensely personalized frustration. 'Midnight' speaks of a native energy that has disappeared from Irish life: 'The wolf has died out,' 'Nothing is panting, lolling,/ Vapouring'. A series of images of emasculation dramatizes a psychic condition brought about by a history of dispossession and alienation: 'My tongue's/ Leashed in my throat'.

The leashing of the tongue in the throat is directly enacted in 'The Wool Trade'. The bulk of the poem is a passionate, mellifluous, vowel-based lament over a lost language and a lost way of life, their interrelatedness emphasized by making the spools, waterwheels, looms and spindles the very forms of language: 'Hills and flocks and streams conspired/ To a language of waterwheels/ A lost syntax of looms and spindles.' The loose and flowing paratactic style, which dissolves those verbal controls whereby reality is normally dis-tanced, classified and subdued, is a version of the 'rambling' and 'unwinding' which characterize the indigenous language; it ex-presses the romantic notion of Gaelic intractability to the require-ments of 'civilization', a notion which fuelled the traditional ideology of Irish cultural nationalism. This is then counterpointed in the last two lines by a harsh, tight-mouthed and heavily consonantal structure reflecting the rational authority of colonial influence:

> And I must talk of tweed,
> A stiff cloth with flecks of blood.

Historically, the poem alludes to the dismantling of the social and political system of Gaelic Ireland following the surrender of Hugh O'Neill in 1603, and to the steady infiltration of colonists, especially of lowland Scots, inaugurated by James I's plantation policy. Heaney takes the wool trade and places it in the context of a highly generalized regime of dispossession: thus, the colonial influence is responsible for replacing a pleasureable, easy-going warmth with authoritarian stiffness, feeling with reason, instinct with efficiency, freedom with coercion, the organic community with violence and alienation. Most conspicuous of all is the much-lamented loss of the Gaelic language. The terms of the various oppositions, however, are ill-defined and so unable to constitute a firm and energetic structure which would save the poem from sentimentality. The root emotion is a nostalgic craving for origins and presence: even more satisfying than Gaelic 'vowels' from the point of view of the mythologist of origins is the pure, unmediated, preliterate expression of looms and spindles into which the Gaelic language metamorphoses half-way through. It is this 'original' language which is then displaced by the planter's 'blood-stained' language, the currency of which is the symbol – the necessarily insufficient word. The contrast is between 'natural' or 'original' language which remains close to its sources in passionate utterance, in feeling, in nature, in the community at large, and 'artificial' or 'foreign' language imposed from outside and governed by the rules and devices of an alien culture. Heaney yields to the Rousseauesque dream of an innocent language and community untouched by the evils of progress, a mythology of presence, which ignores the self-alienating aspect of any language and all social existence.

In 'Linen Town' political disappointment and failure are linked with linguistic loss. The hanged body of Henry Joy McCracken, the Protestant leader of a small insurrection of United Irishmen in Antrim in 1798, is referred to as 'a swinging tongue'. Heaney is contemplating a civic print of High Street, Belfast, 1786, twelve years before the execution of the Irish rebel. The past becomes vividly alive, recreated in the present tense. As the print 'unfreezes' the poet experiences with equal urgency its sensuous reality and the political excitement of the time:

> Smell the tidal Lagan:
> Take a last turn
> In the tang of possibility.

There is an unmistakable poignancy which manages to avoid sentimentality in the best of these poems in which the poet figures as a survivor probing and commemorating 'native haunts', interrogating the 'tints' of a diminished culture, listening attentively for the echoes of a cherished, vital past from which he has been disinherited, and which exists now as 'gleanings and leavings', no more than a 'realm of whisper', almost a dreamworld – but to which he feels indissolubly bound. Its vestigial life, even though bereft of the last 'tang of possibility' and depending for its re-creation on a foreign language, still remains a potent source of nourishment and imaginative freedom.

The poems of place and place-name, Heaney tells us, 'politicize the terrain and imagery of the first two books'.[10] His relationship with the ground he grew up on is complicated by the fact that it is a country of division – historic social, political and cultural divisions that have had a profound effect on the whole psychic life of himself and his people. While he is, naturally enough, principally concerned with defining his relationship with his own community and his own past, 'The Other Side' is an exact and subtly evocative expression of the relationship between Catholic and Protestant as experienced by the poet on the farm where he grew up. The neighbouring Protestant farmer impinges as a large, dramatic presence. Standing amid the sedge and marigolds, he reminds the poet of an Old Testament prophet and the description of him, 'white-haired,/ swinging his blackthorn', subtly hints at the straightforward, black-and-white morality by which he lives. The Puritan aversion to ornament and ritual, the simplicity, sturdiness and orderliness of the man's life, the way in which his every thought is determined by the precepts of his religion, are emphasized in the hard consonantal music and strong accentual rhythms:

> his brain was a whitewashed kitchen
> hung with texts, swept tidy
> as the body o' the kirk.

Even his speech is Biblical, and while the poet may find the grandiloquent high seriousness of his idiom impressive, it is as divisive as the *gh* in 'Broagh'. It does not speak for the poet, for it is the self-righteous 'tongue of chosen people' that is inappropriate to the poet's perceptions of himself and his world. From his less privileged perspective, the poet cannot resist deflating the 'patriarchal dictum', comparing its 'magnificence' to loads of hay too big for his small lanes. The Protestant farmer speaks twice – first to dismiss his neighbour's land as hopelessly barren and then his religion as unscriptural – each remark a blunt, unfeeling rejection that increases awareness of the man's sense of superiority. When he moves off towards his 'promised furrows', he disturbs the weed-pollen which drifts in to infect his neighbour's fields – an image of the unwitting damage which he causes.

Section III moves to the poet's 'side of the house', and he is not uncritical of it either. The rosary is 'dragging mournfully' on in the kitchen, the lack of vitality in Catholic practice contrasting with the obsessive vigour of the Protestant's religion. Now it is the Protestant who is the outsider. As the prayers draw to a close, he is like a stranger in the dark outside, intruding on something intensely personal, forever outside his concern. The gestures of friendship are guarded and embarrassed. The Protestant visitor has to make excuses for calling, and whistle casually to maintain a pretence of disinterest while the family finish the litany and answer his knock on the door. The poet's reaction is equally hesitant and unspontaneous:

> Should I slip away, I wonder,
> or go up and touch his shoulder
> and talk about the weather
>
> or the price of grass-seed?

Even if they strike up a conversation, what degree of intimacy can they hope to achieve? What the poem offers is a picture of two worlds which can never fully meet. The poem marks a considerable development beyond 'Docker' in its balance and emotional complexity.

Faced with the inconceivable horror spawned by Ulster's traditional divisions, the kind of objective dramatization of the relationship between the two communities which we find in 'The Other Side' cannot be maintained. The pain cannot be supported by such a mannerly style. The five poems which constitute 'A Northern Hoard' are amongst the few in *Wintering Out* which turn to the subject of the volume's prefatory poem and take us into the immediate horror of the Troubles in Belfast in 1969. The Northern hoard of history and racial consciousness is filled with blood and death. Actuality mingles with nightmare. 'All shifts dreamily', as Heaney says in the first poem, 'Roots'. Here, the opening stanza's troubled, eerie music introduces the idea of derangement, dissolution and death being deeply embedded in the very geology of the country. It is a quiet, stunned lament over the conditions which make love impossible in the Ulster Gomorrah. Outside are the sounds of gunshot, siren and exploding gas. 'We petrify or uproot now' – the lovers harden to stone, freeze with fear, find themselves cut off from every sustaining thing in their environment. 'Uproot', however, may be active rather than passive, suggesting another alternative – confronting the horror and trying to 'uproot' it. The poet goes on to say he will dream the symbolic release of the evil spirits which plague the lovers:

> I've soaked by moonlight in tidal blood
>
> A mandrake, lodged human fork,
> Earth sac, limb of the dark;
> And I wound its damp smelly loam
> And stop my ears against the scream.

The mandrake-shriek that was supposed to be heard when the plant was uprooted was, according to tradition, the scream of the long-dead murderers buried where the mandrake grew. But there is also the suggestion in these densely enigmatic lines of enwinding oneself with primordial, instinctual forces, returning to the dark, re-uniting oneself with the natural world, thereby assuming the magical, healing virtue that was reputedly attached to the mandrake root, itself a human surrogate because of its resemblance to the shape of the human torso. As in 'Oracle', or in later poems like 'Exposure' or *Sweeney Astray*, the poet is 'Taking protective colouring/ From bole and bark.'[11] The poem expresses an intense desire for exorcism, but the sustained sense of strain in the use of pararhyme and the muted confidence of its exploratory, tentative metres demonstrate that the magical properties of dream and superstitious ritual have not found their aesthetic equivalents in the poetic structure. The poem stands more as a melodramatic expression of need than an imaginative transcendence of it.

In the second poem, 'No Man's Land', the poet, as the title implies, has cut himself off from community and communal consciousness. He has 'deserted', tried to 'shut out' the horror of the violence. He resents having to confront it, but acknowledges that if he doesn't, he forfeits his humanity. Resentment finally gives way to guilt: 'Why do I unceasingly/ arrive late to condone/ infected sutures/ and ill-knit bone?'

The agony of doubt and dividedness is registered in another rhetorical question in the next poem, 'Stump': 'What do I say if they wheel out their dead?' This is the question which burdens Heaney from now on. His response here – 'I'm cauterized, a black stump of home' – expresses a sense of failure and ineffectuality. The crisis of savagery has obliterated the vitalizing and sustaining influences which he celebrates elsewhere as springing from a sense of place and a sense of community. The title of the fourth poem, 'No Sanctuary', anticipates the condition he describes in 'Exposure'. It may be Halloween, the time of harvest celebration and solemn recollection of the Feast of All Souls, but in Ulster 'the turnip-man's lopped head', instead of averting the avenging dead, has an even more sinister meaning – it is the very emblem of the country's horror.

The sequence of poems concludes with 'Tinder' which presents a dark and savage view of human nature and human history. On one level it is an allegory of the underprivileged tribe who light the tinder of revolution and then wonder what to do with their 'new history'. But the prehistoric imagery makes it clear that Heaney is not just thinking of Ireland. He is describing 'the terror behind all', the 'unproductive fury'[12] in human nature. The use of the first person plural emphasizes the continuum of history, the fundamental similarity between primitive man and modern technological man. His concern is with primal consciousness which seems to Heaney to be inclined ineluctably toward destruction. Reference to the 'flames' soft thunder' and facing into 'the tundra's whistling bush', is the apocalyptic imagery of the nuclear holocaust, which further helps to universalize the poem's application. Destruction, desolation and disappointment inevitably seem to attend human 'progress'. 'Canine', the word with which the poem ends, is the essential predisposition, as Heaney sees it, of the human animal. In the picture of the survivors, stunned and silenced, surrounded by the ashes of their own devastation and having to face into desolate psychic tundras, we recognize the anguish of the poet wondering what his role should be.

The question as ever is, 'How with this rage shall beauty hold a plea?' Heaney's answer now is: 'by offering "befitting emblems of adversity"'.[13] Heaney's search for befitting emblems was greatly helped by his reading of P. V. Glob's book, *The Bog People*. It tells of the discovery in Danish bogs of bodies dating back to the Iron Age who had been sacrificial victims to the Mother Goddess, Nerthus, the goddess of the ground, who required new bridegrooms each winter to bed with her in her sacred place, in the bog, to ensure renewal and spring fertility. Heaney uses this archaic, barbarous rite as an archetypal pattern within which may also be contained the tradition of Irish political martyrdom. It offered a way of understanding, of dealing with, a monstrous violence. By presenting contemporary events in Ulster as elements of a timeless continuum they are rendered smaller, more manageable, bearable. It is a technique of assuagement, an effort to find the grounds for endurance and continuance. The realms of whisper are now located in the sucking mud of the bog, whose ancient messengers raised from darkness excite Heaney, speaking to him of a system of reality beyond and behind the visible world.

'The Tollund Man' opens by describing the Iron Age corpse which now 'reposes' in the museum at Aarhus. The details indicate the absorption of the man's pathetic mortality in the timeless processes of nature, their rhythmic organization possessing a narcotic quality which reinforces the 'gentleness', 'mildness' and 'repose' of his appearance, despite the tell-tale sign of the noose. A quiet, reflective wonderment imbues the lines, as the physical particulars are gradually gathered into the larger pattern of meaning: the man is 'Bridegroom to the goddess', the earth is both mother and lover, both fecund maternal principle and demanding lover. In part II the fate of the ancient victim sacrificed to the goddess is linked with that of contemporary victims of Ireland's Troubles whose lives have been sacrificed in the cause of Mother Ireland. Heaney would like to think that the promise of renewal which motivated the Iron Age sacrifice will apply to the Irish situation. The Tollund Man is more than merely a spiritual ancestor of the Irish dead. His union with the Earth Goddess has initiated a transfiguring process ('Those dark juices working/ Him to a saint's kept body') that is paralleled by his imaginative apotheosis effected through the ritual of art. He becomes a possible intercessor to whom the poet would pray to redeem his slaughtered countrymen. The recognition of wishfulness in 'I *could* risk blasphemy,/ Consecrate the cauldron bog/ Our holy ground . . .' (my italics) imparts a special urgency and tension. The long rambling sentence which follows from the words just quoted occupies the entire second part of the poem, but the auxiliary 'could', in 'could risk blasphemy', while still officially controlling the other verbs 'consecrate' and 'pray', acts with increasingly diminished force. It is as if the poet's need is being imaginatively fulfilled in the momentum of the poem's writing. That need takes charge of the second part of the poem as Heaney goes on to make germinate in his own imagination the image of the four young brothers who were victims of an ugly sectarian killing in the 1920s. The rituals of art and religion are closely connected in Heaney's mind, and the whole poem may be seen as an enaction of that pilgrimage to which he pledges himself in the first line: 'Some day I will go to Aarhus.' In language and feeling 'The Tollund Man' is devotional. 'When I wrote that poem', Heaney confirms, 'I had a sense of crossing a line really, that my whole being was involved in the sense of – the root sense – of religion, being bonded to something, being bound to do something. I felt it a vow . . .'.[14] He saw himself quite explicitly as devotee or pilgrim, remarking on 'My sense of occasion and almost awe as I vowed to go to pray to the Tollund Man and assist at his enshrined head.'[15]

The Tollund Man, as well as releasing profoundly religious feelings which for Heaney are connected with his apprehension of the Irish territorial numen and the curious fact of political martyrdom, is also embraced as a kind of ancestor who will perhaps offer the poet a revelation of artistic destiny. The wishfulness of this notion is again acknowledged: 'Something of his sad freedom/ As he rode the tumbril/ Should come to me' (my italics). The poet's bold, leap into a dark, mythic, timeless zone that is also the bog-like depths of self does make available some kind of 'sad freedom' from the contemporary horror. It represents an intellectual distancing of himself from the inchoate pieties that bind him unconditionally to a specific place and past and people. The ancient victim's last journey to his execution merges with the poet's imagined pilgrimage to Aarhus, and as Heaney moves through this psychic territory, chanting the place-names, seeing the people pointing at him but not understanding their tongue, his own complex relationship to the 'man-killing parishes' of Ulster gradually clarifies itself, and the poem reaches toward its climactic, starkly ambivalent recognition:

> Out there in Jutland
> In the old man-killing parishes
> I will feel lost,
> Unhappy and at home.

This tension between allegiance to 'our holy ground' with its sacrificial demands, and the claims of individual values which react against the barbarism of the sacrifice is where Heaney's most intense poetry is located. The discrepancy between communal consciousness and an outsider's sympathy with the victimized individual produces an anguished stance of indirection.

In the poems in Part Two of *Wintering Out* he focuses on personal situations, exploring the tensions which taint marriage, the strange unaccountable forces in life which confuse or pervert love, the hurt and derangement occasioned by social taboo and, beyond that, the cruel imperfections of the human condition itself.

The first poem, 'Wedding Day', begins with the simple statement: 'I am afraid.' It goes on to present the poet's confused emotions on his wedding day, his experience of an eerie sense of unreality, of grief pervading celebration, and remarks on his bride's demented fears. In the gents he comes across the banal popular emblem of romance, 'a skewered heart/ And a legend of love' – even it intimates violence and, in the word 'legend', the unreality of love's promise. But despite the inescapability of taint and vulnerability, the poem ends with an affirmation of simple faith, a gesture of trust and tenderness: 'Let me/ Sleep on your breast to the airport.' The use of the quatrain and the reluctance to stretch or distort its metrical rigidities too severely limit the variety of tunes the poet can play and inhibit the intimacy and complexity of his probing of pain. The form enforces the desire to cling to order and propriety in the face of confusion.

A much more accomplished piece of work, 'Summer Home', appears a few pages further on. Its complex music demonstrates an adventurous expansion of sensibility, an effort to achieve the maximum of individual and personal expression. Using a variety of stanza forms, Heaney stretches the structures and tactics of a rational, orderly conventionalized poetic to reveal intense and fugitive areas of feeling. The freer movement and more 'open' form implies that feeling has not been made to fit into pre-set patterns but that the form has been determined by the dynamics of the subject matter. We are admitted to a terrible privateness in which the movement of the poem is the writhing, anguished movement of consciousness. Discursive and logical language modulates into the invocatory, repetitive and intuitive structures of painful intimacy in which we hear, or rather overhear, the guilt and hurt of marital tension. The source of this pain, we realize, is 'the spirit that plagues us so' in 'A Northern Hoard' – an evil, unidentifiable force in the world which prevents love and pushes us toward self-destruction.

In 'Summer Home' it is a foul and bestial contagion in the 'possessed air'.

Smitten with knowledge of taint and pain, the poet's probing is conducted in an unconfident, querulous voice embodied in the wavering, meditative rhythms, the irregular rhyme and hovering half-rhymes ('summer' – 'sour' – 'somewhere' – 'wondered' – 'inquisitor' – 'air'). His discourse, unified by its olfactory and animal imagery, is, in its terms of reference – summer soured, wind off the dumps, 'something' in heat dogging the pair, fouled nest incubating 'somewhere', larval mat – generalized, oblique and deliberately vague. Part I works its way up to an explosive climax as the poet, proposing a symbolic ritual of self-purgation, vents his desperation in a poetry of the sheer present, a poetry which is, in the words of D. H. Lawrence, 'the insurgent naked throb of the instant moment'.[16]

Part II attempts a more mannerly, fluent movement:

> Bushing the door, my arms full
> of wild cherry and rhododenron,
> I hear her small lost weeping
> through the hall, that bells and hoarsens
> on my name, my name.
>
> O love, here is the blame.

The lines are haunted by a traditional iambic cadence, but their lyricism also depends on an intricately varied, individual and unpredictable musical organization of rhyme (internal as well as end-rhyme), pararhyme and verbal repetition. The long, heavily stressed syllables in the third line intensify pain and desolation, the caesura in the next creating the pause in which the woman's weeping suddenly becomes harsh and ugly, as if for the man's benefit once she is aware of his presence in the hall. Thus the poignancy of 'small lost weeping' becomes quickly inflamed by rancour and revulsion in 'bells and hoarsens'. These heavily-stressed verbs appropriate the emotional focus of the passage, along with the sounds – the forceful *b*, liquid *l*, resonant *r* and the long straining vowels – which had expressed the poet's initial blustering vigour as he approached with a show of confidence, bearing his peace-offering. The isolated last line can direct us forwards to the lesson in love's 'taint' which follows, or backwards – a possibility which is pointed by the 'name' – 'blame' end-rhyme – thus suggesting the poet's awareness that it may be some ineradicable thing about himself that is the cause of pain.

The remainder of the second part takes the form of a meditation on the possibility of ritual healing. The poet's exhortation that he and his wife compose a May altar out of the 'loosened flowers' of their relationship is complicated by recognition of nature's evanescence. Instead, the blooms might more appropriately form a 'sweet chrism' containing the holy unction of their own mortality. The poet is looking for a structure of feeling and a code of practice which will, through required ritual observance, magically bring about a harmonious order out of existence and guarantee love's mystery. Part II ends with the ritual summons: 'Attend. Anoint the wound.'

The liturgical afflatus is abraded and overthrown by the harsh, colloquial irony of the first lines of part III: 'O we tented the wound all right.' Further deflating the high style of ritual confidence is the brutal image of the two of them lying as if winded by the flat of a blade. But watching his wife in the shower, the poet's cadences and vocabulary once again attune themselves to a liturgical music: 'as you bend in the shower/ water lives down the tilting stoups of your breasts'. This is the poet as postulant, struggling to reassert a sexual piety, longing for benediction to offset human imperfection.

Part IV is composed of short, strong pulsations and an imagery of phallic penetration and natural growth, through which the poet seeks to affirm renewed intimacy. The process is 'unmusical' and violent, but contains the possible engendering moment of more honest confrontation. Once again they 'sap' the worn, 'white' path to the heart, 'white' suggesting purity of motive, 'sap' alluding both to the regenerative sources from which the couple, like the maize and vine, draw strength, and, in its other sense of excavate, to the hard work involved to re-open the submerged, blocked channels of love. The short line, 'we sap', is the critical moment of effort and renewal, and leads to the restoration of movement and direction in the longer, though still rhythmically tense, closing two lines of the section.

The tidal ebb and flow which characterizes the poem's structure returns the poet at the beginning of part V to rancour and unease. But the poem does not end until some source of hope and healing has been found. The natural world 'attends' upon them, proclaiming the promise of nurture and fulfilment. In the dark depths of being there survives the possibility – fragile and unconfident though it may be – of love and harmony:

> Yesterday rocks sang when we tapped
> Stalactites in the cave's old, dripping dark –
> Our love calls tiny as a tuning fork.

The ritual affirmation requires none of the extravagant liturgical diction used earlier. After all the metrical strain and uneasiness of the rest of the poem, the poet ultimately contains his hopeful intuition in a quiet, attentive iambic pentameter. Love and lyric ('rocks sang', 'Our love calls tiny as a tuning fork') are modes of resisting the dark.

In 'Shore Woman' marital tension is explored, as in 'The Wife's Tale', through the form of a Frostian dramatic monologue, from the point of view of the woman, and in such a way that the poem becomes an emblem of the opposition between the masculine and feminine principles in life. The epigraph, 'Man to the hills, women to the shore', grounds the poem in the countryman's stock of proverbial wisdom, as many of Frost's poems are grounded in some piece of local knowledge, some small event or folk tale. But in the work of both poets this sense of community, this primitive level of myth-making, is combined with a subtlety of insight beyond the reach of any crudely populist consciousness. The poetry of 'Shore Woman' results from a highly disciplined casualness of tone which comes under increasing pressure to accommodate the barely contained panic; a remarkable actuality of detail developed with delicately allusive logic; and a sophisticated blend of observation and reminiscence, realism and fancy, as the poem moves with assurance from mood to mood, image to image, thought to thought. Devotion to both craft and technique produces a rich texture of sound and meaning – not so passionate and exciting perhaps as that of 'Summer Home' – but one that is finely attuned to the working of this particular mind; the complex drama of a single life, continually revealing itself in its concrete quality, never reduced to a mere interplay of ideas, exemplifying and developing Heaney's sexual myth.

The poem begins with the woman walking along the firm margin between the 'riddling' dunes and the far rocks where 'a pale sud comes and goes'. Here is a severely delimited, phantasmal realm, haunted by suffering and death, and bathed in the light of the moon, the deranging influence of which is suggested in the metaphorical extravagance of the description of the moonlit shore.

In the next section the rhythm and diction are more forceful, as the woman remembers a frightening experience at sea when she

accompanied her husband on a night's fishing. What remains with
her is the memory of the man's absorption, his silence and his skill.
She thinks of her own ignorance of potential danger, registers her
own giddy insouciance: 'He was all business in the stern. I called/
"This is so easy that it's hardly right."' This sense of the drama of
the situation co-exists with an oblique and covert expression as the
fearful moment approaches: they drift 'out beyond the head' – they
have left the safety of the shore and are moving into a symbolic and
psychic realm of hidden terror where the tensions between them are
most strongly focussed. The woman says she is 'conscious' of what
is happening, but her language itself has hidden depths in which we
recognize her unwillingness to confront the full implications of the
situation: drifting beyond the head is drifting beyond rational
control, the drifting apart of their marriage.

In the deep waters they encounter a school of porpoises:

> I saw the porpoises' thick backs
> Cartwheeling like the flywheels of the tide,
> Soapy and shining . . .
> Tight viscous muscle, hooped from tail to snout.

The porpoises are the metaphorical embodiment of a dark, instinc-
tual power lying in the submerged depths. Their relentless physical-
ity, their slimy, secret, absorbing life, like the frogs in the flax-dam
or the eels in Lough Neagh, threaten to engulf and destroy. Insofar
as she associates them with brute male sexuality, they are a
projection of the way the woman perceives her husband. Then
comes the critical moment – the memory of the dunt and slither of
the porpoises against the bottom of the boat. The poem's formal
decorum is pushed to its limit so that we experience at one and the
same time the tense effort to contain and control, and the yawing,
violent rhythms of terror and nausea.

The woman turns to her husband and asks him to return to shore
but he, his 'machismo' awakened, is only interested in pursuing the
physical challenge, and disregards the woman's feelings. He enjoys
an attitude of superiority for, as in 'The Wife's Tale', the poem's
central incident belongs to the male domain. The woman is an
outsider, she has no experience of the routines of fishing; indeed,
according to tradition, it is bad luck for a woman to be in the fishing
boat at all. By allowing her to be there the man defies superstitious
belief. When the woman tells him the porpoises will attack a boat, he

scathingly dismisses her pronouncement as a yarn that has fooled her people far too long. The reference to the woman's people further heightens their separateness, implying a basic tribal distinction between them. Brutally, he refuses her the comfort and understanding she needs. The sea which she finds alien and hateful belongs to him, and its intractibility is reflected in the husband's attitude. The last part of the poem returns to the woman walking the shore:

> I sometimes walk this strand for thanksgiving
> Or maybe to get away from him
> Skittering his spit across the stove.

Her hatred and revulsion surface with a sudden and explicit virulence. The man offends her sensitivity and her piety. Solitariness is a price she is glad to pay for peace and safety. The shore is her 'fallow avenue', the phrase suggesting rest and renewal, and also something with definite direction, something civilized and therefore safe. Counterpointing this faith, however, is the haunting, half-acknowledged awareness of the continued presence of death and danger. She remarks on the shelving sand and notices the abandoned relics of what once were living organisms lying like 'debris' along the shore. More gross and threatening tokens of horror – the gasping carcasses of whales – can be managed for they belong to the realm of hear-say and yarn, to which she and her people are said to be too susceptible. On the shore she feels she has 'rights', but the effort to convince herself of safety and direction is undermined by acknowledgement that she is 'Astray upon a debris of scrubbed shells.' She is anxious to maintain a careful distance from those encompassing forces which threaten destruction, and which she perceives in the 'parched dunes' (spiritlessness, exhaustion, deadness) and 'salivating wave' (bestial, voracious appetite). She is 'a membrane between moonlight and my shadow' – an image of the woman's fragile, marginal existence between madness and death.

In the remaining poems of *Wintering Out* Heaney continues his meditation on the pain and hurt of life. The poems are based firmly on local, rural incident, but continually gesture toward archetypal significance and a perspective of cosmic emptiness. The first three, 'A Winter's Tale', 'Maighdean Mara' and 'Limbo' are about women, 'Bye-Child' is about a child, and 'First Calf' uses the imagery of animal life as an emblem of universal, psychic life. In all of them there is a tender regard for the lost, the outsider, for the deranged, the rejected and the alienated. The tone is elegiac, unsentimentally bleak and desolating.

In 'A Winter's Tale' a young girl, weeping and blood-stained, is suddenly illuminated by a car's headlights on a country road. She is a 'maiden daughter' who roams naked through the countryside at night, often to be found by neighbours, when they return home, lying sleeping by their hearths. The girl's appearance is regarded as good luck, and neighbours are kindly and solicitous towards her. In the course of the poem she accrues larger significance – as an Ulster Perdita, a kind of Vestal Virgin or elemental spirit of the hearth, a female Sweeney fleeing the containments and conventions of civilization, a nature spirit who awakened 'as from a winter/Sleep. Smiled. Uncradled her breasts'. The poem's strength is that these larger implications do not distract from the girl's primary physical actuality which elicits tender concern from family and neighbours and is firmly set amid the realistic detail of 'lanterns, torches/ And the searchers' gay babble'.

'Maighdean Mara' is also a subtle blend of realism and symbolism. It opens with a mesmeric, elegiac but realistically detailed image of what appears to be an actual drowned girl. Her cold breasts are 'dandled by undertow', her hair is 'lifted and laid', sea wracks are 'cast about shin and thigh'. Through the slow, dignified sway of the language and the delicate loveliness of the imagery, the horror of death is dispelled, appropriated by the poet's transfiguring, aestheticizing impulse. The real girl merges with the legendary mermaid who had to leave the sea and marry the man who stole her magic garment, suffer love-making and motherhood, before retrieving her garment and returning to the sea. The legend follows the archetypal pattern of entry into the suffering of human existence, which is endured until eventual release and return to the source. The notion of 'homecoming' offers a form of assuagement in the face of death's inevitability. The poem ends by repeating the lines with which it began thus enacting the legend's cyclical pattern.

The very fine 'Limbo' presents a picture of an unregenerate world. The social order is reductive, authoritarian and responsible for the corruption or denial of natural human feeling; the private life is speculative, repressed and infinitely sad; the natural world and, beyond that, the whole cosmic order, are cold and dead. Consequently, all creation is condemned to a state of inescapable and perpetual limbo.

The poem opens with a precisely defined time and place,

announcing with documentary bluntness that last night fishermen at Ballyshannon found the drowned body of an illegitimate infant in their nets. This is the mode of social discourse. It takes the form of a broadcast, its prime function is utilitarian – to inform; it works by assertive statement, it assumes an audience, and above all it is reductively objective.

The pivotal 'But I'm sure/ As she stood in the shallows . . .' moves us from objective to subjective, from the anonymous to the personal, from public world to private feeling, and from statement to speculation. Focusing on the mother's action, the speaker's language dispels horror and accusation. We concentrate on the mother's pain which is placed against a natural world that is also 'dead'. Ironically, the infant, with his hooks tearing her open, becomes the instrument of her 'death', an idea implying a level of abstraction and play of mind that take us further from the empiricist kind of truth. 'But I'm sure' points the contrast between the opening section which asks to be taken as disinterested, verifiable truth and what follows, which attempts to penetrate the empirical facts, addressing meanings that can only be imaginatively or intuitively apprehended, and which does not try to hide its status as interpretative gesture, even while laying claims to certainty.

The fourth stanza is a continuation of the imaginative re-construction, now seeking to understand the mother's action in a broader social context and gathering to itself the authority of definitive statement as the initial acknowledgement of subjectivism ('But I'm sure . . .') loses force. It is less intimate and more abstract, the shift in the speaker's perspective signalled by the retrospect within a retrospect – the doubling back to re-focus on the point where the woman first enters the water.

'She waded in under/ The sign of her cross' and 'He was hauled in with the fishes' is a conspicuous, localized instance of the poem's ruling structure of parallelism and antithesis. In the first sentence the active voice signifies choice as opposed to the passivity of the second sentence, where the infant is completely in the hands of the fishermen (the social order). But the mother's choice is illusory since social taboo deriving from religious pressure is the main deter-minant of her action. 'In' has two different points of reference: the child is hauled into the safety of the boat, but the salvation afforded by the social order (and the religious order insofar as the fishermen are associated with Christ's 'fishers of men') is cold comfort indeed since it is helpless in the face of death; the mother leaves the safety of the social world and wades into the sea, performing there an action which, we come to see, confirms a human condition of unalterable and absolute degeneracy. 'Under' in the first sentence suggests both subjection and protection; 'with' in the second indicates a more neutral relationship, an association devoid of the mother's hierarchical structure which demands subjection and affords protection: the infant's situation is starkly primordial – he is now one of the fishes. But, despite the mother's ostensible order of signs and symbols and hierarchical structure, that (social and religious) order is eventually revealed as factitious and invalid: both mother and child are, from the very start, lost souls. That her monstrous crime against Life should still elicit our sympathy is a measure of the pathetic absurdity of human existence.

Acting 'under/ The sign of her cross', it is as if her religion initiates and endorses what she does. She is fulfilling a ritual sacrifice at the cost of her own humanity and all natural feeling. In turning to the sea, the eternal mystery, her only framework of address is that provided by her religion. Wading in 'under/ The sign of her cross' suggests the extreme delimiting, formalizing operation of the Christian *disciplina* which seeks to codify and control the vast mystery of the sea. 'Her cross' (as opposed to 'the cross') indicates personal appropriation. If 'under' refers to her subjection by her religion, 'her cross' implies her subjection of religion to her own need. The cross loses something of its original and universal meaning, it is subjectivized, and the view is reinforced that religion, far from being a body of inviolate truth, in instead a structure of belief constructed according to human need.

Allusion to the cross sets up the anticipation of salvation and, indeed, in the next line we read of the infant being fished out of the sea. Salvation, however, is of the most minimal kind since the infant is already dead; and, as the poem sweeps on to its climax, its ultimate statement is that there is no redemption for the soul. The mother's action, even though we have been led to view it sympathetically, is what contradicts the possibility of redemption. Her action is causative: 'Now limbo will be/ A cold glitter of souls . . .' 'Now' indicates an economy of cause and effect. The Christian myth is re-written in the light of actual human nature and actual human action. 'Now' also displaces the concept of limbo as a state existing outside time. Heaney goes on to re-locate and re-define it within a discourse that at least started off as frankly speculative, but, by shaking itself free of the qualifying 'But I'm sure . . .', strains toward unequivocal certainty. Within this discourse the refurbished concept of limbo itself occupies a 'limbo' position somewhere between self-confessed speculation and incontestible truth. Such relativity, the poem demonstrates, is the inescapable condition of all meaning.

Redemption and transcendence of the Christian kind are refuted in the face of an existence which in every way denies them: they are themselves the conceptual products of that existence, framed in unregeneracy. The eternal is predicted on the temporal, a continuity which is expressed in the description of limbo as 'some far briny zone', figuratively composed of the same element as that in which the mother drowned her child. The denial of transcendence demands that the paraphanalia of the Christian myth are de-spiritualized and de-mystified. Hence, there are fishers of men in the poem, but only in the most literal sense; Christ bears his stigmata, but they have no miraculously healing powers; 'her cross' refers to a debased and commonplace 'Passion' – the woman's suffering – and only ironically alludes to the symbol of Christ's redemptive sacrifice as the 'transcendental signifier'.

The 'transcendental signifier' as the term is used by post-structuralists such as Derrida and Lacan implies the possibility of indivisible identity, unequivocal meaning and final truth. The 'transcendental signifier' is the sign which provides the key to all other signs, the 'transcendental signified' the idea, intention or referent to which all signs are subservient and can be seen to point. The post-structuralist critique (part of the larger intellectual effort sponsored by Marx, Nietzsche and Heidegger to extirpate the last vestiges of idealism from western thought) challenges society's 'logocentric' belief in some ultimate 'word', essence, idea, reality which will constitute the grounds of all our thought, language and experience. The notion of a final truth, it is argued, is illusory since it depends on the system of thought and language it is supposed to legitimize. All signification is merely an insistent, endless chain in which the signs have meaning only by virtue of their difference from other signs. There is no necessary correspondence between mind and world, or even between mind and meaning. Transcendental meaning is a fiction.

Heaney reflects the contemporary scepticism, but resists its most far-reaching and radical conclusions. Limbo is a powerfully sugges-tive metaphor for the post-structuralist condition of meaning as a constant flickering of presence and absence, continually eluding the grasp of a full, self-present awareness. The poem itself is an ostensibly transgressive kind of writing in which Heaney's discursive practices may be seen to problematize the notion of fixed meaning and representation. At the same time as he conveys meaning, he indicates something of its relative, artificial status as well, thus hoping to persuade us that he is keeping his distance from an authoritarian or ideological view of the world. Yet, even while acknowledging the arbitrariness and instability of the elements out of which the poem is composed, he does not forgo the will to knowledge and mastery. He is still in quest of the 'transcendental signifier'. The poem as a total structure is in the end what we are asked to take as just that.

Heaney knows, and 'Limbo' shows, that meaning is the product of a particular system, not something that is neutral and natural. And the system on which Heaney ultimately bases his claims to knowledge is one that belongs to a totalizing order of thought, to the poet's own strong imagining, his own creative vision and will to expression and persuasion. The poem's final truth is the product of the complex interaction of its internal meanings and attitudes which, in themselves, are shown to constitute only partial or limited 'truths'. Heaney forces us to acknowledge the rhetorical basis of all 'truth' and, thus clearing a space for his own imagination, confronts a whole prior system of thought and belief, and subverts it through a reinterpretation of its own figurative structures. This reconstructive 'troping' simultaneously disguises and asserts his Romantic will to be self-begotten (a source of unease with Heaney as far back as 'Digging' and 'Follower'). And it is aware of its own liabilities, for it proceeds with sensitivity to the entire range of impulses relevant to the situation (not the suppression of some) and works to integrate all of them – concrete and abstract, subjective and objective, temporal and eternal – so that 'Limbo' can finally achieve its own kind of transcendence, momentary though it may be. The contradiction here, it might be argued, is that the poem rests on assumptions of a knowledge beyond reason and linked to the ineffable certitudes of faith, even while setting out to proclaim the absence or impossibility of these things in the limbo of life. But for Heaney, Art is, as it is not for many modern thinkers, a special, privileged category, wherein 'the limbo of lost words' (the phrase is from 'The Loaning' in *Field-Work*) can be at least momentarily redeemed.

'Bye-Child' concerns another illegitimate child, another reject, who has been confined in a henhouse. The poet is deeply touched by this prisoner of darkness, as he was by the Tollund Man. The image of the moon-faced child remains vividly with the poet, palpable proof of an inconceivable cruelty. It stirs dark fears which lie deep in his mind. Re-activating the earlier moon images, the poem concludes with a poignant description of the boy's removal from the centre of life and love and sanity, into a realm which defies words and all natural human feeling.

'First Calf' reworks the conventions of pastoral. A cow is grazing with characteristic bovine serenity, her calf is hard at her udder. But the first thing to catch the poet's attention is the afterbirth:

> The afterbirth strung on the hedge
> As if the wind smarted
> And streamed bloodshot tears.

The description is realistically vivid, but it is also used as an emblem which complicates the more fluent, euphonious image of nurture. 'The afterbirth strung on the hedge' emphasizes a raw brutishness which the harsh music of the next two lines helps to turn into an image of universal suffering. It is the boldness of the conceit which saves it from sentimentality. Only after these observations does the poet's attention shift to the cow and calf. Pain takes precedence over nurture in the poem's emotional priorities, a point further reinforced by the casual way in which the cow is introduced: 'Somewhere about the cow stands . . .'. The poem ends by returning to the afterbirth:

> The semaphores of hurt
> Swaddle and flap on a bush.

The onomatopaeic ugliness of the last line combines with 'swaddle''s more normal connotations of infant care and its associations with comfort and warmth, to encapsulate the ambivalence of the poet's vision. As always, the natural world is a complex system of signs requiring divination, a 'semaphore' which the poet must articulate.

Wintering Out concludes with a group of poems, mostly based on personal experience, in which Heaney considers the possibility of relief, rediscovery or illumination. 'Good-Night' is a fine, tightly-wrought little poem that makes its impact with a simple, sharply-rendered image. A door opens, 'an edged den of light/ Opens across the yard', the people coming out of the house step into the 'honeyed corridor', then walk off into darkness. The woman on the doorstep remains for a moment in the 'block of brightness', then re-enters the house, closes the door, 'And cancels everything behind her.'

'Fireside' also uses imagery of light and darkness. Around the fireside stories are exchanged about eerie goings-on under the moonlight. One story is about the lamping of fish, and in the atmosphere of heightened imaginative awareness, the poet, imagining himself swinging the moon-like beam of his flashlamp over the stream, suddenly wonders: 'Was that the beam/ buckling over an eddy or a gleam/ of the fabulous?' The real world permits only a fleeting, uncertain intuition of the fabulous: a voice interrupts his reverie bidding him to come to his senses and say good-night.

The concern to escape from rational confinement and experience the 'fabulous' (which is the essential impulse behind Heaney's use of the Tollund Man to explore the contemporary Ulster situation), the desire to protect the private vision against public pressure, becomes a matter of increasing urgency. For Heaney this involves renewing intimacy with nature. 'May' is a quest-poem of this kind, a paen to nature's invigorating, nurturing influence, which the poet longs to re-discover. There is a Hopkinsian lushness in his descriptions:

> Wading green stems, lugs of leaf
> That untangle and bruise
> (Their tiny gushers of juice) . . .

The imagery betrays too great a straining after effect: 'My toecaps sparkle now/ Over the soft fontanel/ Of Ireland'; the desire for union with nature leads to prosaic and sentimental excess: 'I should wear/ Hide shoes, the hair next my skin,/ For walking this ground.'

'Dawn' speaks of the need to 'get away out by myself' – the phrase resonating into the line in 'Casualty', one of the poems in *Field-Work*, where he discovers 'a rhythm/Working you, slow mile by mile,/Into your proper haunt/Somewhere, well out, beyond . . .'. Getting away out, as Heaney explains in the short poem 'Travel', is a quest for psychic release, an effort to transcend routine responsibility, to discover the means to cope with violence and aftermath. In 'Dawn' he is motoring through a town in early morning. The physical world reveals itself as hard, nervous, cacaphonous. Human reason is reduced to a 'tut-tutting colloquy' of pigeons. Everything is dead and empty. There is a 'pompeian silence'. The poet eventually manages to get 'away out by myself', but once on the beach and walking over the cockles and winkles, is suddenly forced into the paralyzing recognition of his own destructiveness: 'Unable to move without crunching/Acres of their crisp delicate turrets.'

In 'Westering', the last poem in the collection, we see that though the poet may be 'away out' in California, sitting under Rand McNally's 'Official Map of the Moon', his imagination is still bound to Ireland. In the space of eight lines he is back in Ireland, recalling his last night in Donegal, in particular the moonlight. What he remembers is the ghostly illumination of his own mortality, and an acute feeling of drifting and emptiness. It is as if Ireland endures the empty stillness and 'falling light' of a continual Good Friday, her people 'bent/ To the studded crucifix', bowed in a posture of perpetual supplication.

At the end, the moon and Ireland merge in imagination:

> Under the moon's stigmata

> Six thousand miles away,
> I imagine untroubled dust,
> A loosening gravity,
> Christ weighing by his hands.

The 'untroubled dust' and 'loosening gravity' are obvious lunar characteristics. The former is an image of desolation (lunar dust that has never been troubled); but also, through its association with the stillness of the Irish town the poet passes through on Good Friday, when everyone is at Mass, it suggests a projected fantasy of a redeemed and peaceful world (terrestrial dust that is no longer troubled). 'Loosening gravity' is ambiguous too. It is connected with the congregation's shedding its burden of guilt and sin, intimated earlier in, 'What nails dropped out that hour?; but it may also refer to a condition of diminished faith, in which case we are given the picture of a society of ritual pretensions but no true centre of spiritual gravity – an ironic image of the communicants' readiness for revelation. All these ambiguities and possibilities are focussed in the last line which brings the poem to its climax by concentrating our attention on the Christian symbol of universal redemption. Significantly, however, the poem refuses to take us beyond Christ Crucified to Christ Risen. We are required to make a connection between Christ's supposedly redemptive stigmata and the dead moon's pitted surface: the whole poem is composed, both literally and metaphorically, 'Under the moon's stigmata'. The earth-bound rituals of deliverance take place within a larger context of cosmic emptiness.

What makes 'Westering' such a subtly and powerfully compelling poem is the fact that its composition is not simply a matter of local materials being illuminated by cosmic perspectives, but rather of internally consistent local material being used to develop a vision of universal application. The poem is characteristic of Heaney's poetic attitude: he does not argue with or attempt to explain the human situation, nor does he subordinate to any specific doctrine his sad longing for an ideal real enough to encompass and transform his experience. Rather, he relies on the momentum and coherence of the creative act itself. Within the poem, a whole set of conflicts which are felt to be insoluble in ordinary life – between subject and object, the universal and the particular, the sensuous and the conceptual, material and spiritual, order and spontaneity – are magically resolved.

The bleak vision which *Wintering Out* has been working towards is a vision of a world beyond redemption, of 'damnation on this earth',[17] as Laforgue described the Baudelairean vision. We can see why one of Heaney's crucial symbols in later work should be Dante's pictured prisoners in the antechamber of Hell, worthy of neither blame nor praise. In releasing his dark, subversive, inward self and exploring a deranged world which, like Eliot's, is 'held in lunar synthesis',[18] Heaney is still seen to be struggling to keep in touch with the springs of joy and vitality. His vision of emptiness is counterpointed by an effort to establish vital continuities with whatever in the past is myth-making, wonder-contemplating and strength-giving, and to discover widened, fresher meanings that can be brought to us through heightened sense-alertness. To validate these findings, there is his faith in the creative alchemy whereby general ideas or feelings are taken, transmuted into aspects of the poet's personality and subjected to the determining influence of his artistic sensibility which makes poetic speech normative – something that at once reveals unregeneracy and the vast richness that is available to us, and thus suggests an ideal.

Hopkins, for whom Heaney had such affection and admiration, regarded composition as a compliance with the will of God, an enactment of the beauty of God's creation, an imitation of Christ, a sign of Grace. Unquestioning faith was the premise of his poetry. Without this external, absolute, validating point of reference,

Heaney's essentially religious sensibility, his longing for transcend-
ence and assuagement, relies – like Yeats's – on the mediation of art
itself. Heaney's faith is in the 'religion of art' allied with a belief in
that other great concept of the nineteenth century post-Romantic,
the 'life-force'. His poetry is a demonstration of Walter Pater's view
that poets desired mainly to bring to life 'a beauty born of unlikely
elements, by a profound alchemy, by a difficult initiation, by the
charm which wrings it even out of terrible things'.[19] Heaney's
fundamental artistic principle is taken from Yeats which Yeats
himself had learnt from Blake:

> Argument, theory, erudition, observation, are merely what Blake
> called "little devils who fought for themselves," illusions of our
> visible passing life, who must be made to serve the moods, or we
> have no part in eternity. Everything that can be seen, touched,
> measured, explained, understood, argued over, is to the imagina-
> tive artist nothing more than a means . . .[20]

This aesthetic liberated Heaney, as it liberated Yeats, from the
bonds of dogma and agnosticism simultaneously by reducing both
to subordinate status in an aesthetically created universe of sym-
bols. It involves placing his art and its motives beyond the reach of
literal-minded morality. It allows him to assert the beauty and
preciousness of life in the teeth of the worst it has to offer. In the
work to follow, however, this is an ideal which Heaney becomes
more and more conscious of as being also an ideological enterprise.
If the old religious ideologies have lost their force and he, like a kind
of Hibernian Arnold, is proposing a more subtle communication of
moral values, one which does not argue openly nor relay beliefs
directly, but which works by concrete enactment rather than
rebarbative abstraction, by sensitive concern with the oblique,
nuanced particulars of human experience – then is not the preoccu-
pation with timeless truths not merely a form of distraction from
immediate commitments? In time of war, how responsible is it of the
poet to cling to the notion of art as a pacifying, assuaging influence,
fostering meekness, self-sacrifice and the contemplative inner life?

4

North

For the Irish writer who, traditionally, has been conscious of political and cultural pressures on creativity – and especially on the Irish writer writing in the middle of a war situation – it takes a remarkably honest, fearless cast of mind to avoid becoming a mouthpiece for opinion and dogma, and sounding hysterical or didactic or narrow-minded. Yeats had warned against the tendency: 'a poet sings in uncertainty', poets 'have no gifts to set a statesman right'.[1] The great thing is to be able to maintain a stance of 'Negative Capability':[2] 'The only means of strengthening one's intellect', Keats urged, 'is to make up one's own mind about nothing – to let the mind be a thoroughfare for all thought, not a select party. All the stubborn arguers you meet with are of the same brood. They never begin upon a subject they have not preresolved on.'[3] But if the 'irritable reaching after fact and reason' is one extreme, there is an opposite temptation. That is to exploit a situation of brutal factionalism for a kind of aestheticism which the poet indulges in for its own sake and without committing himself. Confusion and contradiction, mystery, doubt and uncertainty, can be employed to avoid responsibility.

In the poems in *North* there are times when Heaney succumbs to both these temptations. There are times when the irritable reaching after fact and reason, quite understandable in the teeth of Ulster's horror, is momentarily countenanced as more valuable than the autonomous imagination. And there are times when he succumbs to the attractions of luxurious indolence, when we feel the need for activity, for effort and energy. It is then we feel that sensibility is not fused with intellect and the moral sense. Lacking the discipline of 'high seriousness', the poetry, as Terence Brown has remarked, betrays the poet's indirection and passivity, revealing an abnegation of choice, a quiet acceptance before the goddess.[4] The best poems in the volume are those where Heaney is strict with himself, where the elements out of which a poem is composed are subsumed within the purely aesthetic, impersonal design of art and its source in the 'life-force'. These poems demonstrate a faith in art as man's chief consolation, the prime carrier of tradition, ancestry, civilization and meaning, the tireless opponent of chaos. Political unrest and the daily massacre in Ulster, the more general challenge offered to ancient pieties by the modern world, the claims of the emerging self – Heaney surrenders to all these elements as the infinitely rich resource they are; they enter his imagination and are absorbed and transmuted into the symbolic structure of his poetry. His particular brand of alchemy does not necessitate a radical experimentalism, of the kind which marks the work of many of his American contemporaries with whom he came in contact when he was a visiting professor at Berkeley in 1970–71. Instead, like Yeats, he endeavours to investigate the tradition within which he wrote.

In his poetry after *Death of a Naturalist* there is a growing unease within the culture, a broadening of the fecund world of the free self and, with the concern to place it in relation to the past, an effort to affirm a communal consciousness. The incantatory rhythms and the sensuous language of glut in the early poems gave to their combination of sensation, sexuality and violence an aesthetizing, anaesthetizing luxuriance. The sense of loss often comes across as more self-indulgent than painful. But with the politicization of terrain and sensibility that began in *Wintering Out* – a process in which the relationship between self and communal experience becomes an integral part of his apprehension of universal experience – he opened up the potential for a wider and at the same time more acutely felt pain of loss. And with a more finely tuned alertness to the subtle implications of sound and rhythm, we are more strongly conscious of the poet willing his own survival.

In *Wintering Out* he began the search for a metaphor for Ireland. Ireland is mother and bride, territorial numen and poetic muse. He subjects himself to and rises above the demands of his time through the mutually illuminating interplay of local material and what Michael Allen calls 'specific ironic vantage-points'.[5] By projecting his feelings into sympathetic rapport with other peoples and times he allows freer play of mind, will and sensibility. By freeing himself from all ready-made systems of thought and belief, and facing into the mysterious depths of self, he risks engulfment by all that we protect ourselves from feeling too intensely. By bringing the problems of life into his aesthetic orbit he seeks to transform them in a way which will reveal much more about our whole contemporary meaning then we ever thought possible.

In *North* there is an elaborate development of this strategy of

setting ancient situations, perceived with freshness and immediacy
and with a sensitivity to their disturbing and awe-inspiring mystery,
against contemporary situations. Suspicious of causes and ideal-
isms that will make a man false to himself ('You have to be true to
your own sensibility', he asserts in *Preoccupations*, 'for the faking of
feelings is a sin against the imagination'[6]), Heaney looks for
definitive images befitting our predicament. Hence his fascination
with Iron Age society, the Viking ethos and aesthetic, Icelandic
saga, ancient Celtic ritual and Catholic ritual. They provide him with
a proliferation of malleable images imbued with psychological and
ritual suggestiveness and, as he uses them, relatively free of set
doctrinal associations (it is to avoid sectarianism, for example, that
Catholic ritual is superceded by pre-Christian ritual in 'Funeral
Rites'). His images are often charged with the sexual principle, for
the mystery of sexuality is one of the ultimate sources of meaning.
Heaney's archetypes, cults and rituals are stylistic arrangements of
experience which help him, as Yeats was helped by his 'system', to
hold in a single thought the difficult reality of experience and the
justice of pure vision. They allow a kind of thinking that is free and
hypothetical, yet emphatic and concrete, and he is enabled thereby
to encompass great issues without being swamped by partisanship.
They provide him with points of reference that will not commit him
to any established religion, political system or philosophical school.
They are exotic themes and images – equivalents of Yeats's 'circus
animals' – which, because they are largely and primarily aesthetic,
allow him latitude of thought and statement. They help him to see
his own personality, and they provide valuable clues to the
unconscious life of mind and spirit. He strives for a 'sad freedom' by
insisting on the priority of instinct and emotion, the feminine and
kinship principles, the embodiment of spirit in the symbols of myth,
over the demands of society and over all logical and systematic
thought. However, the desire to evolve a comprehensive myth can
also harden into doctrine and dogma. Myth and ritual help him
toward freedom: the danger lies in becoming their creature. Where
Yeats never lost sight of the objectives of his 'system' and could use
it to speak fully out of his own nature, Heaney reveals himself to be
less flexible in the handling of particular symbols, less concerned
with re-exploring their implications, trying out this solution and
that, ready if need be to discount them entirely.

    These points can be illustrated easily enough by comparing 'The
Tollund Man' in *Wintering Out* with 'The Grauballe Man' in *North*. In
'The Grauballe Man' we find that the tentative, questing, dynamic

mode of the earlier poem has been replaced by something altogether more fixed and finalised. 'The Tollund Man' is composed in answer to a profound, urgent, personal need, indicated in the opening line where the poet pledges himself to a pilgrimage. What the ancient victim means to the poet is a matter of speculation, hypothesis and excited anticipation ('Some day I will go to Aarhus . . .'; 'I could risk blasphemy . . .'; 'Something of his sad freedom. . . . Should come to me'). The Tollund Man is summoned into existence in a probing way. In contrast, the later poem works through constant assertion and celebration of the Grauballe Man's existence. The opening line brings him incontrovertibly before us: 'As if he had been poured in tar/ he lies . . .'. The bulk of the poem is devoted to metaphorical description of the man in a way that tends to erase his human features altogether. He becomes an element of the bog. Similes and metaphors are strung together like solid, beautifully wrought, polished rosary beads. And what this highly figurative language and idolizing incantation does is to register an attitude of ritual obeisance. The whole poem is written in a spirit of tranquil contemplation, of arrival. The religious impulse in 'The Tollund Man' has been transmuted into doctrine and dogma. The dramatic tension of the earlier poem is missing. Reference to the man's 'slashed throat' momentarily reminds us of the horror, but this is quickly dispelled by merging once again man and bog in the image of 'the cured wound'.

There are two restorative, transfiguring forces at work – the bog itself, and the 'perfecting' memory of the poet (compare the use of this word in the early 'Poem'), which are equated in the poet's mind. The Grauballe Man is an object of beauty like the statue of the Dying Gaul, or else he is a human victim arousing pity. In the end the poet would appear to side with the 'victim/ slashed and dumped' rather than art. Life is 'too strictly compassed' in art; the poem's climactic gesture is a forceful, terse expression of life's undeniable horror (though the effect of the culminating image of the hooded victim is limited by its lack of precise, concrete particularity). Art would appear to lose out to life. But this is not what the poem itself enacts. It proclaims the victory of metaphor over actuality.

> Who will say "corpse"
> to his vivid cast?
> Who will say "body"
> to his opaque repose?

Certainly it is not something the poet says readily. The original motivation of the poem is to offer an image of 'beauty' pleading with 'rage', if possible to make them one in the poem's eternal moment, so that we can be carried beyond the desperate moment in which we face atrocity. But there is a literary quality about the poem's consolation which is a mark of its failure to achieve the 'Yeatsian thought' in which is reconciled the beauty of pure vision and the atrocity of real-life.

More extravagant still is the metamorphosing, metaphorical activity in 'Bog Queen'. The girl's dissolution, at first a vague, sinister horror ('My body was braille/ for the creeping influences'), becomes magnificent, marvellous, as she merges with nature's great processes. She is part of an impressive topology of glaciers, moraines, fjords and Baltic amber, the cycle of sun and seasons, the 'floe' of history. In contrast, the masculine human action is brutal and petty: she is 'robbed' of her hair, 'barbered/ and stripped' by a turfcutter's spade, and finally exhumed when the man is bribed by a neighbour's wife. The womb-like bog, which has tried to make good the abuse she has suffered from men ('The plait of my hair,/ a slimy birth-cord/ of bog, had been cut'), at last has to yield up its queen. After she is brought to the surface, re-born into the world of time, the poet's language subsides into a starker, barer idiom, almost as if he recognizes the artificiality of his own imaginative display earlier:

> and I rose from the dark,
> hacked bone, skull-ware,
> frayed stitches, tufts,
> small gleams on the bank.

Imaginative and mythic resourcefulness is dispelled in the moving simplicity of those closing lines.

There is little interest in developing the bog queen's mythical or emblematic function. There are a few gestures towards political allegory: this is the only corpse in Heaney's sequence of poems about the Bog People which had been excavated from Irish soil (probably a Viking found in 1781 on Lord Moira's estate in County Down),[7] and Heaney's description of the queen 'waiting/ between turf face and demesne wall' for the 'rising' in the last stanza may contain some glancing allusion to the emergence of the Irish Free State, once imbued with legendary charisma by the Revivalists, then having to make its way as a viable political entity in the real world of

international affairs. But these are no more than glancing refer-
ences. The poem, turning on a single, self-contained emblem,
sustains a cleanness of line and clarity of shape. Its theme is the
transfiguring power of the bog/consciousness. Heaney restricts
himself to the limited perceptions of the bog queen herself, and this
suggests a kind of avoidance of emotional complexity, a kind of
escapism – escape from the pack, from self, from thought – into
nature's soft textures of decay, the womb's dense mulches of
sensation, the 'realms of whisper' beyond and below the simplifica-
tions of the masculine intellect.

'Come to the Bower' is a further expression of the desire for escape
from the world, and for union with the timeless mystery of nature.
With spring water rising around her, the ancient female victim lies at
the very heart of the life-force, which has embraced and absorbed
death and violence. The poet's approach is sexual, voluptuous –
unhealthily necrophiliac in Blake Morrison's opinion.[8]

> My hands come, touched
> By sweetbriar and tangled vetch,
> Foraging past the burst gizzards
> Of coin-hoards
>
> To where the dark-bowered queen,
> Whom I unpin,
> Is waiting.

The voice speaking is intense with anticipation, hesitant, reveren-
tial, hushed. The lines move with a narcotic solemnity. The hard,
definite *d*'s, *t*'s, *b*'s and *p*'s brace and control the abundance and
luxury of the vowel music which is instinct with mysteries, rituals
and presences. The half-rhyme intimates an uneasy harmony,
something incompletely grasped, that the post strives to conjure
into fuller possession in the last stanza:

> I reach past
> The riverbed's washed
> Dream of gold to the bullion
> Of her Venus bone.

He strives to consummate his loving intercourse with the past, the
land, Ireland, and the effort is enacted in the increasing length and

strenuous, undulating rhythms of the lines. A variety of musical effcts produces greater intensity and resonance of sound: the collocation of long, fully-sounded *e*'s in 'dream' and 'Venus', the *o*'s in 'gold' and 'bone', and the forceful, culminating half-rhyme of 'bullion' and 'bone'. 'Bone' reiterates the straining *n* sound in 'Venus', and with 'bullion' the poet not only plays on the word's normal semantic associations with 'gold', but uses the repetition of the *l* sound in the two words for his own specific, intensifying purposes. In this way the grandiloquent vagueness of 'Dream of gold' modulates into the more specifically and concretely defined imagery of 'bullion/ Of her Venus bone'.

Another poem is entitled 'Bone Dreams'. The title quite frankly indicates detachment from reality and the poet's passive surrender to a process of free association. The white bone found on summer grazing is abruptly transfigured into a miniature Viking ship-burial. The Viking connection directs the poet's attention to England. The poem follows the bone through the trajectory of English linguistic and literary history. Part II begins by sounding the word 'bone-house', then proceeds to trace it back until he comes to the Anglo-Saxon 'ban-hus'. 'Ban-hus' is the human body, and as Heaney savours the word, it evokes the whole ethos of Anglo-Saxon England. 'Ban-hus' is also the necropolis in the bog, which the poet contemplates with a quasi-sexual, quasi-mystical desire to 'ossify' himself by gazing. Part VI is a much more delicately precise little poem about a dead mole he found in a Devon field. Touching it, he 'touched small distant Pennines/ a pelt of grass and grain/ running South'.

Heaney is engaged in plumbing the sensed world, aspiring to the Wordsworthian 'mind sustained/ By recognitions of transcendent power,/ In sense conducting to ideal form,/ In soul of more than mortal privilege'. The 'pondering' that 'illiterate roots' perform in 'Bog Queen' is an exemplary communion and mergence with mystery, which the poet strives to approximate with words. Wordless, like Heaney's revered craftsmen, the bog people are united with mud and they speak its primitive language of the senses. Their bodies are 'braille' for the creeping influences; the white bone on the grazing possesses the 'rough, porous/ language of touch'; in 'Kinship', a little further on in the book, he finds a turf spade buried in the moss and, raising it,

> the soft lips of the growth
> muttered and split . . .

Here, the bog also enunciates itself – its utterance as direct and unimpeded as a vowel – through the illiterate language of sense impression:

> This is the vowel of the earth
> dreaming its root
> in flowers and snow.

The word, however, is also a door into the dark. Even through language Heaney can make contact with the submerged part of his being. One link with the past, as he emphasizes in 'Bone Dreams', is philological. The residual influence of ancient grammars and declensions is like 'a skeleton/ in the tongue's/ old dungeons'. They still whisper dark secrets to the poet. But it is the bog which speaks most eloquently of 'all the realms of whisper' and remains his most potent central symbol, for it is older and more primitive than language ('Come back past/ philology and kennings . . .'). And in 'Bone Dreams' he once again seeks union with its primeval mystery:

> Soon my hands, on the sunken
> fosse of her spine
> move towards the passes . . .

This all sounds rather formulaic now though, curiously, it is a relationship with England, not Ireland, about which Heaney is writing, as the references to Hadrian's Wall and Maiden Castle indicate. The notion of tribal or national ancestry and feeling which is part of the root emotion in other poems about the Bog People is not a part of the mystery in 'Bone Dreams'.

In poems such as 'The Grauballe Man', 'Come to the Bower' and 'Bone Dreams' Heaney continues to work with the relationship between self and landscape, sexuality, language, Ireland and even England. But the terms of the relationship have already been defined and we miss the sense of complex discovery which was present in 'The Tollund Man'. 'The Tollund Man', born of a specific, personal situation, enacts a difficult, dynamic drama of process, in which the poet looks for ways to appropriate his central symbol. But 'The Grauballe Man', 'Come to the Bower' and 'Bone Dreams' tend to rely on a self-sufficient emblem and do not elicit the same excitement. The feeling is much less complicated. In 'Belderg' an ancient site is described as if it were a person, but the feeling is little more than one of archaeological wonderment at the 'congruence of lives' represented by the Irish, Planter and Norse 'growth rings'. We feel that the original motivation for researching into the past – to find emblems of adversity – has been subordinated to an antiquarian interest and a luxuriating, aestheticizing compulsion in which the emblems themselves count for more than what they can be made to mean. Though Heaney does not attempt to explore the myth deeply or develop it (as the similarity between the poems suggests), he attains some magnificent specific effects.

'Punishment', 'Kinship' and 'Strange Fruit' are more ambitious. They reveal a gradual mastery of the impulse merely to identify with, seduce or deify. There is a greater self-consciousness about adopting a posture of surrender or supplication, and a flexing of the masculine muscle of intelligence and will, as Heaney seeks to involve more of himself. The central symbol of the victim in the bog becomes the occasion of an anguished self-analysis. The poetic attitude is complicated, divided, guilt-ridden, self-critical, ironic.

In 'Punishment' the girl hanged and dumped in the bog for adultery is linked (through the reference to her 'shaved head' and 'tar-black face') with modern-day transgressors of the tribal code – Catholic girls who were tarred and feathered for fraternizing with British soldiers. Irish experience is abstracted from its historical and political context to participate in a timeless pattern of ever-recurring and inescapable conflicts. Of course, adultery and going out with British soldiers are not the same thing, but what matters to Heaney is that they are both forms of betrayal of the tribal pieties. The punishments incurred are not viewed as fundamentally moral or political acts but as ritual sacrifices demanded by the indigenous territorial numen. Heaney recognized that this idiom might seem remote from the 'agnostic world' of economic interest and political manoeuvring, but insisted that it is not at all remote from 'the bankrupt psychology and mythologies'[9] of Irishmen who perpetrate atrocity. Here we can see his rational, enlightened humanistic impulse, his desire for larger perspectives than those supplied by the atavisms of his own community. The myth-making sensibility is founded on the wish to overcome chaos, to bring order into the world, to organize phenomena into systems, to distil reality into pure form, not disguised or disfigured by the accidental: reality as the poetic essential. It is expressive of the desire for simplification, for 'understanding' and assuagement. In the suggestion that we are helpless victims of an indifferent deity, that violence such as this is natural and inevitable, we recognize the civilized mind's desire for consolation and absolution, for transcendence through mythic idealization.

'Punishment', however, is a fine example of the incubatory process Heaney called 'technique'. The poem does not rest on the ideas of the myth 'in themselves'. The impersonal claims of mythology are exposed to the pressures of private emotion which he sets out to present and to penetrate in their most irreducible aspects. He shows the relation between theory and experience, between the idea that has been preconceived, that is by its nature general and inclusive, and the tangle of feelings which, in their immediacy and closeness, substantially constitute human experience. He enters imaginatively into his mythic world and looks around, moves about in it, receiving signals from its denizens; he is inside events so that he is not presenting them objectively; he notes them; he is open to contradictory feelings, even more acutely unsure of himself and of what goes on around him than in 'The Tollund Man'. What all this indicates is the imaginative transmutation of the archetypal scheme he has appropriated into concrete experience, the meaning of which is created as he proceeds: the ideas and the words become one. The ideas that lie under or behind the poem are driven into a complex relation with the kinds of experience that resist reduction to formula. Poetically, what counts is not the pre-existing idea, but the activity of vital poetic thought which occurs when the idea is fused with feeling and sense perceptiveness, when the words richly unfold the meaning as it develops. In the end the poem refuses to be dogmatic about barbarism by the way it turns on a central image – the body in the bog – which, followed with strict integrity, forces the poet to shift the ground of his thought, and allows him to transcend the original motive of the poem.

'I can feel the tug/ of the halter at the nape/ of her neck', Heaney begins, stressing identification between poet and victim. By the time we are half-way through, however, a distance has opened between him and the murdered girl: 'I almost love you/ but would have cast, I know,/ the stones of silence.' As the poet takes in more of the situation – the tribal context, the contemporary parallel – the inadequacy of the initial artistic, love-making response to the 'archetype' is highlighted. There is a growing awareness of the difficulty of detaching aesthetics from morality. 'I am the artful voyeur . . .' registers his guilty feeling at having surrendered to a self-indulgent luxuriance (though the offending impulse persists in the description of the 'betraying sisters/ cauled in tar'). Simple

identification with the 'poor scapegoat' who has placed personal
drives above the demands of the tribe and suffered horribly as a
consequence is not possible. Heaney numbers himself with the
silent bystanders of cruelty and ends with reference to his mixed
feelings of 'civilized outrage' and 'understanding' of the tribal need
for it.

There was great mystery in the assuaging image of the 'bride-
groom' united with the goddess in a loving embrace to ensure
renewal. In having to re-work the original mythic scheme of 'The
Tollund Man' to accommodate a female victim who has defied the
tribe, the poet finds it impossible to maintain his role as postulant.
The victims in 'Punishment' cannot command the single-minded
adoration that the Tollund Man or the 'dark-bowered queen' could.
'Punishment' is a complex image embodying opposing elements: its
power lies in the internal tension generated from its ability to give
emotional weight and appreciation to these mutually contradictory
values. It represents the dilemma of the poet whose feelings cannot
easily lodge themselves in either pure aestheticism (the contempla-
tion of the free imagination), rational humanism ('civilized outrage')
or atavistic piety (instinctive understanding). 'At one minute,'
Heaney wrote in 1972, 'you are drawn towards the old vortex of
racial and religious instinct, at another time you seek the mean of
humane love and reason.'[10] And in a *Listener* article the year before,
he wrote of the pain such dividedness causes: 'I am fatigued by a
continuous adjudication between agony and injustice, swung at one
moment by the long tail of race and resentment, at another by the
more acceptable feelings of pity and terror.'[11]

'Kinship' also starts off by asserting unproblematic kinship with
the victim preserved in the bog:

> Kinned by hieroglyphic
> peat on a spreadfield
> to the strangled victim,
> the love-nest in the bracken,
>
> I step through origins . . .

The writing enacts the strain of coming to terms with the past. The
syntactical involution, the consonantal clogging, the priority of the
weight and sound of the words over their sense, demand of the
reader an act of interpretation, an effort of 'divining' the hiero-

glyphics. This exotic word, with the archaism 'kinned' on one side and the colloquial 'peat' on the other, emphasize the complexity of the poet's relation to his 'origins'. The bog requires intensive interpretation and yet it is commonplace. It is ordinary but also macabre; it is a mortuary and a 'love-nest'. The poet knows its frightening, ugly aspect, but treats it with relish, not abhorrence.

The next lines, however, give the identification between poet and victim a defeatedly ironic tone. Recognizing his separation from 'origins' which are, nevertheless, a source of renewal, the best he can hope for is that his experience of them can still take place on an instinctual, pre-conscious level, like the dog's turning on the mat, rather than be a merely purposeful, rationally-pursued quest. His stepping through origins is performed lovingly. It re-awakens his delight in physical sensation, which is all the stronger for his knowledge of the ground's barbaric secrets; and it draws him into the very heart of mystery. The bog is a fathomless, subconscious memory, arousing in the poet a suppliant joy and wonderment. He searches for terms to define it. He takes a primitive, childlike pleasure in playing with onomatopaeia: 'Quagmire, swamplands, morass.' There is no genteel avoidance of the bog's nameless ugly terrors – it is 'the slime kingdoms'. From this, the description modulates into a hieratic movement, where the asyndeton produces a chant-like effect. Probing beneath the physical surface and beneath the literal level of expression, Heaney indulges in a virtuoso metaphorical display in which the bog's contrarieties and mythic capabilities are explored. The direct assertion of the metaphors of stomach, pollen bin, casket, midden, earth-pantry, bone-vault, sun-bank, floe of history, enbalmer, insatiable bride, acquires for the poem a quality of energy and forthrightness; but we have also, in the abrupt displacement of one term by another, a sense of the mind racing, of metaphors endlessly substituting themselves for some direct, complete possession of the bog itself.

The sudden personal appropriation of the bog as 'outback of my mind' leads into the particularized, personal memory of part III. This section tells of the poet finding a turf spade in the moss. He raises it and, in an act of quasi-sexual penetration, thrusts it into the earth. To explore further his relation to the bog, a larger, more capable and more resonant device is required than that supplied by direct experience and personal reminiscence. The craving for the exotic transcendent, for something beyond the domestic resources, but which can yet be absorbed imaginatively, leads to the sudden,

emphatic, repeated intrusion of the anonymous third person plural
('. . . they have twinned', '. . . they raise up') into a discourse
controlled by the first person singular, and the mergence of the
poem's two major discursive modes, that of imaginative re-
construction and identification, and that of direct experience. The
poet's spade standing upright in the ground is 'twinned' by a more
mythically satisfying 'obelisk' – the oak-beam that marked the site of
an ancient sexual union of bog and man. A 'bearded cairn', another
symbol of male (this time patriarchal) authority that has stood over
the 'love-nest' for so long, is at last dislodged and forced to yield up
the female, subterranean secrets. Catkin and bog-cotton tremble as
if apprehensive at the apotheosis of the female principle of Ireland.
The poet approaches the mystery in a spirit of ceremonial reverence:

> I stand at the edge of centuries
> facing a goddess.

Beginning with a description of his own real-life action in the past
tense, the poet moves to a reconstruction of the scene of the body's
exhumation which, though a product of the imagination, loses none
of the immediacy or precision of the earlier first-hand experience,
for it is given present tense status, and comes to occupy the mind so
completely that by the end of the section time and timelessness
converge, and experience and imagination, action and mind, reality
and myth, are one.

Part IV, returning to a generalizing, reflective mode, thus begins
with the assertion that he has discovered a centre that holds and
spreads. This is the literal bog, it is also the bog as his central poetic
symbol, holding within its spread of meaning the paradox of life
itself ('sump and seedbed . . . and a melting grave'), all that has
gone to make the poet what he is:

> I grew out of all this
> like a weeping willow
> inclined to
> the appetites of gravity.

By articulating that maternity he enacts the inclination to the
appetites of gravity. The sources of his strength, like those of
Antaeus later in the book, lie in what he grew out of. The
construction of the stanza is a movement of growing and return. The

middle two lines are composed of high, front, closed and half-closed vowels and semi-vowels. They are in the middle and upper register. Then with the much shorter third line we have energy exhausted, held momentarily in suspension by the break in the phrase at the end of the line, before subsiding into the low, open *a*'s in 'appetites' and 'gravity', and regulated by the aggressive mastery of the plosives which restore the length of the line. In the course of this musical progression we shift from a subject to object emphasis, from the suggestion of aestheticized mortality ('weeping willow') to the heavier ambiguities of 'appetites' (connoting both nurture and insatiable demand) and 'gravity' (which is both an elemental principle of physical order and a suggestion of anxiety and death). The stanza exemplifies Heaney's method throughout Part I of *North* – the moving away to discover parallels and continuities and then, with their help, returning to accept his own, troubled heritage.

Having established his inheritance and his imaginative para- meters, the poet proceeds in part IV to 'deify' the ancient sacrificial victim, as he did the Tollund Man. This is a project of pure imagination, a 'growing out', a process of letting the mind expand and enjoy itself, before it complies with the reality principle, with the appetites of gravity, to produce the poem's final, dark medita- tion on the graves of the 'fearful dead', and the appetites of the goddess who 'swallows' the faithful, reclaiming them for her ruminant ground. Though this is the fate of his 'kinsman', Heaney first seeks to affirm beauty, pride and plenty in the shadow of death. The turf-cart the man rides might recall the tumbril that would have taken him to his place of execution (an image 'The Tollund Man' leaves us with), but this ominous suggestion is displaced by the reminder of the man's sexual desire and pride of life, implied in the association of the cart's tail-board with a cupid's bow and its cribs with lips. The cart-wheels are 'buried' in turf-mould, the mordant implications of 'buried' juxtaposed with the bog's plentiful nurture. The man is pictured at a time when summer 'died' and the fields were deserted, but again there is nothing sinister or desolating about this. The scene is an evocation of pastoral tinged with a romantic melancholy, against which the man's vigour, like the haws in the darkening hedges, stands out all the more strongly. This section is in the narrative mode, with a relaxed rhythm, and the containment of each narrative unit in a stanza produces a sense of order and power. At the centre is a buoyant, self-hypnotic, mystical identification between the man and the poet, a dream of freedom.

The man's robust, primitive nobility, his healthy physicality and sturdy independence, his practical skill (seen in the description of the tail-board, cribs and felloes, underlined in Heaney's adoption of the technical terms), the respect he commands from the rest of the community (he is saluted, given right-of-way) constitute Heaney's ideal of manhood. He has found in one of 'the faithful' whose blood is to merge with 'our mother ground' a spiritual ancestor. The celebratory intensity belongs to the same order of feeling that can be traced back to early poems like 'Follower'.

The structure of the whole poem is a process of opening and closing, which is the shifting, sucking movement of the bog itself, a version of the 'growing away' before succumbing to the appetites of gravity. 'Kinship' begins with the literal bog, the 'spreadfield'; this quickly generates a more and more elaborate play of mind until in part IV the mode of experiential reality is controlled entirely by the dynamics of imaginative projection. The last part of the poem, though its primary mode of discourse is still dream-like, incorporates a movement of reversal: the braking, demystifying action of personal realism. The glowing aura and inspired, exultant tone of the previous part, are replaced by a fatalistic stasis. The psychological mechanism has been triggered which moves the poem out into new dimensions. Part VI shows that there is another aspect of kinship which Heaney cannot elude. The poem dives suddenly into the heart of terror:

> And you, Tacitus,
> observe how I make my grove
> on an old crannog
> piled by the fearful dead.

A guttural, cacophonous music takes over as the poet accepts his kinship not only with romantic victim but barbaric tribe. The insistent first person plural emphasizes concern with tribal identity. And tribal identity can only be apprehended by considering the tribe in relation to the wider world. The goddess co-exists with another kind of power – the imperial legions who stare from the ramparts, indifferent to the immolation of the 'faithful' who lie gargling in the 'sacred heart' of the bog. The present continuous tense emphasizes the unalterable, timeless nature of this configuration. The directness and candour with which this part begins in its address to Tacitus leads to self-deprecating acknowledgement of perpetual defeat; and this, in turn, leads to a concluding statement of the basic horror of life, the primal reality of the insatiable goddess, which is set against the meanings discovered earlier in the poem. The tragic condition of man – the Baudeleirean 'damnation on this earth' – is thus encompassed in all its painfulness as well as potential for heroism – and accepted, as the poet urges Tacitus to accept it:

> report us fairly,
> how we slaughter
> for the common good . . .
> how the goddess swallows
> our love and terror.

Kinship does not simply inspire comfortable feelings of manliness and pride; it is also acceptance of a desolating heritage of brutality and defeat. In the poem, that elation is nurturing and assuaging: that burden is assumed in a spirit of self-deprecating bitterness and melancholic irony.

That Heaney himself felt uncomfortable about his obsession with the past and knew how easy it was for him to be seduced by it is seen in the sonnet 'Strange Fruit', and in his comment about the writing of the poem: '"Strange Fruit" had ended at first with a kind of reverence, and the voice that came in when I revised was a rebuke to the literary quality of that reverent emotion.'[12] The octave is a precise and carefully observed description of a girl corpse, with a tendency toward rather trifling absorption in 'lovely' effects: the girl's head is 'Pash of tallow, perishable treasure'. But the hammering directness of the closing lines dispels any luxuriating complacency:

> Murdered, forgotten, nameless, terrible
> Beheaded girl, outstaring axe
> And beatification, outstaring
> What had begun to feel like reverence.

The corpse rebukes the poet's inclination toward deification.

'Viking Dublin' also starts off with a display of the resourceful imagination, in this case playing over and animating a Viking trial piece. The trial piece is a 'cage' or 'trellis' in which to conjure. Its shape is like a child's tongue moving to his own calligraphy, it is like a writhing eel, a bill in flight, a nostril, the prow of a ship, a long sword, a worm of thought the poet follows into the mud. The poem is composed of fluid images and associations evoked by the line incised on the trial piece. Some of the connections are much too fractionally or arbitrarily achieved, as when Heaney invites us to see a longship's 'clinker-built hull/ spined and plosive/ as *Dublin'*. Since it is hard to see how his correspondences proliferate dynamically from any centre of deep emotional involvement, the poem tends to generate a cult of arbitrariness and self-indulgence. As in 'Bone Dreams', the poet stands in very self-conscious imaginative relation to his mythic territory:

> My words lick around
> cobbled quays, go hunting
> lightly as pampooties
> over the skull-capped ground.

At one point he suddenly pulls himself up short for his anthropological, archaeological and philological tendency. He caricatures himself as 'Hamlet the Dane,/ skull-handler, parablist,/ smeller of rot/ in the state, infused/ with its poisons,/ pinioned by ghosts/ and affections,/murders and pieties.' Like Hamlet, he is 'sicklied o'er with the pale cast of thought' which paralyzes will and stimulates guilt. The last poem in *North*, 'Exposure', returns to the agony of conscience, but in 'Viking Dublin' he proceeds with a glib defence of his morbid preoccupations as 'a coming to consciousness', and immediately resumes, with renewed vigour and confidence, his search for 'Old fathers'. (Heaney's apostrophe is an echo of Stephen Dedalus's call, 'Old fathers, old artificer, stand me now and ever in good stead'.[13] which had been a part of Joyce's effort to 'forge the uncreated conscience of the race',[14] through bringing the present into significant relation with the past.)

Heaney's ancestry is with

> neighbourly, scoretaking
> killers, haggers
> and hagglers, gombeen-men,
> hoarders of grudges and gain.

The effort here is to capture something of the stark outline and vitality of the Anglo-Saxon alliterative tradition. The alliterative terseness, scattered stop-sounds, the sharp breaks in movement forced by the punctuation and the short irregular lines, create an impression of life choked off from fruitful meaning, and channelled into bursts of violence. Ancestry does not register itself in any more profound way than through this cramped and artificial catalogue of shorthand abstraction. The consonantal forcefulness and constricting, short-lined quatrains are intended to provide the narrow, compacted drive, turning with the enjambment of line and stanza, that will enact the movement of a drill. But such passages lack subtlety and refinement. Instead of flexible soundings, we recognize the constraints and lack of variety imposed on the poetic attitudes by a rhythmic movement that has degenerated into mannerism. The short-lined, unrhymed quatrain traps the poetry into a uniformity of tone and a regularity of pattern, which give the reader no sense of a sharp distinction between one poem and another. The mood is limited to a vaguely melancholic nostalgia or solemnity, even when the feeling would naturally lead elsewhere. And not only is there this prevailing uniformity between many of the poems, but within a single poem Heaney rarely varies tone, pace and intensity in a way that quickens our attention.

We hear the familiar cadences in 'North' – and with no more success in generating interest, in combining the power of the eye, the sound of the words and a rhythmic excitement, to stir and satisfy us. 'North' begins with the poet searching for revelation as in 'The Tollund Man'. The longship's swimming tongue speaks, achieving a sweeping historical summary to prove its relevance as a theme for the poet. That history is a demoralizing catalogue of lust and feud. Once again Heaney relies on a vocabulary of paired abstractions (geography and trade, couplings and revenges, hatreds and behind-backs, lies and women), some with an archaic cast, rather than vivid images. The rhythmic and syntactic structure quickly becomes monotonous. A civilization is reduced to a litany, litany being one of the most extreme forms of repetitively uniform verse. It inhibits variety, excitement and subtlety. Heaney is writing in apparent disregard of the advice urged upon the poet in the last stanza:

> Keep your eye clear
> as the bleb of the icicle,
> trust the feel of what nubbed treasure
> your hands have known.

These lines stress the poet's need to remain faithful to his instinctive, sensuous intimacy with the world. They are also spoken by 'the

longship's swimming tongue', as part of the aesthetic it recom-
mends to complement its earlier assertion of an ethos of pettiness
and violence.

> It said, 'Lie down
> in the word-hoard, burrow
> the coil and gleam
> of your furrowed brain.
>
> Compose in darkness.
> Expect aurora borealis
> in the long foray
> but no cascade of light.

   The images reiterate the poet's concern with excavating the
hoards of history and language, probing the dark, secret depths of
nature and consciousness. Commit yourself to art, the longship
advises, but don't expect it to give you immediate solutions. There is
a restrained confidence in this kind of art, which contradicts the
avowed uselessness of the poet in 'Ocean's Love to Ireland'
('Iambic drums/ Of English beat the woods where her poets/ Sink
like Onan'), or the sense of failure and disappointment in 'Exposure'
(where the poet, languishing in darkness, feels he has 'missed/ The
once-in-a-lifetime portent/ The comet's pulsing rose'), or the picture
of the poet in 'The Unacknowledged Legislator's Dream' (as a
blindfold prisoner), or the poet's caricature of himself in 'Viking
Dublin' (Hamlet 'dithering, blathering' in a rotten state).
   Heaney's predilection for 'jumping in graves' (as he put it in
'Viking Dublin'), his taste for 'the appetites of gravity' (seen at their
most self-indulgent, perhaps, in 'Come to the Bower'), his idea that
darkness is the element in which the poet must compose (going as
far back as 'The Forge' and 'The Peninsula') represent an important
impulse in his work. It lies behind his use of the Antaeus myth.
'Antaeus' is the first poem in Part I of *North*. The poet's sympathies
are with dark, native Antaeus, whose strength depends on his
intimate contact with his mother, Earth. But 'Hercules and
Antaeus', the last poem in Part I, tells of how Antaeus, the 'mould-
hugger', is overcome by Hercules. Picking up the image of
childhood in the first poem, the second describes how Antaeus is
'weaned at last', as Hercules lifts him away from the earth, into the
air, cutting him off from what sustains him and casting him into 'a

dream of loss/ and origins'. Hercules is the man of action – 'snake-choker, dung-heaver'. He is no ditherer and blatherer. His action exposes Antaeus as 'a sleeping giant/ pap for the dispossessed'.

Hercules and Antaeus may be seen to represent two different kinds of poet, two opposing tendencies which Heaney recognizes in himself. Antaeus is the instinctual, feminine, artesian, assuaging principle: his 'black powers' feed off 'the territory'. Hercules, 'sky-born and royal', is a rational, masculine, architectonic, aggravating intelligence, associated with technology and imperialism. Antaeus, Heaney seems to imply by the arrangement of poems in the book, prevails in the symbolic, mythicizing approach of Part I of *North*; his defeat in the last poem of Part I prepares for the emergence of the rational and personal explicitness of Part 2. 'The two halves of the book', Heaney has said, 'constitute two different kinds of utterance, each of which arose out of a necessity to shape and give palpable linguistic form to two kinds of urgency – one symbolic and one explicit'.[15] The two parts, however, do not divide up as neatly as Heaney implies. There is much in Part I which, displaying effects that are very consciously striven for, is more the work of Hercules' architectonic intelligence manipulating artesian resources, crafting words in the service of an idea that precedes the poem, than of Antaeus's instinctual, involuntary activity that intimates a sense of natural release like the ooze and nurture of the gum tree. What can be more cogently argued is that the strategic placing of the two poems suggests Heaney's conscious intention to adopt the role of man of action, to make his art *do* something – something, I believe, other than what it is naturally suited to do.

The transition from Part 1 to Part 2 is provided by a series of poems on Anglo-Irish relations in which more open declarations of resentment accompany a note of growing pessimism. These poems, 'Ocean's Love to Ireland', 'Aisling', 'Act of Union' and 'The Betrothal of Cavehill', are meditations on the process of historical and linguistic conquest, worked out in the indirect terms of symbol (that of violent sexual union), but from the point of view of the 'slightly aggravated young Catholic male'. 'Ocean's Love to Ireland' (the title an allusion to Ralegh's poem to Queen Elizabeth, 'The Ocean's Love to Cynthia') presents an incident recorded in John Aubrey's *Brief Lives*. The story is of Ralegh 'getting up one of the Mayds of Honour up against a tree in a Wood'[16] and raping her. Heaney uses the incident as an emblem of Ireland's exploitation by the English colonist.

In 'Act of Union' England and Ireland are once again pictured as a man and woman lying together. England is the 'tall kingdom', 'imperially male', lying over the shoulder of Ireland. From their 'act of union', England's 'legacy/ Culminates inexorably'. The offspring is 'an obstinate fifth column' of Ulster Protestants, who are savagely criticized in the reference to the child's 'parasitical/ And ignorant little fists'. The terms of the metaphor are a little odd. After all, it is not just Ulster Protestants who wield parasitical and ignorant little fists, and it is hard to see them as the ones who are beating at borders or threatening England. Perhaps it is the entire situation in Northern Ireland which Heaney is treating as the offspring of the Act of Union. The speaker can see no hope for the future: 'No treaty/ I forsee will salve completely your tracked/ And stretchmarked body.'

The symbolic framework of 'The Betrothal of Cavehill' is less sharp in outline. The Irish landscape, in particular the environs of Belfast, has both a male and a female aspect. There is the hidden Ireland, the landscape of secret places, the mysterious lover to whom the bridegroom poet is betrothed: 'The morning I drove out to bed me down/ Among my love's hideouts, her pods and broom.' Presiding over his love-act is the 'profiled basalt' of Cavehill, 'proud, protestant and northern, and male'. The male presence is watchful and militaristic. Its rituals are the rituals of power, symbolized by the coercive, phallic gun ('They fired above my car the ritual gun').

Clearly, Heaney's myth is not without contradiction. Elements overlap. The soft, female bog entombs the warrior male: Mother Ireland is of course female, her sacrificial victims, male. But the male figure incorporates not only all Irishmen sacrificed to the goddess, but the colonizer like Ralegh, with his 'superb crest' which 'drives inland', and the Ulster Protestant 'fifth column'. England is 'the tall kingdom', 'imperially male', who lies down to 'caress/ The heaving province' of Ireland. The female figure is Kathleen na Houlihan, the Irish maid ravished by Ralegh, the consciousness of the oppressed group, the contemporary Catholic sensibility. The poet is a member of this oppressed minority, but he is a man. The overlapping categories are part of the complicated reality of Northern Ireland. The challenge is to reconcile them.

In terms of Heaney's myth, Ireland is female, its destiny decided by others. 'Servant Boy' presents an image of the boy who has learnt how to please. In 'Midnight' the poet is silenced, can speak only in obscure and acceptable ways. 'Hercules and Antaeus' describes the defeat of the earth-lover by the man of action. In 'Ocean's Love to Ireland' the 'Irish' of the 'ruined maid' is overcome, and Ireland's poets 'sink like Onan'. There are further erosions of manhood for the Northern Irish Catholic in a society where the master's role is assumed by the Protestants, as 'The Betrothal of Cavehill' indicates. And the church's authority is an added burden: 'I was under that thumb too like all my cast', Heaney writes in 'Freedman'. '"What's your name, Heaney?"' he remembers being asked as a schoolboy (in 'The Ministry of Fear'); and his reply: '"Heaney, Father."'

The Irish Catholic sensibility, bound to immolation, takes on a notably modern cast. It is representative of what we have come to know as 'the modern malaise', associated most strongly with many of Heaney's American contemporaries. There are Lowell's confessional impulse, Jarrell's acute feeling of violated sensibility, Eberhart's theme of injured vulnerability, Shapiro's terror of the 'nameless hurt'. The notion of a world locked in a grisly dream of the endless victimization of man controls such contemporary novelists as Bellow, Malamud, Ellison and Kesey. The pariah and the victim are central metaphors of modern literature. Heaney's Irish suffer the fate of the colonized. They are passive, emasculated, no longer masters of their fate. Ireland is 'the ground possessed and repossessed' ('Ocean's Love to Ireland'). The question is, what kind of manhood is there for one who is simply asked to obey? What kind of manhood is there for an Irish Catholic in the North, especially when he is a poet?

The opening line of 'Funeral Rites' engages this question: 'I shouldered a kind of manhood.' The association of poet and pallbearer indicates the way in which Heaney seeks to assert himself while having to bear the heavy burden of loss and death. It is by assisting in funeral rites, the paying of last respects, adopting a posture of supplication. In this way the spirit of continuance and human dignity is affirmed. The same impulse underlies his fascination with the exhumed corpses, his canonization of the Tollund Man, his 'deification' of the sacrificial victim in 'Kinship'. And it is continued into *Field-Work* where he very explicitly assumes the role of elegist and anointer of the dead. The ceremony and rhythms of his art are poetic forms of a social strategy, but more sophisticated, perhaps even more efficacious, for the ritual of art is less rigid than the rituals of life. Ritual has a positive, assuaging function:

                    we pine for ceremony
                    customary rhythms.

These 'customary rhythms' are what Heaney celebrates in two
poems which lie outside the two parts of *North* and serve as a kind of
preface to the collection. Their statement of faith and transcendence
provides an important perspective on the bleakness of what follows
in the book. In the first, 'Sunlight', he describes a scene from the
peaceful, remembered world of childhood. His aunt, bathed in
sunlight, is in the kitchen baking. Her blessing radiates out over the
whole poem. This is the goddess in different guise. No longer a
doom-laden deity but a real-life person in a domestic situation. The
poem contains a kind of love which hitherto Heaney had found
difficulty in expressing. It is to strengthen significantly in *Field-Work*
and *Station Island*. There is about 'Sunlight' a deeply sustaining
quality – the sunlight, the aunt's firm stance, the ample flour-scoop
and the general sense of space and love and ritual activity. The
domestic commonplace is hallowed by the loving detail of the poet's
remembrance. The aunt, who does not appear till the third stanza,
demonstrates a kind of love and nurture that is unassuming and
self-effacing. Like the gleam of the flour-scoop sunk in the meal-bin,
her love lies in and beneath the routine and the commonplace. Like
the sunshine, it illuminates the entire scene and transcends time:

                    here is a space
                    again, the scone rising
                    to the tick of two clocks.

The lines offer a poetic model too. What the poet wants is 'space', a
space in which all his feelings, in all their complexity, can exist;
spaces which he can create for the expression of self, love and
cultural inheritance, without pushing them into ready-made
moulds of dogma.

   The second poem, 'The Seed-Cutters', presents the work of seed-
cutters as a 'calendar custom', a seasonal ritual which is also an
emblem of continuance and transcendence:

                    O calendar customs! Under the broom
                    Yellowing over them, compose the frieze
                    With all of us there, our anonymities.

'Sunlight' and 'The Seed-Cutters' are humble, deeply-felt asser-
tions of 'custom' and humanity, relying on nothing more from the

poet than recording and celebrating what he sees by 'getting them true'. But in the other poems in Part I, the tendency is towards elaborating large-scale ritual activity that goes beyond the world of childhood and seeks to deal with 'neighbourly murders', the hooded victim/ slashed and dumped'. Ciaron Carson praises 'Funeral Rites' for the poem's initial evocation of remembered funerals and adds: 'All too soon we are back in the world of megalithic doorways and charming noble barbarity.'[17] The criticism is echoed by Edna Longley: 'The root emotion is that of "The Tollund Man" – Heaney's passionate desire to "assuage," but he goes to such ritualistic lengths as to obliterate his starting-point.'[18]

In 'Funeral Rites' Heaney's central concern is to find a ritual that will take the place of Christian burial traditions which he can no longer accept. Their failure, he makes explicit in an earlier draft of the poem, made 'the confirmation of manhood useless'.[19] Out of this state of hopelessness and disaffection he turns to ancient burial ritual. 'The world of megalithic doorways' is motivated by the desire to find a ritual model that would make the experience of death by extreme violence bearable and dignified, and at the same time pre-date Christian ritual which lies at the root of the contemporary conflict. Thus Heaney imagines the funeral cortege moving south towards the Boyne, a river associated with both pre-Christian Celtic ritual and the assertion of Protestant supremacy. The procession is a 'black glacier', suggesting not only the cortege of cars, but also the poet's feelings of overwhelming and depressing bleakness as he contemplates the looming presence of death. As the mourners enter 'the megalithic doorway' another striking image is used. They are like 'a serpent quiet'. The sexual connotations of this richly evocative metaphor harp back to Heaney's notion of death as a sexual union of man and female earth. 'Serpent quiet' also has a Biblical connection which reminds us of the context of doom and insidious evil in which the ritual activity takes place. The poem ends with another ancient model for acceptance: the ancient Celtic burial at Newgrange is linked with the burial of the Icelandic hero, Gunnar.

One of Heaney's great talents is for accurate, sensuous evocation of object and process and, as the five drafts of 'Funeral Rites' demonstrate, there is a discernible process of replacing abstractions with concrete, evocative metaphors. The use of mythological/ archaeological material, he knows, could inhibit his poetic power. The other danger, as we have also noted, was that the mythological/

archaeological material could seduce him into a dream of beauty and love and adoration, into a notion that a corpse, thousands of years old, is not really dead ('Who will say "corpse"/ to his vivid cast?'), in fact seems just born ('a head and shoulder/ out of the peat/ bruised like a forceps baby'), a fantasy of 'germination' or resurrection, in which the 'murdered, forgotten, nameless' emerge as pure as saints, as innocent as newborns, their wounds 'cured'. 'The Tollund Man', 'Punishment' and 'Kinship' are too honest to indulge these dreams, and Heaney goes on to use the mythological/archaeological material to explore his uncertain, equivocating feelings about himself as a man and a poet in the midst of atrocity. He does not have any neat message for his people, he does not subscribe to one political extreme or another; but neither does he 'stand dumb' and 'cast the stones of silence'. He confronts that other great challenge, the most difficult of all – the creating of a space in which to manipulate and shape the complexities of feeling without having recourse to the simplicity of a dogma. And this is Heaney's other major strength – his handling of equivocation, his capacity for orchestrating nimble shifts of tone, which keep in balance various possibilities. Past is linked with present in order to dramatize the present situation.

In 'Funeral Rites', however, he clearly wants to do more than provide continuities and parallels. 'Funeral Rites', more than any of the other poems in Part 1, attempts to reconcile the poet and the man of action. It does so by emphasizing the need for communally held ritual. Heaney seeks to bring together his personal experience and his social concern to provide consolation for a civilized culture now become barbaric. 'Funeral Rites' does not contain the wishful hope that something good, some kind of renewal, might emerge from the violence, which was a part of the complex, personal feeling in 'The Tollund Man'. He accepts the reality of death. A dead body is a dead body; there is nothing hopeful about it. But there is a minimal idealism still present in his faith in the power of ritual to enable us to cope with that reality. Ritual is treated as an expression of therapeutic, elemental forces in human nature. It is an indomitable, sacred embodiment of the life-force principle, which Heaney would urge us to re-discover for ourselves. Rationally speaking, the limitation of Heaney's proposition lies in his assertion of ritual without consideration of the need for a whole, underlying, unifying system of belief (so conspicuously absent in Ulster society), which is the only thing that could give the ritual transcendent meaning.

Ritual is inevitably tied to particular social and religious values (as the first section of the poem recognizes). An Ulsterman could hardly be expected to assent to ancient Celtic and Icelandic ritual any more than to the validity of a Hopi Indian rain dance. Obviously, Heaney thinks the example of long ago is what matters to us. He derives deep comfort from the demonstration that such a course of action was once possible. Its relevance to the contemporary situation depends on unearned assertion. And this is symptomatic of a terrible vulnerability to the reality of death, the great disaster against which the secular sensibility has no weapon.

What we miss in 'Funeral Rites' is the hypothetical, tentative, nervously uncertain, moment-by-moment immediacies of the sensibility that informed 'The Tollund Man' and gave to its attempt to wring a positive feeling out of atrocity a piercing emotional authority. 'The Tollund Man' is humbler and more yielding, in style and rhythm as in frame of thought. Heaney's presentation of the doomed man carried us into consciousness of the mystery of death and re-birth with the most delicate, sentient accuracy, the ending of that poem flattened out, a quietist handling of terror that does not lack intensity. Throughout 'The Tollund Man' we are kept uneasily alive to all the uncertainties of Heaney's position and direction, the feeling deepening cumulatively. 'Funeral Rites', by contrast, works with statement and assertion, with convictions that we are asked to take on trust. All can be well, Heaney tells us, but we have it only on his own wishful authority. Merely to contradict agony is not to undo it. The poem ends on an image of peace and beatitude wherein all human tensions become irrelevant. But it is not the momentary peace that is achieved with opposing forces tensed in equal balance: it is spurious and contrived because it is presented as revealed dogma. There is not the same uncompromising self-exposure in a poem like 'Funeral Rites' as in, say, 'The Tollund Man'; not the same integrity of balance. Lacking tough-mindedness, 'Funeral Rites' seeks to gain our assent through the intoxication of sound and image, but in the end convinces us less successfully of the validity of the poet's triumphant vision than of the desperate crisis that motivated the attempt. The poem is indicative of the effort to make poetry solve problems. The poetry suffers as a result.

The poet's relation to immediate social problems becomes the central preoccupation of Part 2 of *North*. To be a man is to act, and if your form of action is to create art then let it be the art of direct political statement, even though it will be more exacerbating than assuaging. Poetry must now speak out on the rights and wrongs of social issues. It must come down on one side or the other (though secretly Heaney knows this kind of 'exaltation' may well be his 'fall'). In Part 1 the wish for meaning compelled a return to the sources of significance and implication which myth and ritual had to offer, to the powerful heritage of ancient pieties which shone over the troubled present like the moon over Gunnar's tomb. This imaginative repossession of the moods and modes of the past, often tinged with a glamorous exoticism, was a way to get beyond the moment's crisis and give it the focus of distance. It put him in touch with 'all the realms of whisper'. The ancient, pagan earth cults were more clearly informed by an awareness of the mystery of the 'life-force' than the contemporary consciousness. In the best of these poems, the merging of the historical and the personal was accompanied by devotion to a perfectionistic and aesthetic-centred poetry, aspiring to a durable music of elegance, grace and precision, a solemn, quiet intensity of phrasing. In the aesthetic mode his poetry looks to the encompassment of opposites, the breaking down of dogmatic formulations, and affirmation achieved through symbolic argument. Political thought, rhetoric and action, on the other hand, demand partisanship. Life assumes priority over art.

Part 2, then, is more overtly political, outspoken and direct. It is composed of poems which provoke rather than secrete controversy. Few indications are given of any confidence in the art of poetry. The first poem, 'The Unacknowledged Legislator's Dream', is an inert prose piece; 'Freedman' and 'A Constable Calls' were originally prose pieces appearing in Padraic Fiacc's anthology, *The Wearing of the Black*. 'Freedman' has undergone some shaping and stylization, but still relies on a prose paragraph to point its meaning. 'A Constable Calls' is virtually the same piece divided into stanzas.

'Whatever You Say Say Nothing' is one of the most politically direct and vigorous of the poems in Part 2. It is a kind of serious verse-journalism that probably takes its main impetus from Auden – a combination of witty and knowledgeable commentary with panicky looks at the world's terror. The verse form is no longer the artesian drill of short-line quatrains but a more expansive, rhyming quatrain of iambic pentameters that are sufficiently flexible to accommodate political commentary and reflection as well as description, dramatic action and dialogue – the utterance of a public, willed, contemporary voice.

The Bog poems hinted at the possibility of renewal resulting from violence, but there is no such optimism in 'Whatever You Say Say Nothing.' To 'diagnose a rebirth in our plight', Heaney says, 'would be to ignore other symptoms'. In this exacerbated condition, journalistic jargon and liberal cliché are inadequate; but so, too, has been the poet's own previous aesthetic response: 'Yet for all this art and sedentary trade/ I am incapable.' He, like his countrymen, is a victim of 'the famous/ Northern reticence, the tight gag of place/And times'. Relying heavily for its effects on tone and rhythm, the poem registers Heaney's exasperation with the deceit and duplicity of the Ulster consciousness which he recognizes in himself: 'Whatever you say say nothing.' He feels like the silent bystander in 'Punishment', looking on while atrocity takes place all around.

'Freedman' is prefaced by a patronizing comment from R. H. Barrow's book, *The Romans*, which Heaney uses as a reflection on his own emasculation: 'Indeed, slavery comes nearest to its justification in the early Roman Empire: for a man from a "backward" race might be brought within the pale of civilization, educated and trained in a craft or a profession, and turned into a useful member of society.' Despite his own education and training, Heaney resists this 'justification'. The principal agents of his own enslavement – the Catholic Church and colonial hegemony – are gently mocked in the poem's arcane and exotic vocabulary. It was only when poetry 'arrived' that he believed he had found the means of his emancipation from the tight gags of cultural and religious repression. With poetry, he believes, all that counts is the validity of his own language and his own insights.

The quotation from Wordsworth which prefaces 'Singing School' is an acknowledgement of the usefulness and relevance of the English tradition. And it is an affirmation of the nurture received from rural, childhood experience:

> Fair seedtime had my soul, and I grew up
> Fostered alike by beauty and by fear.

This is Wordsworth's child 'drinking in a pure organic pleasure'[20] and 'under the impressive discipline of fear',[21] that 'fear' which works him into a sense of the mysterious 'sentiment of Being'. For both Wordsworth and Heaney the prior, most profound influences shaping the moral sense lie in their childhood relationship with the natural world, rather than their social relationships as a function of developed intelligence. The Yeatsian quotation which follows is another statement about childhood, but in terms of a political and cultural division which, though it means nothing to the child, is the unique and inescapable heritage of any Irish poet. What Yeats's statement emphasizes is the power of poetry to move – to move in unpredictable and possibly dangerous ways. It was the 'pleasure' he got from reading a book of Orange rhymes which led to Yeats's boyhood dream of dying while fighting the Fenians. The poet has a moral obligation, for upon it depends the humanity of the individual and the quality of civilization. In pursuing this obligation, the 'English lyric' of Wordsworth can be adapted to the Irish poet's own special purposes. As Heaney asserts in 'The Ministry of Fear' (his title a phrase from Wordsworth):

> Ulster was British, but with no rights on
> The English lyric: all around us, though
> We hadn't named it, the ministry of fear.

The rural childhood world with whose mystery the poet had communed in a spirit of Wordsworthian intensity had its dark and frightening aspect. Now that world is seen in strictly political terms. The poet's task is to set the darkness echoing by 'naming' a different kind of terror. And that 'naming', if it is true enough, will bear the watermark of the writer's own origins.

Much of 'The Ministry of Fear' is taken up with a consideration, based on autobiographical fragments, of the political and social implications of tribal 'naming'. There are carefree recollections of how, as a young poet, Heaney experimented with the dialect of his tribe. This leads to another memory of being told as a schoolboy that Catholics don't speak as well as Protestants, a notion which is scathingly dismissed by the older Heaney: 'Remember that stuff? Inferiority/ Complexes, stuff that dreams were made on.' The Shakespearean allusion is a kind of childish proof that he is adept in the English tradition as well as his own. But the differences between Catholic and Protestant 'naming' can be a source of discrimination and danger in this 'land of password, handgrip, wink and nod'. The policemen with their torches and sten-guns who crowd round his car at a road-block echo the priest's question earlier:

> 'What's your name, driver?'
>   'Seamus . . .'
>   *Seamus?*

The policeman's response is that of suspicious, sinister Authority. The priest is happy with the young Heaney's reply ('"What's your name, Heaney?"/ "Heaney, Father."/ "Fair/ Enough"'), but this priestly authority is equally destructive of personal identity and free expression.

Half-way through the poem Heaney rebukes himself for 'shying as usual'. Surrounded by the emasculating influences of church and state, it is all the more necessary for him and his fellow Irish poets to develop those social and poetic strategies which would allow them to express their own most authentic experience. Prompted by a more recent memory of policemen at another road-block reading the 'hieroglyphics' and 'svelte dictions' of one of his letters, he makes his final defiant assertion about the possibility of an Irish lyric, one based on the English model, that would be capable of 'naming' the truth about the Hidden Ulster.

'A Constable Calls' describes another childhood experience of the ministry of fear. Heaney describes how he watched, petrified, as a little boy while his father cheated the constable in his tillage returns. The sinister symbol of the policeman's authority – his revolver – fascinates the child. The fear of the child is reflected in the harsh sounds and rhythms which pervade the poem, and in the imagery which constantly relates to the gun (the policeman's bike has 'fat black handlegrips', its dynamo is 'gleaming and cocked back'; the policeman is seen 'snapping the carrier spring/ Over the ledger'). The dominant impression is of a temporarily restrained but potentially unimaginable violence, imaged in the pedals 'hanging relieved/ Of the boot of the law' and the tick, tick, tick, of the wheel at the end.

The violence in the next poem, 'Orange Drums, Tyrone, 1966', is not so understated, and through it the poet registers his disgust at the savage power of Protestantism. Written earlier than most of the poems in *North*, this one lacks the clarity and precision of the mature work. Individual elements have the surprising force of an original perception: the air is 'pounding like a stethoscope', the drums are 'like giant tumours' – suggestive of the cancerous nature of such sectarian spectacle. But do 'tumours' resound like this? Can they 'preside' ('the drums preside, like giant tumours')? Loosely related images are not brought together to create an emotionally and imaginatively coherent total impression. The poem strains to turn the drummer, who is depicted as a deformed and ugly monster, into an emblem of Protestant supremacy:

> The lambeg balloons at his belly, weighs
> Him back on his haunches, lodging thunder
> Grossly between his chin and his knees.
> He is raised up by what he buckles under.

Again, the imagery is out of control: the double-meaning of 'what he buckles under' refers satisfactorily to the self-destructiveness of Protestant bigotry (an idea taken up later in 'The pigskin's scourged until his knuckles bleed'), less satisfactorily to the effects of Protestant supremacy on the Catholic community which then becomes incongruously identified with the Orange drum.

'Summer 1969' sees the poet withdrawn from the ugly immediacies of life in Northern Ireland which keep battering at him. At a time when sectarian savagery has once again gripped his country, he is holidaying in Spain. Friends there urge him to 'go back'. Uncertain about what to do, he withdrew to the cool of the Prado, the museum where Goya's 'Shootings of the Third of May' is exhibited. Goya's mural depicts the horror of the Napoleonic firing squad which executed Spanish patriots who had staged an unsuccessful rising against the French in 1808. There are other paintings also relevant to Heaney's situation: Saturn drenched in the blood of his own children, and one in which two beserks club each other to death 'For honour's sake, greaved in a bog, and sinking.' The poem ends with a couplet describing Goya's response to his country's troubles – he dealt with them head on:

> He painted with his fists and elbows, flourished
> The stained cape of his heart as history charged.

This response contrasts with the advice Heaney remembers being given by an old friend and mentor, Michael McLaverty, in the next poem, 'Fosterage'. McLaverty's own stories are notable for their observation of great modesty and delicacy which, as one of his commentators, John Foster, says, possesses 'the nearsightedness of childhood and love'.[22] It takes on the character of presentiment – 'a kind of revelation where we least expect it, amidst the daily and the commonplace'.[23] Public surface and private vision merge. McLaverty's racial myth is essentially poetic, a far cry from the more public myths of Irish political life. His priority, as Foster further remarks, is 'the human heart whose corners are inaccessible to the affairs of kings and state'. This is what makes him 'a diffident champion of the

Ulster Catholic heritage'.[24] His people are the poor, the deracinated and the forgotten – kin to Heaney's 'mound-dwellers' – not generally obsessed with their social condition. At the centre of a McLaverty story beats an intensely personal consciousness, pre-occupied with private losses and the mesmeric past. The writing is elegiac and soliloquizing, uncontaminated by any obvious, 'masculine' effort on the part of the author to shape or transmute the recorded experience. It demonstrates McLaverty's continual alertness to 'the realms of whisper' which are personal and unique to him.

It is no surprise, therefore, that the advice Heaney remembers in 'Fosterage' is '"Description is revelation"'; '"Go your own way./Do your own work"'; '"Remember . . . that note of exile."' The poem is far from being among Heaney's best. In the very act of telling how he was fostered and sent out with words 'Imposing on my tongue like obols', he disregards another piece of advice from his old friend: '"Don't have the veins bulging in your biro."' What 'Fosterage' does importantly represent, though, is a continuation of that troublesome debate about what a poet's role should be, especially in time of war. Here, McLaverty's advice is very similar to that of the longship, and it is echoed by the shade of James Joyce in 'Station Island'. However, as other poems in Part 2 of *North* demonstrate, Heaney's faith in art and the aesthetic tradition was going through a crisis of confidence. The last poem in *North*, the tense and anguished 'Exposure', is the climactic expression of his divided feelings.

In 'Exposure' he is still worrying over his responsibilities as a poet, still wracked by guilt at having departed from roots. His dilemma as a poet is now complicated by the physical fact of having opted to 'escape from the massacre' in the North and go and live in the peace and quiet of County Wicklow. His present state is defined in terms of dripping branches, last light, cold, damp leaves, husks, spent flukes of autumn. These carefully observed details are drawn from the immediate environment which registers itself minutely and intimately. They contrast with a more abstract, less well-defined, quasi-mystical imagery of 'diamond absolutes' and 'comet's pulsing rose'. The former is related to the poet's longing for indefinable perfection, the latter to his wish for some kind of externally bestowed revelation. His sense of failure and frustration is unmistakable. He thinks of someone small and inconspicuous, like David on his muddy compound, who was yet a hero championing the cause of his tribe. The idea of art as a weapon in the political struggle – like David's slingstone 'Whirled for the desperate' – has great attraction. It leads him to mock his own careful attitude as pretentious and literary: 'As I sit weighing and weighing/ My responsible *tristia.*' At times the frustration is insupportable and he wonders how he ever came to this impasse. He caricatures himself as an ancient anchorite or perhaps the stereotypical liberal intellectual with long hair and thoughtful mien. He sees himself as one who has withdrawn from the public world to engage in an inner journey: 'I am neither internee nor informer/ An inner émigré.' The earlier castigating description of himself (in 'Punishment') as 'artful voyeur', as a mere self-gratifying observer of atrocity, is deepened and dignified by this suggestion of a more responsible, self-exploratory motive. And though he may have 'escaped from the massacre' he does not deny his heritage – he is still a 'wood-kerne', he is still a soldier enlisted in his country's cause. But the battle is to be fought on his terms, the terms of art.

Like Sweeney, Heaney has defied the pressures of the world. As a consequence, he is condemned to suffering, isolation and exposure. Like Sweeney, too, he seeks protection, a bleak form of freedom, in his intimacy with elemental things: 'Taking protective colouring/ From bole and bark, feeling/ Every wind that blows.' If by turning his back on the North he has missed the 'once-in-a-lifetime portent,/ The comet's pulsing rose', he has, by lying down in the word-hoard, committed himself to the 'diamond absolutes' of art, no matter how imperfect he may feel his attainment of those absolutes may be. Refusing to enter the sensational arena of public affairs, he has preferred instead the inward journey in quest of what nubbed treasure lies buried in his own most intimate experience.

The result is what he calls, in the poem 'Casualty' in *Field-Work*, 'a tentative art'. There may be the persistent, niggling longing for another kind of poetry, one that would have the power and status of prophecy, but at the same time he acknowledges that only poetry which springs instinctively and intuitively from the well of inspiration that is personal and unique to him can even 'recall' the 'diamond absolutes'. The truth he confronts is that no one can issue orders in art as one does in politics, that art must be inspired and shaped by the artist's own unmistakable personality, not by an abstract dogma. The poet must listen to the voice of his own conscience, not because he is always sure to be 'right', but because if he does not, his poetry will immediately reveal the presence of a foreign, spurious element and will cease to be effective. For Heaney, truth lies not in his friends' 'Beautiful prismatic counselling', nor in the inhuman authority of 'the anvil brains of some who hate me'. Instead, it is carried in the elemental rain, the voice of the land, its philology and history. It is borne in to him from 'all the realms of whisper'. To the extent that he is attuned to these spirit-voices, he can hope to fix the raindrop's ephemeral, fragile beauty in the indestructible 'diamond absolutes' of art.

> Rain comes down through the alders
> Its low conducive voices
> Mutter about let-downs and erosions
> And yet each drop recalls
> The diamond absolutes.

The lines echo 'Gifts of Rain':

> Soft voices of the dead
> are whispering by the shore
>
> that I would question
> (and for my children's sake)
> about crops rotted, river mud
> glazing the baked clay floor . . .
>
> a mating call of sound
> rises to pleasure me . . .

In both poems there is a whole history of suffering and disappointment calling on the poet, but also an intimation of beauty ('diamond absolutes') and 'pleasure'. In both poems he resists the life of politics, direct action and confrontation and instead embraces the role of 'Dives,/ hoarder of common ground' – the assuaging, preserving role of mediator and artist. However, the contrast between the tone of exultant affirmation with which 'Gifts of Rain' concludes, and the bleak sense of failure at the end of 'Exposure' is a measure of the doubt and uncertainty about his art which have latterly afflicted the poet.

5
Field-Work

Field-Work, as the title indicates, involves a conscious scaling-down of Heaney's vision. His imaginative parameters are now those of a field, not the international time-warps of *North*. The scope and ambition of *Field-Work* are reduced. It does not range so freely in the boglands and along the shorelines of cultural history; the tone is more confessional and intimate. Heaney's muse is no longer the mythological goddess of Irish history, the implacable 'black mother'. Instead, he develops the image of the domestic muse or sibyl. She was the personalized goddess of 'Sunlight' and reappears in a variety of guises in *Field-Work*. She is the young girl in 'Triptych', one of the 'small-eyed survivor flowers' of his country's troubles. She is the 'girl in a white dress' associated with the 'doctor fish', the tench swimming 'in touch with soft-mouthed life' in 'The Guttural Muse'. She is the old woman whom he remembers in 'A Drink of Water'. And she is the poet's wife who inspires a renewed interest in love-poetry as the consummation of the domestic. Heaney, no longer content to explore the dark depths of the imagination or the mists and drizzles of the past, engages the community in terms of its individual members.

One of Heaney's major concerns is to evolve a poetry which will unite the extremes of Hercules and Antaeus, the explicit and the symbolic, humanism and atavism. A poetry relying on humanism alone would fail because humanism is a rational construct of the atavisms out of which it initially arises; and while it may be welcome from a rational point of view, it would render the utterance inadequate and irrelevant, especially when bigotry and irrational feeling are so much a part of the Northern psyche. Equally, a poetry that is composed only of atavisms loses out too, for it encourages easy thoughts and lacks any ironic point-of-vantage from which the intimate and local materials might be viewed.

Heaney wants a poetry that is not just private, arbitrary and occasional, nor just schematic mythologizing. The great task is to find a point of balance between Yeats's concern with ordering structures for his psychic materials and energies, and Kavanagh's

116

immersion in the day-to-day in a spirit of unpredictable susceptibility and lyrical opportunism. Heaney has of course already demonstrated his concern with this kind of synthesis in poems like 'Punishment', where the customary denunciation of tribal violence is set against acknowledgement of a reverberation in himself of the instinctive undercurrent of prejudice. But this poem depends on an elaborate, far-flung, mythological apparatus, the treatment of which continually threatens to degenerate into escapism and mannerism in his less successful poems. What is happening in *Field-Work* is the effort to discover a poetic form embedded in the daily and the domestic for the expression of archetypal forces located in daily and domestic material. Crucial to this task is the advice of Michael McLaverty, which Heaney celebrated in *North*: ' "Description is revelation!" ' He strives for a poetry in which 'there are elements . . . which are capillaries into the large brutal scheme of things, capillaries sucking the whole of the earth'.[1] This is reminiscent of Joyce's method in *Dubliners* or Faulkner's use of his Yoknapatawpha County.

There is a sense of new beginnings in *Field-Work*, and a conscious readjustment of poetic style which is designed to embody what Heaney calls 'a more social voice':

I wrote a fairly constricted freeish kind of verse in *Wintering Out* and *North* in general, and then in the new book *Field Work*, I very deliberately set out to lengthen the line again because the narrow line was becoming habit. The shortness of a line constricts, in a sense, the breadth of your movement. Of course, a formal decision is never strictly formal. I mean it's to do with some impulsive things, some instinctive sense of the pitch you want to make. And with *North* and *Wintering Out* I was burrowing inwards, and those thin small quatrain poems, they're kind of drills or augurs for turning in and they are narrow and long and deep. Well, after those poems I wanted to turn out, to go out, and I wanted to pitch the voice out; it was at once formal but also emotional, a return to an opener voice and to a more – I don't want to say public – but a more social voice. And the rhythmic contract of metre and iambic pentameter and long line implies audience.[2]

A number of poems in the Glanmore Sonnet sequence in the middle of *Field-Work* are about poetry. In the second sonnet the poet, newly landed in the 'hedge-school' of Glanmore, speaks of himself as hoping 'to raise/ A voice caught back off slug-horn and slow chanter/ That might continue, hold, dispel, appease.' Poetry no longer depends on elaborate mythologizing, but on sensitivity to 'sensings, mountings from the hiding places'. 'Thought' or 'theory' which is the Herculean systematizing, generalizing element, is an indispensible one, for it rescues first impressions from all that is gross and erratic, extends consciousness and promotes the grasp of principle. But poetic activity begins with a sense of the particular and concludes again in a heightened, more penetrating sense of the particular. It is its closeness to the essential object or process and its ability to contribute to a significant whole which transforms description into revelation. We have already noted that there was a part of Heaney's nature which was infatuated with the narcotic and escapist, and that this was a tendency which dimmed his clear eye for the object and betrayed him into dreaming and self-indulgence, an unduly passive and 'feminine' attitude. In the second sonnet, however, he re-dedicates himself to what Keats called 'sensation and watchfulness'.[3] Heaney's guarantee of the wholeness of the act of knowing is a language of 'words entering almost the sense of touch'. Taking up the theme of the title of the book, and making a connection with early poems like 'Digging' and 'Follower', he re-asserts the poet/ploughman identification: 'Vowels ploughed into other, opened ground,/ Each verse returning like the plough turned round.' These, the concluding lines of the second sonnet, are a repetition of the opening line of the first ('Vowels ploughed into other: opened ground'): the poetry returns like the plough turned round. Rhyme and rhythm and the use of the highly disciplined sonnet form reflect the ploughman's steady, careful movement. The poetic voice is modelled on Wordsworth's, about which Heaney had this to say in connection with the suggestive etymology of the word 'verse': ' "Verse" comes from the Latin *versus* which could mean a line of poetry but could also mean the turn that a ploughman made at the head of the field as he finished one furrow and turned back into another. Wordsworth on the gravel-path, to-ing and fro-ing like a ploughman up and down a field, his voice rising and falling between the measure of his pentameters, unites the old walking meaning of *versus* with the newer, talking sense of verse.'[4]

The new beginnings we sense in *Field-Work* are exhilarating because, with Heaney's move to County Wicklow, there is renewed contact with nature. In the first sonnet the good life is crossing a field. Art is compared to new earth from the lathe of a plough. The opening of the poem is quiet, misty, static. In the background, though, there is a threatening, disturbing presence: a distant gargling of tractors which troubles the deep silence of the countryside. The poet ploughs the field and waits to receive the approaching inspirational 'ghosts'. The ploughing analogue emphasizes a traditionalism in poetic practice much prized by Heaney. He himself demonstrates how traditional forms can liberate more than confine, can disclose insights as new and powerful as the rank, steaming furrows turned up by 'old ploughsocks'. By slight modulations within and away from conventional verse, he gains the emotional freedom he needs while retaining the great advantages of a recognizible line that need not be wearyingly 'regular'. The writing evokes the mystery of poetic creation yet remains rationally controlled and orientated. There is a restraint, a toughness and elegance, a silence, in the poem, which is enormously expressive. The description pushes towards a dramatic intensity when, after careful tillage, the poet is 'quickened':

> And I am quickened with a redolence
> Of the fundamental dark unblown rose.
> Wait then . . . Breasting the mist, in sowers' aprons,
> My ghosts come striding into their spring stations.
> The dream grain whirls like freakish Easter snows.

The poem describes a Wordsworthian method of composition.

In the third sonnet Heaney tentatively connects himself and his wife in the pastoral surroundings of County Wicklow with Dorothy and William in Dove Cottage. The poem emphasizes the creative influence of nature's 'strange loneliness': the evening is 'crepuscular and iambic', the breeze 'is cadences'. The fifth sonnet develops this sense of the inextricable connection of language and nature in a way that is reminiscent of the earlier 'Oracle'. 'Oracle' has the poet hiding in a willow tree, wanting to be the 'lobe and larynx/ of the mossy places'. In the sonnet he remembers hiding in a boortree's trunk, but now the childhood idyll incorporates more threatening elements: 'It was our bower as children, a greenish, dank/ And snapping memory as I get older.' The sheer beauty and plenitude of nature are suffused with intimations of pain and violence, which still intensify rather than diminish its appeal: 'I love its blooms like saucers brimmed with meal,/ Its berries a swart caviar of shot,/A bouyant spawn, a light bruised out of purple.' There are echoes of

'Blackberry Picking' here, but the emotional response is more complicated. The longing to recover the instinctual feeling of childhood is accompanied by awareness that his means of expressing it are hybrid and 'learned'. Yet the adult experience of language, instead of promoting a painful dream of loss, is 'quickening'. It is as exciting as the game of 'touching tongues' he played as a child. As 'etymologist of roots and graftings', he is devoted to probing the organic processes of linguistic and experiential evolution which parallel those of nature. Nature, language, the 'leavings' of childhood and the racial past – these provide a sense of sanctuary and continuity. They are a vital source of nurture: 'I fall back to my tree-house and would crouch/ Where small buds shoot and flourish in the hush.' Happiness is the shelter from the world he finds when, in the words of another poem ('Homecomings'), he is 'occluded' by the whispering leaves and branches of his 'tree-house'. The insistent past tense in which the fifth sonnet is cast, and the connotation of wishfulness in 'would crouch' imply an awareness that the shelter which was once there is there no longer. For the adult Heaney, as we recall from 'The Tollund Man', 'home' is being 'lost' and 'unhappy'. The sonnet conveys this sense of exposure, but also reveals what the shelter had been.

The majority of poems in *Field-Work* confront the public world of political violence and turbulence. Heaney's best poetry emerges from the dialectical relationship established between the claims of that public world on one hand, and private vision and domestic feeling on the other. Personal experience assumes a communal relevance. And what we find is that as the feeling of exposure is intensified, so too is the effort to re-create a sense of the lost shelter. Beginning in the imbalance of violence and evil, the typical *Field-Work* poem struggles toward poise and balance. The poem itself becomes the poet's 'home'. Acknowledgement of the public world forbids a comforting retreat into the protective arms of dream: the newly-conceived muse does not seduce him from communal responsibilities. The question he asks of her (in 'Sibyl', one of the 'Triptych' sequence) is: ' "What will become of us?" ' And her answer (as the 'Triptych' poems as a whole demonstrate) does not have the simplicity of political statement, but the indirectness and complexity of the poetic symbol. Those who destory art for politics are doomed. Thinking of Thomas Cromwell in 'Leavings', of his dissolution of the monasteries, his banishing the Mass and his 'threshing' the Church clear of its sumptuous artifacts, Heaney wonders to which circle of the Inferno Cromwell has been consigned. Yet in the midst of barbarism the artistic spirit persists, like a ghost or 'sheaf of light' in a blackened stubble field.

'Oysters', the first poem in *Field-Work*, takes up the questions which had preoccupied Heaney in *North*. He feels guilty at surrendering himself to sensation and beauty – the 'glut of privilege' – when there is always the niggling awareness of the historical and political context from which such 'privilege' derives. Thinking of the Romans making their way home across the Alps with their spoils of conquest, he turns the oysters into symbols of imperialist plunder. But where in 'Exposure' he feels frustrated and despairing because of a lack of political commitment, in 'Oysters' he is angry that he cannot shed social conscience, free himself from the darkness of the past, and 'repose/ in the clear light, like poetry or freedom/ Leaning in from sea'. This is wishful thinking, of course, for neither poetry nor freedom is to be found 'Leaning in from the sea'. They both have to be striven for. Poetry and freedom do not exist as divinely bestowed gifts, nor as things arising outside society. Poetry cannot be divorced from an attitude to or a philosophy of life. It is, implicitly if not explicitly, a critical evaluation of individual and social values. Only by an act of conscious will can the poet allay, even temporarily, the stirrings of social conscience and surrender to the enlivening pleasures of the present:

> I ate the day
> Deliberately, that its tang
> Might quicken me all into verb, pure verb.

Here, the poet dedicates himself to the word, to art, in the face of those perennial, inescapable pressures from everyday life which threaten to distort or obliterate what is unique, irreducible and most intimate in his negotiations with the world. Politics inevitably colour the emotional life; but for Heaney poetry is rooted in a sacramental regard for the 'life-force' rather than in political opinion. The poet's first job is to trust the tang he has tasted, the nubbed treasure his hands have known. It is only the tension of the poet's own most authentic experience that has 'quickening' authority. As Heaney writes at the end of 'Badgers':

> How perilous is it to choose
> not to love the life we're shown?

'Badgers' re-works the familiar theme of the encounter between artist and some haunting, fugitive thing that is redolent of place and past (like the 'strange noises' in 'The Given Note', or 'the dead' in 'Bog Oak', or the muttering voices in 'Gifts of Rain' and 'Exposure'), and embodies those dark, instinctual forces Heaney recognizes in the world and himself (like the eels in 'A Lough Neagh Sequence'). It is another poem in which he attempts to explore his complex relationship with nature, the past, nation, language and self. 'The Badgers', like Hughes's 'The Thought-Fox', uses natural scene and image to describe a mental process. Like the 'dawn sniffing revenant' in 'Casualty', the poem immediately preceeding, the badgers' 'soft returning' under the laurels is the night-time visitation of troubling daemons, dark atavisms, which rise to haunt and 'badger' the poet's mind. The thing which lies beyond the poet's jurisdiction is, as Heaney described Hughes's 'thought-fox', 'characteristically fluid and vowelling and sibilant':[5]

> When the badger glimmered away
> into another garden
> you stood, half-lit with whiskey,
> sensing you had disturbed
> some soft returning.

The echo of 'glimmered' in 'half-lit' suggests the identification between animal and human, between the external visible world and the hidden emotional life. In the ghostly hush created out of the poem's music, the badgers first evoke thoughts of the murdered victims of the Troubles, then of the unfortunate dispossessed. The community's response of being 'vaguely honoured' by the badgers' visits is tested on the pulse of the poet's own feelings, and he is forced to conclude that it is 'fear' not pride which the badgers prompt in him. Like the 'thought-fox' the badgers are granted 'a dilation of their mystery'[6] before their Gaelic vowelling music is fully possessed by an authoritarian consonantal voice formed from the Anglo-Saxon:

> Last night one had me braking . . .
> the bogey of fern country
> broke cover in me
> for what he is:
> pig family
> and not at all what he's painted.

The poet's sudden 'braking' is reflected in the inverted mirror-image of the badger which 'broke cover in me': the former is both the cause and the effect of the latter. 'Braking' arrests the proliferation of hypotheses, and the badger finally emerges, caught with jolting, de-mystifying precision, in the quelling, defining action of the con-sonants and the colloquial directness of ordinary speech. That longer last line suspends the badger's movement, fixes and holds its identity. It is recognized as one of the shadowy daemons lurking beneath the self's acceptable surfaces. The poet becomes civilized man confronting the atavisms of 'unaccomodated man', probing the issues of loyalty and responsibility to origins. He recognizes violence and terror in the ghostly presentiment of the past, and he recognizes these things in the depths of his own being, however far he may have tried to remove himself from the dark outside. Violence and terror are a part of his ancestry of servitude and dispossession; they co-exist with a more positive inheritance of sturdiness, intelligence and endurance. The badger suddenly recalls 'The Servant Boy':

> The unquestionable houseboy's shoulders
> that could have been my own.

In that ambiguous 'could have been' there is recognition and reserve. The reserve has to be placed alongside the awareness, rhetorically expressed, of 'How perilous is it to choose/ not to love the life we're shown?' to appreciate the complexity of Heaney's feelings about fidelity to origins, kinship with the tribe and acceptance of the self. He acknowledges the impossibility of escape from elemental, shaping influences which are reductive as well as sustaining, and at the same time retreats from wholehearted acceptance of them.

The role of inheritance is the subject of 'The Harvest Bow'. The harvest bow made by the poet's father is the emblem of the traditional skills the poet celebrates. It is an emblem of the past, the record of a harvest. It is 'the spirit of the corn', 'a throwaway love-knot of straw' – a symbol of hope, love and continuance. Like the servant boy's eggs, the harvest bow is 'still warm'. The simple strength, skill and growth it signifies live on, indeed are 'burnished' by time's passing. Its creation is a paradigm of artistic activity. The old man works at the bow 'with fine intent/ Until your fingers moved somnambulant'. The bow is woven without conscious effort, just as poetry should spring naturally and inevitably from deep wells of being. It is 'a frail device', as poetry is a device, and the motto it evokes is Coventry Patmore's dictum, *'The end of art is peace.'* The harvest bow is a gift to future generations who may learn from the lesson it contains and 'glean the unsaid off the palpable'. Similarily, the poet's task is to bring order and 'peace' out of an exhausted world; to create something that 'does not rust'.

Poetry is to have a therapeutic effect. This idea is further suggested in 'The Guttural Muse' where Heaney writes enviously of 'the slimy tench/ Once called the doctor fish because his slime/ Was said to heal the wounds of fish that touched it'. Heaney as poet would like to possess the same healing power:

> I felt like some old pike all badged with sores
> Wanting to swim in touch with soft-mouthed life.

This role gives rise to a poetry of peculiar intensity when Heaney turns to contemplate the recent deaths by terrorist violence of three people whom he knew.

'Casualty' is about an acquaintance, Louis O'Neill, a harmless old alcoholic, who defied the curfew imposed by the IRA three days after thirteen people were killed in Derry and, on his way to a pub late at night, was killed by a bomb. The man's death is used by the poet to explore his own relationship with the tribe. The problem of loyalty which had preoccupied Heaney in poems like 'Punishment' becomes a matter of even greater intimacy and urgency.

The man, out for his customary night's drinking, behaves in accordance with a more primitive dictate than the social strictures of the tribe: he drank 'like a fish' we are told, 'naturally/ Swimming towards the lure/ Of warm lit-up places'. We discover that he was, in fact, a fisherman, and Heaney, aligning himself with the victim, recreates an occasion when he accompanied O'Neill in his boat. Description of the mesmeric pace of the man's funeral cortege flows into the rhythm of the man fishing and the sound of his purling boat-engine. The ritual of the victim's death merges with the rhythms of his life. The poet passively enters the fisherman's world and finds that, as with the Tollund Man, he 'tasted freedom with him':

> As you find a rhythm
> Working you, slow mile by mile,
> Into your proper haunt
> Somewhere, well out, beyond . . .

The poet, like the fisherman, lays claim to the grace of a domestic rhythm, to the quick and the purity of the inward act that must be preserved at all costs, and lies beyond the outward structures imposed by the community. Yet if the power of the writing in the final section, which holds before the poet's mind the memory of the fishing-trip, indicates his obvious sympathy with the dead victim and puts the poet outside the tribe, he refuses to be dogmatic.

The affinity Heaney feels is evident from the beginning. Just as strongly felt is the poet's guilt which, ironically, the fisherman also arouses. Heaney knows that his poetic vocation has occasioned an alienation from his people more profound than that of the man who defied the curfew. The poet's awkwardness in the company of the fisherman is nearly as incapacitating as that in the encounter between Catholic and Protestant farmer in 'The Other Side'. The fisherman ultimately confronts the poet with the question of how culpable he was in defying the tribe. The strength of the poem lies in Heaney's refusal to settle for a single answer. The sense of community may be supportive and maternally consoling (like a 'swaddling band'), but it is also restrictive and stifling ('Lapping, tightening/ Till we were braced and bound'). The poem ends by turning back on itself. The dead fisherman, a ghost of the landscape, returns to confront the poet once more with the question of his culpability. On an explicit, intellectual level, the question is posed and left unresolved: this is counterpointed by the incantatory power of Heaney's language (its meditative cadences alternating skilfully with a colloquial directness), which is the poet/fisherman 'finding a rhythm working him'. It enacts the primacy of mysterious, elemental forces, carrying him beyond the time-bound politics of the tribe.

'The Strand at Lough Beg' is about another victim of the Troubles, this time Heaney's second-cousin, Colum McCartney, who was the innocent victim of a random shooting one Sunday when he was coming home from a Gaelic football match in Dublin. The setting of the killing is quickly established as a landscape of legendary barbarity, in which Colum McCartney becomes another victim of an ancient cycle of pursuit and sacrifice. The attack takes place 'out, amongst the stars'. Like Louis O'Neill, Colum McCartney has found himself outside the safety of the tribal pale. The authority that confronts him is as 'fake' as that which Heaney writes about in 'The Toome Road'. But even in Colum's own, familiar territory there are ominous tokens of violence and death. Nature is suffused with foreboding: there is the soft treeline of yew, the firing of the guns behind the house, the duck shooters who 'haunted' the marigolds and bulrushes, their spent cartridges 'Acrid, brassy, genital, ejected.' After the jabbing harshness with which this connection is made between violence and perverted sexuality, the poem relaxes into the vowelling calm of a longer line in which Heaney recreates the rhythm of the farm, then moves on to celebrate the tribe of strong, tough watchful men from which he and his cousin sprang. The poet's relationship with these men of action has been uneasy and ambiguous from the moment when he first took up the pen instead of the spade. The ambivalence is acknowledged in poems like 'Casualty' or 'The Badgers', but suppressed in this poem about one of the poet's own relations. Colum McCartney is presented in an even more personalized, intimate way than Louis O'Neill, so that his death is all the more poignant.

Heaney pictures himself accompanying Colum, as he had accompanied the fisherman, going about his daily work:

> Across that strand of yours the cattle graze
> Up to their bellies in an early mist
> And now they turn their unbewildered gaze
> To where we work our way through squeaking sedge
> Drowning in dew. Like a dull blade with its edge
> Honed bright, Lough Beg half shines under the haze.

The soft, pastoral mood, emphasized by the long vowel sounds, the comforting chime of the end-rhymes and the meandering, co-ordinate syntax, is gradually infiltrated by a more ominous note – the effortful 'work our way' and cacophonous 'squeaking sedge', the consonantal dunting of the *d* sounds, the defeat that is sounded in the word 'drowning', strategically placed for maximum emphasis at the beginning of a line and controlling the falling cadence enforced by the caesura. The accumulation of threatening portents reaches its climax in the heavily-stressed, consonantal monosyllables of the next line and a half describing Lough Beg. Wrenching the syntax to obtain the inverted simile first creates a sense of blunt, brutal force, then allows the second half of the comparison to modulate into a more relaxed cadence as it picks up the pastoral rhyme ('graze' – 'gaze' – 'haze') and prepares for the quiet, ritual observance with which the poem ends. The dream-like atmosphere is suddenly intensified, past merges with present, and the poet is kneeling beside his murdered cousin:

Then kneel in front of you in brimming grass
And offer up cold handfuls of the dew
To wash you, cousin. I dab you clean with moss
Fine as the drizzle out of a low cloud.
I lift you under the arms and lay you flat.
With rushes that shoot green again, I plait
Green scapulars to wear over your shroud.

The language has the power of incantation while remaining colloquial and tender. In these exquisitely poignant lines we have the poet as anointer of the dead, performing the rites which seek to transform his friend into a spirit of this barbaric place. Heaney toyed with this role in 'The Tollund Man' and aspired to it in 'Funeral Rites', as the nearest the poet can come to *doing* something. The concern with doing something indicates a lack of faith in the religion of art, in the transcendent efficacy of its symbolic resolutions to enable us to cope with death and terror. 'The Strand at Lough Beg' is poetry of reaction, poetry with palpable design, poetry with intention. It is shadowed by what Kavanagh called a 'kinetic vulgarity': 'all action', Kavanagh said, 'is vulgar'.[7] It fails – a magnificent failure, admittedly – because personal feeling has not been transmuted into the purely aesthetic, impersonal, self-contained public ritual of the poem's own 'action'. As Keats remarked, 'The genius of Poetry must work out its own salvation in a man.'[8] Poetry which works like a charm or spell can never be entirely satisfying.

The third of Heaney's elegies to dead friends, 'A Postcard from North Antrim', voices the same desire to resurrect his social-worker friend, Sean Armstrong, whose 'candid forehead stopped/ a point-blank teatime bullet'. 'Get up from your blood on the floor', Heaney commands him. The poem, however, remains disappointingly unresolved. The celebratory impulse is developed within a strictly nostalgic structure of feeling rather than submitted to the transcendent, saving power of the aesthetic imagination. 'Elegy' (for Robert Lowell) has Lowell speak of 'art's/deliberate, peremptory/ love and arrogance', in a poem which may be considered, along with another tribute to a dead artist, 'In Memoriam Sean O'Riada', as demonstrating the opposite extreme from 'A Postcard from North Antrim': in 'A Postcard', the substance of life is valued too much for itself and has not been transmuted into art; in 'Elegy' and 'In Memoriam Sean O'Riada', a willed, peremptory aestheticism devotes itself to the word rather than the person. The subjects which prompted these two poems are grossly 'poeticized'; art loses touch with life. The third of Heaney's elegies to fellow artists, 'In Memoriam Francis Ledwidge', is a stronger poem than any of these. Here the poet finds the form in which life and language are more nearly one. There is an interaction between the two (which is theme as well as method): life nourishing art and art illuminating life.

But first, 'Elegy', the background to which is the conflict between art and life, which Heaney could see played out all through Lowell's work.[9] Not a great poem itself, 'Elegy' registers Heaney's tender feeling towards the life of anguish and crisis that lies behind Lowell's poetry, his gratitude for the art that Lowell could not or would not separate from life. Heaney's 'life study' of his subject presents a poet of great power and passion, an embattled and alienated spirit who plunged 'boldly' ('boldness' is also a key word in Heaney's review of Lowell in *Preoccupations*) into dangerous waters – a 'course set wilfully across/ the ungovernable and dangerous'. Heaney responds to the plight and pain of the lost self which guiltily feels itself to proclaim all the degradation and violence of the contemporary American waste land. But he responds, too, to the holding fast to a moral perspective, to the conservative, sturdy faith in the creative spirit which struggles to absorb the shock of personal and cultural breakdown. Where others (John Berryman and Sylvia Plath, for example), as Heaney says in his review, 'swam away powerfully into the dark swirls of the unconscious and the drift towards death . . . Lowell resisted that, held fast to conscience and pushed deliberately towards self-mastery'.[10] Master, welder, bully, inveigler, groom, ward, amphibian, armourer, father, risk-taker – these are the powerful, masculine terms in which Heaney describes his subject in 'Elegy', and the poem echoes Lowell's own aggressive imagery, his energetic language and strong rhythms, which were the driving force of his aesthetic of anguish. The poetry that is most valued is 'not the proud sail of your great verse' – not the poetry of direct personal utterance with epic ambitions that we find in *Notebooks*, for it is vitiated by a failure of form; instead, it is the poems where he has struggled for a form – a narrative drawn from life, or an image he has found – which he can use to transform the raw materials of life into the precise, hard-working, public vehicle of art. Then, when he is in control of his experience, his work speaks for more than himself:

Not the proud sail of your great verse . . .
No. You were our night ferry
thudding in a big sea . . .

In the end, the bond between the two poets is their shared belief in art as what will redeem a fallen world.

The subject of 'In Memoriam Sean O'Riada' was born James Reidy in Cork, in 1931. Though trained in classical music, he is remembered by Heaney for his interest in the indigenous musical heritage[11] and his contribution to Irish traditional music. O'Riada was, in fact, responsible in the 1950s for founding Ceoltoiri Cualain, a group of traditional musicians, some of whom went on to achieve international fame as the Chieftains. Other groups such as Planxty and the Bothy Band owed their success to the new directions that Irish traditional music took under O'Riada's influence. He wanted to see it elevated from its dependence on ceili band treatment and informal session performance in pubs and houses. He gave traditional music formal arrangement, took it into the concert hall and recording studio and introduced it to a much wider audience. He helped make it respectable. In O'Riada, the two traditions – classical and Irish – are brought together. This combination of the hieratic and the folk, the civilized and the natural, is reflected in Heaney's diction and imagery: conducting the Ulster Orchestra, O'Riada is like a drover herding them south with an ashplant in his hand; he is formally suited, yet 'springy'; the 'black stiletto' of his baton metamorphoses into a quill; his inspiration comes from the natural world – the call of the cuckoo when he is out fishing (the cuckoo significantly being the bird which lays its eggs in other birds' nests). Continuing one of his favourite metaphors for the creative process – that of fishing – Heaney describes how the mackerel 'shoaled from under', displaying their 'barred cold': this swarming vitality, echoing Yeats's 'mackerel-crowded seas', is 'conjured' into the formal control of the composer/arranger. O'Riada is proof that Ireland has as many rights in classical music as the Irish poet has in the English lyric. Like the radicalism of a Burkean sub-text underlying what is ostensibly a masterpiece of conservatism (say, Burke's *Reflections on the Revolution in France*), there is, beneath the classical decorum of O'Riada's music, a submerged political force, an indomitable nationalism, the sound of the jacobite:

he was our jacobite,
he was our young pretender
who marched along the deep

plumed in slow airs and grace notes.
O gannet smacking through scales!
Minnow of light.
Wader of assonance.

This showy high style is used to convey O'Riada's actual
performance and, out of that, to force a climax; but the poem
founders under the strain of the poet's effort to 'conjure' his subject
into his net. The jumbled imagery gives him away. Its looseness and
diffusiveness betray his uncertain grasp of the complexity he finds
in his subject, the failure of his integrating power. Images which at
best are isolated, flashy units, give the impression of fanciful,
literary manufacture. O'Riada as drover, then fisherman, then
falconer, then underwater jacobite, then swooping gannet, then a
fish in the water, then a wader – it's too haphazard a pile-up. Jostled
abruptly from one to another of these proliferating images, we begin
to flounder for want of a reassuring structure and an organic
expression. 'Gannet smacking through scales' conveys natural
energy penetrating classical discipline, but the image relies on a
forced, affected word-play. The 'minnow of light' image comes too
abruptly after the gannet's violence and has to compete with other
altogether contrary images (such as that of the proud, plumed
jacobite absurdly striding the deep). There is, presumably, some
strong, characteristic attitude of the man which Heaney wishes to
indicate, but his image is so arbitrary, its sensible meaning so vague,
that it is little more than a gesture toward a kind of serenity and
arrival achieved through music. The best thing about it is the
mesmeric stillness that blooms off the mellifluous vowelling of the
short line. The parallelism in this concluding section gives the
feeling of complete certainty, as if the appositional statements all
confirmed each other; and the last line moves with a finalizing
gravity and deliberation. Yet the poem ends in bathos. A swift,
concretizing power still eludes the poet. He chooses to round off the
poem with the impressiveness of a summarizing abstraction (which,
if we were feeling generous, we might think of relating to O'Riada's
project of bringing together the sounds of two traditions, or, since
'assonance' is a literary term, to an affinity between musician and

poet, both of whom sought to keep alive the ghostly whisper of ancient tradition, one in classical music, the other in the English language): such is the degree of abstraction that the image of the wader loses all precision and vividness, so that it, along with the subject it is supposed to illuminate, sink without trace.

Heaney's engagement with the Irish poet, Francis Ledwidge, is more rigorous. Ledwidge was a poet drawn from the momentous events in Ireland in 1916 to fight in Flanders fields for the British. The poem, 'In Memoriam Francis Ledwidge', opens with a recollection of a trip to Portstewart when Heaney was a boy. The memorial statue on the Promenade fascinates him. Though it meant little to the 'worried pet', he perceives the difference between art and life: it was a windy day and in such conditions the bronze soldier's bronze cape would not in reality sit the way it was cast. The reference to the 'loyal', fallen names on the embossed plaque is ironical in the light of soldiers like Ledwidge who made the supreme sacrifice in the service of a foreign cause. The contemporary meaning of 'Loyalist' adds a further irony. The poem continues with the young Heaney gripping his Aunt Mary by the hand and the two of them walking out to the strand and seeing the pilot sailing out to the coal-boat, the courting couples among the dunes, a farmer sunning himself, the coloured lights along the sea-front. A peaceful, holiday scene. However, the repetition of the word 'pet' in the conversation of the country people talking about a great litter ('"We'll pet the runt"') and their reference to the barbed wire that had torn a cow's elder signal a darker undercurrent making itself felt. Ledwidge, it is implied, shared the same childlike innocence, which is gradually touched by the reality of the wider world – but only partially, for it is in the language of the poem itself that the full meaning of his career is inscribed.

Heaney's treatment of his subject is circling and indirect. The poem's fragmented, loosely associative structure belongs to the subjective mode of private vision: controlling that structure is a pervasive ironic perspective which betokens the pressure of the public world. Events, scenes, objects, people from Heaney's own experience speak to him, and it is through them that he approaches Ledwidge. Heaney begins by discovering in himself the central conflict which was sensationally proclaimed in Ledwidge's life and work. Ledwidge is not an historical curiosity but a representative figure – representative of the difficult negotiations between the public and the private worlds in any man's life. Everything about his own childhood trip to Portstewart has a subtly latent relevance to what Heaney has to say about Ledwidge. He is obviously thinking of the soldier-poet when he describes the memorial statue, but no explicit mention is made of Ledwidge until we are six stanzas into the poem, by which time the memory of Portstewart has taken on a life of its own and Heaney has moved away from the statue altogether and is remembering the courting couples along the beach. The connection with Ledwidge is made a little too bluntly in the poem, but carries an appropriate emphasis: a rural Irish courtship is the context in which he belongs, not that of the battle-fields of Europe.

With Ledwidge now the declared focus of the poem, a series of increasingly violent contrasts follows, in which Ledwidge's Irish idyll, like the poet's childhood illusion, its disrupted by a vicious realism. Heaney's image of the typical young Georgian poet 'literary, sweet-talking, countrified', at home 'among the dolorous and lovely' is counterpointed with another disturbing vision – Ledwidge 'ghosting' the trenches in his Tommy's uniform, a 'haunted Catholic face', unnaturally placed on the battle-fields of Flanders and the Dardanelles when spiritually he is more attuned to the bloom of the hawthorn and the silence of a Boyne passage-grave. Then another shift: Heaney, an adult now, is looking at another memorial – a photograph of his Aunt Mary when she was a girl in 1915. Aunt Mary was the source of comfort and reassurance when the bronze soldier stirred the poet's childhood anxiety: now, the photograph evokes thoughts of her peaceful, routine, farm-life in Ireland from which the horror of war cannot be excluded. The simplicity of 'She still herds cows' is juxtaposed with the bumpy, clichéd understatement, 'But a big strafe puts the candles out in Ypres', a line which speaks poignantly of the difficulty of managing inconceivable horror. Within Heaney's statement of life's absurdity, there is Ledwidge's own dawning awareness of fundamental contradictions in his situation – his understanding that his soul is in the Irish countryside, that there is a troublesome discrepancy in fighting for Britain at a time when Ireland was coming of age and struggling for a place among nations. But his understanding is far from complete. He does not appreciate the feeling that lay behind the 1916 Rising. Heaney treats his failure with savage irony: 'You were rent/ By shrapnel six weeks later. '"I am sorry/ That party politics should divide our tents."'

Ledwidge gradually achieves emblematic status. Heaney deconstructs the opening symbol of the memorial statue and composes a more complex image with special relevance for Catholic nationalist Ireland:

> In you, our dead enigma, all the strains
> Criss-cross in useless equilibrium.

The poem's loose criss-crossing of strains (the various 'strains' of Ledwidge's music, of his inheritance and make-up, the 'strains' involved in coping with diversity and contradiction) tightens and resonates in the last two stanzas. Heaney finds in Ledwidge's 'useless equilibrium' the substance of his own transcendent expression. Caught between the Boyne and the Balkans, both scenes of defeat, one for Irish nationhood, the other for British imperialism, Ledwidge had no way of reconciling the conflict which disabled him as a poet and destroyed him as a man – the conflict between action and contemplation, realism and idealism, life and art, British sympathy and Irish origins. By entering the world of action and following the British fife and drum – the music of 'these true-blue ones' – he missed the 'twilit note' to which his Irish flute was naturally pitched and keyed, and which might have been tuned to his country's 'confirmation' – as Heaney himself feared that by escaping from the Irish massacre he had 'missed the once-in-a-lifetime portent/ The comet's pulsing rose'. Heaney is not simply advocating a nationalistic music. Ledwidge's 'twilit note' has connotations of romantic decadence, and it refers to a music which has been shown in no uncertain terms to be disastrously out of touch with the brutal realities of life. But it is still the natural pitch and key of Ledwidge's music, and what Heaney implies above all, is that the artist's talents, his imaginative vision, the sources of his creative energy – all may be perverted or dissipated if his writing does not spring, instinctively and intuitively, from those deep levels of being that are personal and unique to him. To deny them is to follow a 'sure confusing drum' – the word 'sure' functioning as a straightforward intensification of 'confusing', and subtly indicating a certainty that is socially validated but ultimately unsatisfying ('confusing') at the deep levels of personality. In the end, the poetry which counts is the same kind as the drama which Arthur Miller said counted: '. . . the drama of the whole man. It seeks to deal with his differences from others not *per se*, but toward the end that, if only through drama, we may know how much the same we are'.[12] This is the ultimate reality enforced by Death, the great leveller, who nullifies all patriotic sentiment, British, German or Irish. The musical imagery of strains, tunes, drum, note, flute, sound, keyed and pitched culminates in the poem's last line: 'Though all of you consort now underground.' The sense in which Ledwidge is consorting with the enemy (British and German) is absorbed by the larger meaning of a Wilfred Owen-style 'strange meeting'. The art which Heaney recommends is rooted in a common, fundamental ground of humanity beneath the convulsions of sectarian or nationalistic conflict.

Heaney's interest in Ledwidge is divided between the man's life and his work, but in none of the three elegies for dead artists does the terrifying reality of death enter the poem with the same heart-felt immediacy as in 'The Strand at Lough Beg'. Their primary concern is with the subject's role as an artist rather than the intimate details of his life or the personal tragedy of his death. That the poet is not so uncomfortably close to his subject in 'In Memoriam Francis Ledwidge' as, say, in 'The Strand at Lough Beg', is doubtless a factor in promoting a greater formal control. Indeed, the Ledwidge poem inclines away from elegy altogether and edges toward parable.

The usual impulse behind the elegy is to celebrate and affirm, despite loss and sorrow, and it is this impulse which permeates nearly all the poems in *Field-Work*. The elegy is an appropriate genre for a poet preoccupied with 'leavings' – 'leavings' not only in the sense of deaths, but also inheritances that are precious and sustaining. The elegy is a declaration of faith as well as an expression of loss, a formal enactment of the admonishment written on the cup in 'A Drink of Water': '"Remember the Giver" fading off the lip.'

In this haunting little poem Heaney re-dedicates himself to the life-giving sources, to his role as diviner through whom the water used to broadcast its secrets. The female of his poetry has grown old. She is 'like an old bat staggering up the field'. The imagery suggests difficulty, noisy effort, disease and decline: the pump's 'whooping cough', the bucket's 'clatter/ And slow diminuendo', its 'pocked' enamel, the 'treble/ Creak' of the old woman's voice, the moon that 'fell back' and then 'would lie/ Into the water', the inscription 'fading off the lip'. But despite all this, and despite the poet's faithlessness, the old woman still provides the drink of water. At the end the poet has 'dipped to drink again to be/ Faithful'.

Struggling to hold on to his faith, he confronts the violent facts of Ulster. 'After a Killing', the first of his 'Triptych' poems, written after the murder of the British Ambassador to Ireland, Christopher Ewart-Biggs, in 1976, is composed of two contrasting sets of images. The first is sinister and demonic – two young men with rifles on a hillside. They are dark figures of nightmare, incarnations of 'unquiet founders', hatched from the collective memory. They 'profane' the landscape's beauty, but there is still something 'Bracing' about violence and terror. Despite death's ominous imagery all around, a different kind of vision is still able to re-assert itself. Amid harsh conditions a delicate loveliness survives – 'small-eyed survivor flowers/ The pined-for, unmolested orchid'. The poet thinks of his own stone house on the coast surrounded by nature's beauty and bounty:

> And to-day a girl walks in home to us
> Carrying a basket full of new potatoes,
> Three tight green cabbages, and carrots
> With the tops and mould still fresh on them.

The two young males with their guns are ultimately replaced by the female principle, the bearer of love and life. The structure of feeling is very similar to that in early poems like 'At Ardboe Point' or 'Night Drive', where the pressures of mortality serve to heighten and validate the positive force of love. In the midst of darkness the poet is, to use Wordsworth's phrase, 'surprised by joy'.

In 'Sibyl', the second of the 'Triptych' poems, Heaney addresses his muse. His tongue, 'a swung relaxing hinge', asks her what will become of his people. Another door opens into the dark.

> And as forgotten water in a well might shake
> At an explosion under morning
>
> Or a crack run up a gable,
> She began to speak.

She is the voice of the neglected life-force in its social mode, the 'sensible', forward-looking voice of 'home', concerned with communal order and safety, the future of the race. But she has been 'forgotten' and 'shaken', her authority exploded and undermined by the forces of violence and materialism. Her language is the language of rational humanism, warning that things will only get worse unless 'forgiveness' can re-assert itself. She uses the imagery of resurrection – Ireland is doomed 'Unless the helmeted and bleeding tree/ Can green and open buds like infants' fists' – but the re-birth she speaks about depends on the eminently prosaic and practical 'forgiveness'. There is a big difference between this and the mystical, wishful kind of poetical 'germination' Heaney had entertained in *North*. Out of sympathy for the slaughtered Irish he had sought to turn them into saints and heroes and fertility gods, and their deaths into a manifestation of the 'life-force' rather than a defiance of it. The Sibyl strips Ireland of the least vestige of romance and glamour. Its people are hypocritical and materialistic, they have sought to substitute a brittle future based on material and technological exploitation for nature's slow, rich processes; what should be the deep, strange wells of nurture are now exhausted, filled only with 'silence'. Heaney's Sibyl is detached from all the traditional female representations of Ireland, especially in the last stanza, where the traditional territorial numen, the insatiable goddess, is held responsible for engendering atavisms that flout the life-force principle and leave the country 'full of comfortless noises.'

In the third poem, 'At the Water's Edge', one of the 'comfortless noises' is the army helicopter patrolling overhead. The scene is Newry in 1972, a week after the infamous Bloody Sunday massacre in which British soldiers shot thirteen civil rights marchers. Newry is a spiritual waste land. The values, both pagan and Christian, of old Ireland are dead and gone. At the cathedral carved monastic heads were crumbling like bread on water; on Boa the 'god-eyed, sex-mouthed stone' was silent; the basin reserved for holy water held only rain water; a hammer and a cracked jug full of cobwebs lay abandoned on a windowsill – the hammer symbolizing power, industry, technological progress, the male principle, and the cracked jug, no longer able to hold the life-giving water, connoting the female principle. The poet looks skyward for a supernatural sign. But all he sees is the icon of the new secular order – the 'god-eyed' helicopter.

There is a longing for a new start, for renewed contact with elemental things, for a world in which the religious impulse could find expression:

> Everything in me
> Wanted to bow down, to offer up,
> To go barefoot, foetal and penitential,
>
> And pray at the water's edge.

Religious regeneration at the water's edge finally merges with political regeneration in Newry where the first faltering steps were taken in defiance of a shadowy, repressive authority.

Heaney groups these poems into a 'Triptych' because each turns on a different kind of response to Ulster's Troubles: each represents a crucial impulse in Heaney's total, complex relationship to his country. 'After a Killing' emphasizes the aesthetic, 'Sibyl' the rational humanist, 'At the Water's Edge' the pietistic and nationalistic. Coming at the very beginning of the book, 'Triptych' introduces the three strands that make up the 'love-knot' of Heaney's art. That he uses the unusual 'Triptych' form suggests that, as yet, he is unable to write out of all these impulses simultaneously.

In *Field-Work* we can trace the effort to create a synthesis of the elements which inform 'Triptych'. It is the effort to evolve an organic form that will acknowledge the dark Antaean, spontaneous energies of the creative act, the inchoate pieties engendered by a sense of 'home', with its language of instinct, sensation and personal feeling, and, at the same time, provide the outward organizing structures that are rooted in the daily and domestic materials out of which they arise, and capable of bringing about increased power over the particular. It is an effort to take account of the poet's own world and intellect and voice on the one hand and, on the other, to satisfy the need for communication, community and universal significance. For Heaney, there must be a dialogue between 'all the realms of whisper' and 'the obstinate voice of rational humanism'.[13] Out of that encounter he finds a form for that primary, unspoken world.

Field-Work constructs an Irish landscape at once politically-charged, communal, relevant: but it is a kind of cultural landscape moulded out of Heaney's own psychic disposition. He deals with the contemporary crisis, not by accepting the formulation it is given in the public world, but by making his own domesticated imagery, his own terrain, take the colour of it. Hence, the countryside which had once meant bulls and blackberry-picking, forges and furrows, is now constantly under threat – from the 'charioteers' in 'The Toome Road', the two gunmen on a hill in 'After a Killing', the 'comfortless noises' in 'Sibyl', the defeat and decay in 'At the Water's Edge'. The poet may move away from Ireland but the psychic landscape remains the same. In 'High Summer' the hot, still heaviness of a farmhouse holiday in the Basque country is infused with intimations of pain and unrest – the baby crying at night, the ugly sound of a tractor, the ominous bag of maggots which are compared to a 'newsreel of a police force run amok', the flies which are 'the

barristers and black berets of light', the crossroad shrines. Beneath
the surface of summer's fecund indolence lie dark and troubling
demons. On the riverbank fishing rods lean out, 'nodding and
waiting, feelers into quiet', an image which is intensified by the
neurotic, disjointed attention to snails in the grass, bat-squeak and
darkening trees. Typically, the lines reaching down into the dark are
juxtaposed with the act of writing: the poet has found a barn an
'ideal place' to write. The poem itself, however, is a demonstration
that the poet's 'ideal place' – his 'space' – does not go untouched by
the evil in the world. He slept that night only when 'mists'
obliterated the fearful mementoes of mortality and goatbells pro-
claimed a comforting pastoral reassurance.

As well as the refreshing influence of nature, Heaney celebrates
human values in his love poems, or marriage poems, as he prefers to
call them, in the Glanmore Sequence at the heart of the book. These
poems take full account of all that is disquieting, but while love may
be tainted by nervousness and forboding, he always manages to
affirm its enduring and rejuvenating power. In the fourth sonnet he
waits for the sound of an approaching train, presumably bearing his
loved one to him. As he listens patiently for vibrations along the
track, it is the noise of 'struck couplings and shuntings' which
echoes across the trees. The agitation of a horse by a 'cutting' and the
'small ripples' shivering across the drinking water as the train
passes are projections of the poet's own nervous anticipation. In the
last line the ripples 'vanished into where they seemed to start': there
is no permanent relief from unease. It is an integral part of the
human world of 'seeming'. Nevertheless, it is with the image of the
stilled drinking water on the table – an affirmation of the life-force
principle, that the poem ends.

The eighth sonnet, rather than developing a central image,
presents a more diversified, more generalized impression of the
world's dark and nameless evil. The atmosphere of the poem is
borrowed from *Macbeth*. Big raindrops are 'lush with omen' and
'spattering dark on the hatchet iron'. A sleeping horse evokes
thoughts of 'armour and carrion'. The poet fearfully expects to meet
some bloody apparition in the dark, weltering hush of the country-
side. He senses the evil presence of a toad in the depths of a
woodpile. The series of rhetorical questions emphasizes his help-
lessness and hopelessness before such indescribable horror. Then
comes an image of love and succour – the memory of an old woman
in a French pension rocking and singing her mongol child to sleep.

The resources of memory and imagination are restorative as well as terrifying. They re-galvanize the poet's paralysed will. The last two lines take the form of impassioned personal address, in which the poet, retreating from the world's blast, calls upon his loved one to join him:

> Come to me quick, I am upstairs shaking.
> My all of you birchwood in lightning.

'Quick' suggests the urgency of the poet's need: but also his faith in the 'quickening' power of love.

In the sonnet immediately following, corruption and evil is a black rat swaying on a briar 'like infected fruit'. The rat has been a favourite image of Heaney's to evoke the horror of a child. 'Something slobbered, curtly close,/ smudging the silence: a rat/ slimed out of the water and/ my throat sickened,' he writes in 'An Advancement of Learning'. The rat is 'this terror, cold, wet-furred, small-clawed'. The barn is full of bats, birds and great blind rats which threaten to engulf the child. The blissful memory of blackberry-picking is spoiled when he recalls the 'rat-grey fungus glutting on our cache'. He remembers one particular well which 'was scaresome for there, out of the ferns and tall/ foxgloves, a rat slapped across my reflection'. Heaney's poetry is an effort to confront these things. The totems of civilization like the 'burnished bay tree at the gate/Classical' can offer no protection. The tree itself is infected. A contrast is drawn between passive, reflective poet safely immured in his house, observing, and the men of action, the labourers in the field who are so intent on their husbandry that they remain untouched by horror or evil. What, then, the poet asks, is the justification for art? His answer is obliquely stated:

> The empty briar is swishing
> When I come down, and beyond, your face
> Haunts like a new moon glimpsed through tangled glass.

The poet's action has a much less sensational effect than the field workers' unceremonial violence. Neverthless, the poem ends with horror dispelled. Having confronted the evil of the rat, a new vision of love 'beyond' becomes available to him. It is linked with the moon, symbol of cosmic order, of divinity and purity. But we are never allowed to forget the tentative nature of Heaney's affirmation:

the briar still bears the traces of the rat's presence, the new moon can only be 'glimpsed', and the glass is incapable of returning an undistorted image.

The last of the Glanmore Sonnets is another version of Heaney's 'exposure' theme. He and his loved one are compared to Lorenzo and Jessica 'in a cold climate', and to Diarmuid and Grainne, all fugitive lovers. He sees himself and his lover as sacrificial victims of some pagan earth cult. The sestet completes the poet's 'dream' by affirming the redemptive power of love. Switching from the legendary to the contemporary world, he goes on to describe another transfiguring, ritual act performed in a hotel bedroom. The note of triumph is restrained. Their intimacy brings a stronger knowledge of their 'separateness'; it confers a 'respite' – something more temporary than rest.

A similar emotional structure shapes the other sonnets where the focus is less personal. The seventh sonnet gives us a forceful, impressionistic description of a stormy Atlantic sea-scape. The physical conditions are made palpable in the relentless battering of the consonants, the hiss of sibilants, the irregular, heavily-accented rhythms, the insistent pounding and graphic bluntness of the Anglo-Saxon compounds ('eel-road, seal-road, keel-road, whale-road, raise/ Their wind-compounded keen'), the imagery of 'swift upsurges', 'flux', 'collapse', 'midnight and closedown'. Then, after the Nordic violence of the octave, the sestet introduces a soft, romantic contrast. He lists the names of the boats which have found a haven from the storm: '*L'Etoile, Le Guillemot, La Belle Hélène.*' The languid rhythm, long vowels and liquid, lateral *l*'s emphasize calm and relief. The boats 'nursed their bright names this morning in the bay' – the language re-affirming hope and recovery, tenderness, composure. The flatly unromantic simile now used to describe the sea – 'toiled like mortar' – gives us a quiet reassurance of its containment and defeat. With growing confidence the sway of the voice, equable, sustained, internal, moves on, eventually resuming the list of shipping areas with which the poem began. Now the rugged sounds of the opening line ('Dogger, Rockall, Malin, Irish Sea') are replaced by a gentler insistence:

> It was marvellous
> And actual, I said out loud, 'A haven,'
> The word deepening, clearing like the sky
> Elsewhere on Minches, Cromarty, The Faroes.

The music of these lines is a music of coming to rest, of understanding. Like the 'North Atlantic flux' itself, the poem flows, shifts, drifts and comes to rest with the poet composed into a stilled consciousness, emphasized by the penetrating assonance in the penultimate line. The sestet, like the octave, is a cumulative movement; as it moves on to conclude the poem it does not press toward a climax, but intensifies the lingering meditation. Yielding to the appeasements offered by the music's potential for euphonious self-reproduction, the poem arrives at an entranced state in which the turbulence is allayed by apprehension of a longer, deeper tranquility. The love-act of naming and listing constitutes a kind of 'chaunt' that intones relief, thankfulness and joy. The lift of the poem, the moment of equilibrium, is prolonged in that last line. 'My own voice cheered me',[14] Wordsworth once said, at the same time knowing that his spoken music was but the 'imperfect sound' of 'the mind's internal echo'. So, too, Heaney exults in the sound of his own voice, even though it can only be a shadow of 'all the realms of whisper'. He is drawn into himself at the very moment he speaks 'out loud'. A comment Heaney made about Wordsworth says as much about himself: 'It is this mesmerized attention to the echoes and invitations within that constitutes his poetic confidence. . . . The more attentively Wordsworth listens in, the more cheerfully and abundantly he speaks out.'[15] This listening in so that more can be revealed is, in the end, what constitutes Heaney's 'apology for poetry'. The personal reality is not merely a matter of commonly received precept and principle: it is substantially constituted through surrender to energies that spring within the centre of the mind. The ninth sonnet carries the implication of a causal connection between the dispersal of evil and the function of poetry, in the juxtaposition of 'empty briar' with the immediately preceding question: 'What is my apology for poetry?'

In the sixth sonnet the artist is figured as a wild white goose 'Heard after dark above the drifted house', one who lived in the 'unsayable lights'. Like Hardy's darkling thrush, he is the one who enshrines the spirit of hope. The country is so cold things crystallize or founder, but it is also 'bright as a studio', the simile representing the nexus of nature, art and illumination which lies at the allusive heart of the poem. The artist's role, far from following the worm of thought into the mud or allowing himself to be infused with his country's poisons or pinioned by its ghosts, is to oppose paralysis and defeat with a 'story' that will 'quicken us'. Anomalous, 'wild', silly creature that he is, he stands for life against death. He is the one who is still sensitive to the vestiges of brightness and beauty: 'He saw the fushia in a drizzling noon,/ The elderflower at dusk like a risen moon.' His function is not just to 'glaze over' or 'perfect'. Like the adventurer/poet in 'The Plantation' or 'The Given Note', he is pledged to 'break through', to go beyond the safe limits into those realms of consciousness fraught with risk, to retrieve whatever is life-enhancing.

At the root of Heaney's work is a belief in the power of the 'story' and 'song'. That faith is more plainly expressed in 'The Singer's House'. The soul of a people is enshrined in their language and song; 'music' and 'belief' cannot be separated:

> People here used to believe
> that drowned souls lived in the seals.
> At spring tides they might change shape.
> They loved music and swam in for a singer . . .

Heaney urges a renewal of the artist's hoarding instinct (which ensures that a tradition is 'crystal and kept') and of imagination (which ensures freedom from the bondage of routine): 'Raise it again, man. We still believe what we hear.' The artist's 'wildness' works its will, not by imprecision, but by the freedom of its images from common associations or conformity with known general laws. What Yeats called 'the filthy modern tide' has all but swept away the tradition of imagination and installed instead a cult of empiricism, the small and squalid soul of the modern.

The view of art's social function implied here is one that recognizably belongs to that current in the Irish literary tradition seized upon by the Revival writers: committed to the nationalist enterprise, they elaborated a Romantic mystique of Gaelic spirit and imagination to oppose the deadening habits of an industrial and utilitarian ethic which they took to characterize the English and indeed the whole cultural mainstream of the western world. Synge, as concerned as Heaney with the idea of 'nourishment', proclaimed that art is made serious, 'not by the degree to which it is taken up with problems that are serious in themselves, but by the degree in which it gives the nourishment, not very easy to define, on which our imaginations live. We should not go to the theatre as we go to a chemist's or a dram shop, but as we go to a dinner where the food we need is taken with pleasure and excitement'.[16] Heaney's singer and his wild white goose are the source of 'the rich joy' of which Synge spoke, which is 'found only in what is superb and wild in reality'.[17]

The title-poem of the collection, 'Field-Work', fuses many of the themes of the book. It is a rich, imaginative exploration of the poet's relationship to the natural world, to his wife and to his artistic vocation. The poem opens with a precise and vividly drawn picture of a rural scene, that combines the reminder of Edenic perfection with intimations of mortality:

> Where the sally tree went pale in every breeze,
> Where the perfect eye of the nesting blackbird watched,
> Where one fern was always green.

The poet is watching his wife take in the washing and notices the vaccination mark on her arm. The perfect natural circle of the blackbird's eye is transmuted into the protective stigma of modern living. The slow passing of a train full of big-eyed cattle being carried to the slaughter-house momentarily separates the poet and his wife. The contrast between lines and circles becomes a major organizational principle of the poem. Part II further extends and manipulates the symbolism of rings and circles. His wife is metamorphosed into a 'wounded dryad' in a 'mothering smell of wet/ and ring-wormed chestnuts'. She bears her stigma, 'an O that's healed into the bark'. Merging with the natural world, she becomes a part of a great mystery that encompasses opposites: her 'wound' that is both disfigurement and innoculation is mirrored in the condition of nature which is both nurturing ('mothering') and diseased ('ring-wormed'). Her symbol of continuance and healing is the 'O'. This section ends with reference to the elemental image of the moon which overhangs them both, a contrast with the linear image of the train that separates them at the end of Part I. The moon which is small and far but still brilliant is associated with longing for the absolute, which they share in common with all mankind. It is compared to the coin long gazed at on the 'Pequod''s mast – another gleaming little circle pressed on wood (further suggesting the conjunction of male and female, the aspiring and the mundane) – which was the prize for capturing the elusive, mysterious white whale.

Part III presents a kaleidoscope of seasonal vignettes, culminating in the image of the sunflower. Each stanza begins with a 'No' or a

'Not' as the poet works through the things he does not want to be or
to do. He settles on the sunflower, its long straight stem connecting
it directly to earth, its heart a burning circle like the sun. The
sunflower, with its receptive senses of mouth and eye, is a model of
strength, beauty and stillness, drawing its sustenance from earth as
well as sun. Braced to a pebble-dashed wall, it represents a freedom
rooted in the earth and achieved through acceptance of the earth's
restraints and irregularities. It is 'dreaming umber', umber being the
brown earth pigment that is used to colour and beautify. Since
'umber' could be the object of 'dreaming' or 'dreaming umber' could
be an appositional phrase further defining 'sunflower', Heaney
achieves an effective double-meaning: the sunflower *is* what it
dreams about – a version of poesy as the gum which oozes from
whence 'tis nourished. But it is also transcendent, opposed to the
black weedy water full of 'pock-marked' leaves, the winter cow
parsley with its 'old whitened shins and wrists', and summer's 'tart
green shade'.

The word 'umber' appears again in Part IV, when Heaney
describes how he pressed a leaf onto his loved one's hand and then
daubed it with mould:

> my umber one,
> you are stained, stained
> to perfection.

This 'birthmark' signifies acceptance of and redemption from mortal-
ity. It signifies union with nature. It is 'staining' but, as the lesson of
the sunflower showed, the way to 'perfection'. Like the vaccination
mark, it is a disfigurement, but also the token of health and
wholeness. The mergence of human and natural is a ritual act ('I
anoint the anointed/ leaf-shape') through which life and love are
guaranteed and the loved one is blessed ('crossed/ criss-cross'),
anointed, innoculated against life's fever and fret. Once again
Heaney affirms for himself the role of healer and assuager. His field-
work is a kind of primitive earth magic.

In 'Field-Work' circles symbolize perfection – artistic, personal,
domestic, marital. In 'Casualty' they represent artistic perfection,
but also a kind of self-absorption that excludes the tribe. In 'An
Afterwards' the circle of art is a 'rabid egotistical daisy-chain' which
is bitterly resented by the poet's wife: 'She would plunge all poets in
the ninth circle' of Dante's inferno. The poet's self-absorption has

led him to neglect his family: ' "Why could you not have, oftener in our years/ Unclenched, and come down laughing from your room/ And walked the twilight with me and your children?" ' The allusions to Dante in this poem and in 'Leavings' prepares us for the last poem in *Field-Work*, a translation of Cantos xxxii and xxxiii of *The Inferno*. Heaney's poem, 'Ugolino', describes the ferocious savagery of Count Ugolino's revenge against Archbishop Roger for the latter's cruelty against Ugolino and his four sons:

> For the sins
> Of Ugolino, who betrayed your forts,
> Should never have been visited on his sons.

Ugolino's story of treachery, hunger, hunt-downs and hallucination could be an image of the vicious circle of violence that has constituted Irish history. Watching Ugolino tearing at Roger's head 'like a famine victim at a loaf of bread', the poet asks:

> Is there any story I can tell
> For you, in the world above, against him?

Confronted by a nightmare vision of cruelty, the poet presents himself as observer and intermediary. His self-appointed task is to try and understand the savagery, to 'report the truth' (the same concern Heaney made explicit in 'Kinship').

Heaney's characteristic method in *Field-Work* is to sustain a sometimes Dantean close-up of minutely detailed, realistic horror which then modulates into a sense of coming through into calm, mature reconciliation. The poems are a statement of the poet's faith that the harshness of the world is significantly less than the whole picture. 'September Song' has him 'in the middle of the way', poised between joy and melancholy, relief and unease, collapse and celebration: 'We toe the line/ between the tree in leaf and the bare tree.' But in 'Ugolino' the monstrous violence which the poet confronts seems to be all there is. Listening to Ugolino's story of injustice and seeing the ferocity of his revenge, the poet, like the Sibyl, adjudges the whole country hopelessly accursed: 'Pisa! Pisa, your sounds are like a hiss/ Sizzling in our country's grassy language.' Its people are unable to escape their tortured inheritance, condemned for all time to an Inferno of cruelty and hatred.

6

Sweeney Astray and *Station Island*

Heaney's continued troubling awareness of the conflict between the pull of the free exhilarated imagination on the one hand, and the claims of social responsibility on the other, is one of the things that prompted a special interest in the medieval Irish story of King Sweeney. In his Introduction to his own version of the poem, Heaney writes: 'Insofar as Sweeney is a figure of the artist, displaced, guilty, assuaging himself by his utterance, it is possible to read the work as an aspect of the quarrel between free creative imagination and the constraints of religious, political and domestic obligation.'[1] The Sweeney story, Heaney goes on to explain, provided him with the outward, mythologizing structure, an epic framework, for his own psychic materials:

> In this Sweeney story we have a Northern sacral king, Sweeney, who is driven out of Rasharkin in Co. Antrim. There is a sort of schizophrenia in him. On the one hand he is always whinging for his days in Rasharkin, but on the other he is celebrating his free creative imagination. Maybe here there was a presence, a fable which could lead to the discovery of feelings in myself which I could not otherwise find words for, and which could cast a dream or possibility or myth across the swirl of private feelings: an objective correlative.[2]

The figure of Sweeney had been haunting Heaney's imagination for a long time. He tells us that for over thirty years he had lived on the verges of Sweeney's ancient kingdom, in sight of many of Sweeney's places – Slemish, Rasharkin, Benevenagh, Dunseverick, the Bann, the Roe, the Mournes. When he began to work on his translation he had just moved to County Wicklow, near Sweeney's final resting place at St Mullins. 'One way or another,' Heaney writes, 'he seemed to have been with me from the start',[3] the connection between Heaney and Sweeney existing, as he once playfully remarked, even at the level of rhyme. Metaphor thus becomes a manifestation of the whole structure of the poem, not just a localized occurrence.

Significantly, however, the sheer power of the poetry first fired Heaney's interest. He had been working on the poem for many years:

> My first impulse had been to forage for the best lyric moments and to present them as poetic orphans, out of the context of the story. These points of poetic intensity, rather than the overall organiza-tion of the narrative, establish the work's highest artistic levels and offer the strongest invitations to the translator of verse. Yet I gradually felt I had to earn the right to do the high points by doing the whole thing: what I was dealing with, after all, is a major work in the canon of medieval literature.[4]

The Sweeney saga satisfied an essentially lyric impulse and at the same time offered an epic structure, not native to modern Irish conditions but essential to Heaney's poetry. It represented another kind of nurture. By using it Heaney forged another kind of relationship – with a literary tradition now half submerged in a forgotten language. Like Kinsella's Tain cycle and Montague's interest in Gaelic lore, it allowed Heaney to affirm a specifically Irish tradition that went beyond Yeats and Kavanagh. With *Buile Suibhne* Heaney could bring ancient mythic shapes into conjunction with his own psychic disposition, his own essentially artistic consciousness. He could think of his poetry as belonging to a larger Irish whole while embodying the private, creative moment.

Heaney follows the original story in telling of how Sweeney, the sacral king of Dal-Arie, comes into conflict with the distinguished ecclesiastic, Ronan Finn. The trouble starts when Sweeney discov-ers Ronan marking out a church in his territory. Sweeney takes Ronan's psalter and throws it into a lake (it is miraculously recovered, unharmed, by an otter). Then, when Ronan's psalmists come to bless Sweeney's army before battle, Sweeney thinks the gesture has been intended as a mockery and kills one of the acolytes. He throws a second spear at Ronan, piercing the sacred bell he wears round his neck. The peremptory cleric curses Sweeney, prophesying that he will take the form of a bird and eventually die by the spear. After the Battle of Moira, Sweeney is metamorphosed into a bird and the bulk of the story describes his subsequent wanderings and hardships until he is wounded by the spear of a jealous herd. Before he dies, however, Sweeney is reconciled, somewhat unconvincingly, to Christianity.

Heaney's version of the story is based on J. G. O'Keefe's bilingual edition which was published by the Irish Texts Society in 1913. This edition is based on a manuscript written in County Sligo between 1671 and 1674. The Sweeney story had, however, been taking shape in the ninth century, and was probably a development of traditions dating back to the Battle of Moira in A.D. 637 Heaney points out that the imagination which fastened on Sweeney's story was 'clearly in the grip of a tension between the newly dominant Chritian ethos and the older, recalcitrant Celtic temperament'.[5]

Buile Suibhne is a virtuoso lingusitic display. It is, says Heaney, a 'primer of lyric genres – laments, dialogues, litanies, rhapsodies, curses'.[6] It employs eleven different verse forms, some with highly complex metrical disciplines, exploiting the resources of alliteration, assonance and rhyme, and the quibbling ambiguities that arise from the use of words and phrases with multiple sense possibilities. Heaney adopts the only feasible approach – that of rendering the spirit of the original in his own way. Even the literal meaning of the original title (The Frenzy of Sweeney) is changed. Heaney tells us that, even though his title lacks 'the bursting sound of the original Irish', which something like 'Sweeney's Spasms' would have caught more expressively, he settled on 'Sweeney Astray' so that he could highlight the notion of derangement in both its physical and mental sense.[7]

To demonstrate how this double-focus is embedded in the 'deep structure' of the language of the original poem, Ciaran Carson, in his review of Heaney's translation, directs attention to these lines:

cian om eolus-sa
crioch gusa ranag-sa

They are from Section 45 and are omitted in Heaney's version. O'Keefe renders them as 'far from my home/ is the country I have reached'. Here we have the crucial concept which runs through all of Heaney's poetry – the ambivalent concept of 'home'. Home is the source of consolation, it is presence and possession, inheritance and nurture; but it is also authority and conformity, ritual observance of incontestible law and precept. All these things are more strongly signalled by the Irish word *eolas* which O'Keefe sometimes translates as 'home'. With the help of Dinneen's Irish Dictionary Carson adduces the following meanings: '"Knowledge of direction, way, guidance, bearings; knowledge, learning, skill; a habit, especially of frequenting a place; a recipe, a prescription or formula; an incantation.' And for *crioch* he finds these definitions which give frightening dimensions to the isolation of the adventurous, poetic spirit: 'furrow, boundary furrow; limit, end; region, territory; a definite end or object; business; *ceithre criocha deidheannacha an duine*, the "four last things" (death, judgment, heaven, hell)"'.[8]

The original text, like many early Irish compositions, consists of alternate prose and verse, the latter constituting the bulk of the work. The prose is devoted to the outward events of Sweeney's journey while the more stylised expression of the verse renders the inner, psychological journey. The poem is composed out of their dialogue. One of the rules of the Irish verse forms was that they must begin and end on the same word, and this may be seen as a fortuitous formal enactment in Sweeney's private utterance of the circular pattern followed by the outward events of his career: his original sin was caused by a spear, his life is ended by the spear. The Irish for spear – *beann* – also means horn or spire – emblems of Sweeney's original, royal, sacral position; but *beann* also means antler, wing, mountain-peak, crest, branch – all the things which obsess Sweeney in his deranged condition. Thus, in Section 40, where Sweeney's praise of trees and animals – especially the antlered stag – is intermingled with a rehersal of his own hardships and sorrows and thought of past glory, the word *beann*, its variants and homophone *binn* ('sweet, melodious') are used, according to Carson's count, forty-three times. In the original Sweeney calls himself *fer benn* – man of the peaks or antlers or spears (O'Keefe retains the original phrase as a proper noun, Heaney glosses it as 'Peak-pate, stag-head'): Sweeney is consciously dramatising himself as one who is his destiny. The verbal organisation is dense with possibility, a constant process of interchange where none of the elements is absolutely definable, 'pure' or fully present. Everything is caught up and traced through by everything else. Meaning is always somehow dispersed, divided and never quite at one with itself. Ambiguity and circularity form a complex tissue which is Sweeney's schizophrenia. His failure to dominate language enacts his inability to be in full possession of himself.

We can see why Flann O'Brien should have been attracted to the Sweeney story. When O'Brien revived Sweeney in *At-Swim-Two-*

Birds he was drawing on a work that not only exhibited an imaginative and verbal exuberance which matched his own, but also demonstrated an imprisoning structure, the elements of the story always mirroring or returning on themselves. This was the basis of O'Brien's experiment with the demoralising modernist notion of infinite regress. In *At-Swim-Two-Birds* Sweeney joins Finn McCool, a couple of cowboys and a group of modern-day Dubliners in a landscape of hilarious chaos and helpless, unchanging unreason. O'Brien's exploration of imaginative imprisonment is an immensely elaborate fictional excursion that delights in the observation that art cannot rescue us from our limitations. It is a novel about writing a novel, in which each story becomes a story within a story, each character a bewildering set of selves.

In their different ways, Heaney and O'Brien have found *Buile Suibhne* useful in their explorations of what we might call 'levels of reality' and the kind of relationship that might exist between them. Both writers are concerned with the limits of art, but also the enormous freedom that is possible within those limits. For O'Brien this is a matter of aesthetic metaphysics that he treats with ingenious playfulness. For Heaney the arbitrariness and innocence of the artistic impulse have serious social ramifications. It raises painful questions about the relationship between the artist and his 'home', questions of responsibility. O'Brien's procedures are those of encyclopaedic parody and promiscuous pastiche: Heaney's tone is serious.

Some of the heightened prose passages in the original Heaney renders in free verse. This is what happens in Section 11 describing Sweeney's transformation into a bird. The manic, strongly-alliterated sound patterns of the original are matched by the aural strenuousness of Heaney's rendering. The original is:

> . . . rolion nemhain & dobhar & dasacht & faoinnel & fualang & foluamain & udnhaille, anbsaidhe & anfhoistine, miosgais gach ionaidh ina mbiodh & serc gach ionaidh noco roichedh; romheir-bhlighset a meoir, rocriothnaighsiot a chosa, roluathadh a chroidhe, roclodhadh a chedfadha, rosaobadh a radharc, rotuitset a airm urnocht asa lamhuibh co ndeachaidh la breithir Ronain ar gealtacht & ar geinidecht amail gach n-ethaid n-aesdha.

O'Keefe's translation:

. . . whereupon turbulence, and darkness, and fury, and giddi-
ness, and frenzy, and flight, unsteadiness, restlessness, and
unquiet filled him, likewise disgust with every place which he had
not reached. His fingers were palsied, his feet trembled, his heart
beat quick, his senses were overcome, his sight was distorted, his
weapons fell naked from his hands, so that through Ronan's curse
he went, like any bird of the air, in madness and imbecility.

Heaney's version:

> His brain convulsed,
> his mind split open.
> Vertigo, hysteria, lurchings
> and launchings came over him,
> he staggered and flapped desperately,
> he was revolted by the thought of known places
> and dreamed strange migrations.
> His fingers stiffened,
> his feet scuffled and flurried,
> his heart was startled,
> his senses were mesmerized,
> his sight was bent,
> the weapons fell from his hands
> and he levitated in a frantic cumbersome motion
> like a bird of the air.
> And Ronan's curse was fulfilled.

Comparison with O'Keefe's translation highlights the tremendous
investment of energy in the manipulation of sound, rhythm, syntax
and metaphor in Heaney's effort to repossess the vigour of the
original. The intoxication of sound and phrase engages us at once,
catching us up in the strenuous metamorphosis taking place. The
lines constitute a kind of metaphorical enactment of the action. As
we take the meaning, re-create the action, respond to the syntax and
sense-movement against the verse structure, make the succession of
efforts necessary to pronounce the words, we perform in various
modes a continuous analogical enactment.

O'Brien's version lacks the immediacy of Heaney's. Tending
towards parody, it contrasts with Heaney's more severe idiom,

which is a blend of the homely and the formally dignified. Here is
O'Brien:

> . . . he was beleagured by an anger and a darkness, and fury and
> fits and frenzy and fright-fraught fear, and he was filled with a
> restless tottering unquiet and with a disgust for the places that he
> knew and a desire to be where he never was, so that he was
> palsied of hand and foot and eye-mad and heart-quick and went
> from the curse of Ronan bird-quick in craze and madness from the
> battle.[9]

Heaney's rendering of the original Irish also involves a revitaliz-
ation of the compact, short-lined, drill-like quatrain. It accomodates
both extremes of jubilation and lament, which are the poles between
which Sweeney's mood is continually swinging. And it is a useful
vehicle for the remarkable precision, concreteness and clarity of
Sweeney's perceptions of the visible world. Emphasis on the details
of the natural world makes the poetry alive with symbolic inward-
ness. The natural world impresses by its severity as well as its
beauty. Heaney's version of Section 45 draws on the battering
vitality of the Anglo-Saxon alliterative tradition to give utterance to
an imagination informed by the austerity of cold, plastering rains
and sharp-toothed winds. It is a landscape which the Anglo-Saxon
Wanderer or Seafarer would recognize. It is also King Lear's
untamed heath where 'unaccomodated man' sees himself as a poor
bare forked animal, like all the other animals. Heaney's version is on
the left, O'Keefe's on the right:

Without bed or board	Gloomy this life,
I face dark days	to be without a soft bed,
in frozen lairs	abode of cold first,
and wind-driven snow.	roughness of wind-driven snow.
Ice scoured by winds.	Cold, icy wind,
Watery shadows from weak sun.	faint shadow of a feeble sun,
Shelter from the one tree	shelter of a single tree,
on a plateau.	on the summit of a table-land.
Haunting deer-paths,	Enduring the rain-storm,
enduring rain,	Stepping over deer-paths,
first-footing the grey	faring through greensward
frosted grass.	on a morn of grey frost.

But Sweeney's utterance does not spring only from animal recognitions. He is sustained by a primeval landscape that he apprehends with religious force. Loneliness and despair are kept at bay by the natural magic of the countryside and by the intellectual force of Christianity. The trees and flowers and animals are hallowed by a vague lore, half-pagan, half-Christian. Heaney's most sustained lyric moment is found in the fifty-eight quatrains of Section 40. The section opens with a description of the trees of Ireland, after which Sweeney recounts his own sorrows and sufferings. This leads into a re-affirmation of his love of the woods, their birds and badgers and stags, and the section ends with Sweeney resuming his jeremiad. O'Keefe speculates on 'this lack of artistic coherence',[10] reminding us that, while characteristic of many medieval manuscripts, it may be due to an incomplete text. Or, he further suggests, it may be 'the author's way of representing the incoherent mind of the madman'.[11] As both the original and Heaney's version stand, the tensions of asceticism, Sweeney's guilt and melancholy, weave in and out of his paean to nature's beauty and abundance, and this combination brings out the pathos of Sweeney's condition. Here is Heaney's version of Sweeney's praise of the trees; beside it O'Keefe's:

Briars curl in sideways,
arch a stickle back,
draw blood and curl up innocent
to sneak the next attack.

O briar, little arched one,
thou grantest no fair terms,
thou ceasest not to tear me,
till thou hast thy fill of blood.

The yew tree in each churchyard
wraps night in its dark hood.
Ivy is a shadowy
genius of the wood.

O yew tree, little yew tree,
in churchyards thou art conspicuous;
O ivy, little ivy,
thou art familiar in the dusky wood.

Holly rears its windbreak,
a door in winter's face;
life-blood on a spear-shaft
darkens the grain of ash.

O holly, little sheltering one,
thou door against wind;
O ash tree, thou baleful one,
hand-weapon of a warrior.

In comparison with O'Keefe, Heaney's greater expressiveness is immediately felt. Heaney's lines are tauter, more subtly modulated. All the realms of whisper are given their voice in the sough and sigh of his sibilants and ricocheting vowels, and in the varying inflections of the rhythmical organization. Sense and sound commingle to convey the distinctive mood and movement of each stanza, the unique being, the proper quality of each tree. The slightest hint of abstraction is resolutely eschewed. We are not given an elaborate or sustained description of any of the trees, but rather a succession of pictures and images which the poet impressionistically calls before us by light and skilful touches. The half-said, the hint, the fleeting perception, is what is valued. Kuno Mayer has already made the connection between Japanese *Haiku* art and early Irish nature poetry. The eye is washed miraculously clear, the voice is content and eager with a simple joy and a young revelation. 'We are nearer the first world in that first poetry,' Heaney says, 'nearer to the innocent eye and tongue of Adam as he named the creatures.'[12] In his version, Heaney remains acutely sensitive to this kind of keen and unaffected delight in the beauty of the natural world. His panegyric style imitates the strictness and conciseness of the original. He tends to use metaphor instead of simile; he is bolder and more barbaric in his terms and figures than O'Keefe; his images are as vivid as they are precise and restrained, contributing to the original strange vision of natural things in an almost unnatural purity. He relishes the childlike, open-eyed attentiveness to the small and familiar. It is the kind of poetry Keats called 'great and unobtrusive' – 'a thing which enters into one's soul, and does not startle it or amaze it with itself, but with its subject'.[13] Impressions stand free, each to itself, eluding entirely all learned or literary intelligence. The poem, relying on the power of sight and sound, is a series of flashes of the actual. The images are 'actual', redeemed by the careful composition of the words, so that they are not literary, and they are not 'photographic'. What might lurk beneath the surface defies meaning, is infinitely less compelling than the words themselves. And this is so because the imagination functions in a world of things, not ideas. Heaney's interest in this kind of poetry amounts almost to an act of defiance. Educated and knowledgeable comment on the contemporary situation, the habits of everyday speech and thought, what most people would like poetry to be about – all of this is rejected for a poetry of great sensuous freshness and verbal purity, a poetry intent on revealing the power of a thing to be itself. His interest is in a language that will cut beneath the formulated, the stereotype, the incantation, to yield a moment of insight. His witness brings the trees into existence in a new way; it is a birth of new life, a release of possibility, an increment to being. It affirms the miraculous variety of the world. Through the refinement of his musical effects, he looks for an immediacy that will transform merely descriptive verse: it is not just the trees but the emotion which matters. In comparison with O'Keefe, Heaney's expression is more subtly personal. Sweeney's mind is the centre, the sensitive focus of the interest. The intricate lacework of sound, rhyme and rhythm reveals the lively humanity behind this curious fabric, helping to turn literal exposition into evocation. Two main strands of image inform Sweeney's utterance. They are the two opposing forces which have driven him astray. On the one hand there is the *pagus*, the pagan wilderness, lush, barbaric, unrestrained, severe, to which he responds as unregenerate natural man. On the other hand there is the arch and the door and the churchyard, the dark hood and the crown, the spear-shaft and the queen, attacks and blessings – the social world with its hunts and battles, its civilization and its Christian *disiplina*. Like much early Irish nature poetry, the writing here belongs to the anchorite tradition which combined praise and penitence. *Sweeney Astray* is a poem grounded in a deep affiliation to the old mysteries of nature, in the direct, simple, trusting perceptions of a child, even while ultimately proclaiming its fidelity to the new religion. Sweeney, Heaney comments, 'is at once the enemy and the captive of the monastic tradition',[14] as Heaney himself is divided between the claims of illiterate piety and the pressures of the contemporary, public world, and desperately trying to reconcile the two.

In *Station Island*, Heaney's recent collection,* the poet's role continues to be a matter of urgent and tormented inquiry. The title poem in twelve parts, placed at the centre of the book, is composed of a narrative sequence set on Station Island in Lough Derg in County Donegal, which has been a site of pilgrimage in Ireland for over a thousand years. The island is also known as St Patrick's Purgatory because he was supposed to be the founder of the penitential vigil of fasting and praying which still constitutes the basis of the three-day pilgrimage. Each unit of the pilgrim's exercises is called a 'station' and involves walking barefoot and praying round the 'beds', stone circles which are said to be the remains of early medieval monastic cells. As the poet wanders among the worshippers there is enacted a series of dream encounters with familiar ghosts, some of them writers who have exerted an important influence on him.

---

* Heaney's *The Haw Lantern* (London: Faber, 1987) appeared after the present book had gone to press.

The poem is the chronicle of an inner, circular journey, a search for coherence and integrity. Like Kinsella's dream journey to the underworld and the land of the dead in 'One', 'Finistere' or his river journey poem 'Downstream', 'Station Island' takes its mythic structure from Dante's *Commedia*. 'Station Island', Heaney says, is 'a purgatorio in itself . . . involving a dark night and a bright morning, a departure from the world and a return to it'.[15] At first he says he was put off the idea of setting his poem on Lough Derg because other writers had been there before him – Carleton, O'Faolain, Kavanagh, Dennis Devlin. But with Dante's example, he thought of using actual people to dramatize his own crisis of conscience, and making Carleton 'a sort of Tyrone Virgil', and Kavanagh 'a latter-day Co. Monaghan Cavalcanti'.[16] Most useful of all, however, was the model Dante provided of the poet who had managed to reconcile the contrarieties which bedevilled Heaney: historical and political consciousness with free, exhilarated imagination, values and judgements with local intensity, personal realism with dramatic creation. These strains Heaney sought to present 'by meeting shades from my own dream-life who had also been inhabitants of the actual Irish world. They could perhaps voice the claims of orthodoxy and the necessity to refuse those claims. They could probe the validity of one's commitment'.[17]

The first meeting is with Simon Sweeney, the Sweeney of whom Heaney writes in the Introduction to *Sweeney Astray*: 'I was in a country of woods and hills and remembered that the green spirit of the hedges embodied in Sweeney had first been embodied for me in the persons of a family of tinkers, also called Sweeney, who used to camp in the ditchbacks along the road to the first school I attended.'[18] The Sweeney of the 'Station Island' poem is such a genius of the woods, a free, pagan spirit. Heaney's memory of him is tinged with fear: in the warmth and safety of his 'bedroom dark' the ghostly presence of this 'mystery man', drenched with natural magic, would haunt the child's imagination. Sweeney, who lives exposed to elemental influences, dismisses the child's 'civilized' learning and silences his presumption with the colloquially ambiguous, '"Damn all you know."' Sweeney is a druidical figure, the denizen of a dark archaic world before history and before Christianity. The description of him amongst the trees 'with a bow-saw, held/stiffly up like a lyre' connects the barbaric life of the woods with the lyrical imagination. This suggestion may not be without some historical basis, for there are those scholars who tell us that the *fili*, the formal poet of Celtic culture, was continuous with the archaic 'druid', the root of the word 'druid' being *doire*, meaning an oak grove. The spirit of place moves in the poem's vocabulary of breathing, whispering, brushing, rustling, sensing, saddening and conjuring. This is an eerie music, sibilant and vowelling, and it contrasts with the hard urgency of the 'quick bell' which summons the pilgrims to their devotions. Despite Sweeney's warning, ' "Stay clear of all processions!" ' the poet is unable or unwilling to resist communal expectations. He follows the crowd's 'drugged path' and, as past dissolves into present, the bell that awakened him from his dream of Sweeney years ago, rings again to call him to his prayers.

In Section II Heaney meets William Carleton, the nineteenth century novelist and short story writer from County Tyrone. Carleton is presented as a vigorous peasant figure, anti-clerical and common-sensical. Heaney describes him as 'bareheaded, big, determined/ in his sure haste along the crown of the road'; he is an 'aggravated man'; at the end he 'headed up the road at the same hard pace'. Details such as these reflect the real-life Carleton's pesonality and style: spontaneous, careless of form, improvised, utilitarian, rapid, colloquial. Carleton's work was the product of an instinctive realism, of close feeling for the textures of Irish peasant life, and in his stories of Lough Derg pilgrims, of hedge-schools, flax-pullings, dances and local characters, Heaney recognizes an affinity with his own rural experience. Heaney's image of him hastening 'along the crown of the road' neatly encapsulates the story of a life spent seeking the middle of the road between the extremes of its Catholic origins and those of its adopted Protestant-ism.

Poetry, Keats believed, should come as naturally as the leaves on the trees. Such natural efflorescence has, historically, not been at all easy for the Irish poet to come by. Unless the generative force is indeed a strong one, how can there be natural growth without benefit of an enduring and recognizable culture? With no contin-uity, no shared history, no reliable audience, the Irish writer's experience has typically been one of exposure and alienation. His is, as Thomas Kinsella says, a divided mind.[19] Carleton is a con-spicuous example of an Irish writer trying to make his way without the vital sustaining force of an available tradition. With nothing in his inheritance to help him towards an identity, he must improvise one for himself. 'Carleton had to become a partisan of one group or another', writes Seamus Deane, and Deane's further comment that Carleton 'would have liked to be free of the need for his consistent adversarial status'[20] pin-points the special relevance to Heaney of this 'aggravated man'. Not only aggravated, but absurd too, as Heaney suggests in the picture he gives of him 'flailing between the attitudes of his adopted faith and the affection of his deserted tribe',[21] in 'A Tale of Two Islands', an essay published four years before *Station Island*.

Carleton's defensiveness stemmed from his rejection of Catholicism, motivated partly by the frustration of his early priestly ambition, partly by his anxiety to secure an audience as well as a livelihood. So it was that this 'pure-bred Catholic if ever there was one',[22] as Kavanagh calls him, allowed his precise and intimate knowledge of the Irish peasantry to be exploited by the fanatical Rev. Caesar Otway, editor of *The Christian Examiner*, an organ of the Protestant evangelical revival in the 1820s and 1830s. In the pages of this magazine, Carleton made his literary debut with melodramatic sketches excoriating Catholic superstition. Recognizing the limitations imposed by Otway's polemical requirements, he set out to provide a more faithful picture of the manners of his people in his best-known work, *Traits and Stories of the Irish Peasantry* (1830).

Carleton values what he can in the peasant subculture, but his living tradition is in English. His work marks the transition from the tale of oral tradition to the literary mode of the modern short story: entrapped by history, he contributed to the demise of the culture which he wanted to preserve. He can no more fully possess his origins than he can the larger world. The double-consciousness produces a curious literature. In the interests of keeping faith with the realities of peasant life, he (like Kavanagh after him) resists turning the intimately known 'truth' of the hidden Ireland into an ennobling myth; yet there is an ambivalence, a necessary distancing of himself from roots in order to impose an order, deriving from one polemic or another (he wrote for every shade of opinion in Ireland), upon the swarm and tumult of memory and passion. As Heaney comments in his essay: 'Synge's discovery of his subject involved an escape: Carleton's involved a denial'.[23] This denial is at the bottom of the waste and dissipation of energy which characterize Carleton's career, in the end leaving him, in Thomas Flanagan's harsh words, 'a hack whose pen was for hire in Dublin's ugly literary wars'.[24] The guilt and self-criticism Carleton voices in 'Station Island' sound very like Heaney's own in 'Whatever You Say Say Nothing': the bigotry of Orangemen and Ribbonmen, Carleton says, have made him into the 'old fork-tongued turncoat/ who mucked the byre of their politics'.

Like Heaney, Carleton lived in turbulent times: in the poem he says he 'smelled hanged bodies rotting on their gibbets/ and saw their looped slime gleaming from the sacks'.[25] But Carleton's politics, as Flanagan also says, was ultimately 'a politics of the spirit'.[26] He could lay bare the raw nerve of peasant passion, but could not come to terms with the formal ideologies which shaped contemporary Ireland and gave it meaning. He had complete confidence in his peasant material, but his treatment of it betrayed his divided feelings, torn as he was between love and loathing of his country, his people and their religion. In him the old Gaelic values and those of the modern public world clashed, and he never found a way to master the resulting confusion. Documentary truth and moral purpose were more important to him than aesthetic considerations. There is no more profound and sympathetic rendering of the Irish character in the nineteenth century, but it comes to us in fragments, in the tales and sketches, in the novels out of a morass of amorphous narrative, incredible characterization, crude melodrama, rhetorical excess and persistent editorializing. In the absence of a properly considered aesthetic, the real source of his power – his imaginative sympathy with his people – was continually being disrupted and diffused.

For Heaney, Carleton represents the plight of the artist in Ireland, his difficulty in clearing an imaginative space for himself – that 'sunlit space' of which Heaney was so appreciative in *North*. In the 'Station Island' poem, sound and image intensify the poet's sense of clamour and clogging. Born within earshot of an Hibernian Hall, yet 'always Orange drums'. The natural world which once had been his inspiration is dark and heavy – not with fecundity, but despair. Confessing that he has 'no mettle for the angry role', Heaney feels lost. This dejected reverie is interrupted by the brisk, sensible voice from the nineteenth century, the voice of a man whose instinct it was always to play safe in the interests of respectability and reputation. There is the middle road, the way of not remaining subject to the forces which, at the other extreme, impel Joycean flight. Life, Carleton says, '"is a road you travel on your own"'; tribulation is purifying. In hard times it is necessary to become hard too – even traitorous. Acceptance, keeping your head, making sense of what comes – these are the golden rules:

'We are earthworms of the earth, and all that
has gone through us is what will be our trace.'

In his essay, Heaney discovers in Carleton's work itself corrobor-
ation for this assertion of a level beneath the surface at which mind
and milieu are one, at which the energies of the dialect are released
and an inner freedom is realized.

Carleton's world, 'instead of being described and idealized from
without . . . is welling up from within himself'. Will has not
subdued imagination: 'what remains most potently in the mind is
the substance of what is being condemned'. In 'The Lough Derg
Pilgrim', the sound of the pilgrims at prayer 'was the sound of that
underworld that made Carleton': his 'country Catholic being
responds in complete harmony to the humbled melodies of his own
patient tribe'. It is 'the music of his own humanity'.[27] For Heaney,
Carleton is the instinctual artist.

And yet, however reassuring Carleton's assertions in 'Station
Island' may be to the despondent poet, there is a naivety in the
aphoristic confidence, which Heaney uses to mark the limits of
Carleton's success as an artist and his value as a mentor. Carleton's
image of primitive worm-like digestion underestimates the stresses
and strains of accommodating the larger world: it does not begin to
take account of the complex processes of mediation which are
involved in the artistic enterprise and which crucially determine the
quality of the artist's 'trace'. (As far as his own 'trace' was
concerned, what mattered most to Carleton was its closeness to life:
that was justification enough for his polemic.) More sophisticated
than Carleton's notion of digestive process is Heaney's twin
emphasis on 'incubation' (technique) and 'mastery' (craft). The
combination of these two enables him to see conflict, to understand
it, as Yeats did, at the deepest levels of the personality, and to turn it
into the substance of his poetry. This is what happens in the
whispering, ghostly dream-realm of 'Station Island', for Heaney
knows – what Carleton did not – that until the quarrel is internalized
we make rhetoric and not art. Heaney's sensibility is attuned to the
sacral, to the archetypal and mythic resonances of experience:
Carleton is political, historical and realistic. Heaney submits all to
the dark: Carleton pursues the crown of the road.

Another meeting (in Section IV) is between the poet and a
disillusioned priest who, in his mid-twenties, had gone to the
Phillipines as a missionary. The priest's life of renunciation and

service is one of the blurred memories that swim into the pilgrim-
poet's mind just at the moment when, on Station Island, he is about
to utter the 'dream words, "I renounce."' The phrase 'Dream words'
immediately signals a good deal about Heaney's attitude. What
follows is an exploration of the relationship between the inner and
outer worlds through the dramatized interplay of the poet (who
places the inner life above the public one) and the priest (who places
the public above the private). Both poet and priest are seen to
embrace and renounce simultaneously their Catholic origins. The
poet embraces them as material he can use as a poet, but renounces
them as a man in the world; years ago the priest embraced
'convention' and though he continues to do so it is only for the sake
of his people not out of deeply felt religious conviction, for as far as
he is concerned, '"the god . . . has withdrawn"'.

The poem details the priest's private disaffection. Recounting his
missionary experience, he is conscious of how oddly out of place his
vocation and the arcane ritual of his church are in the steaming
luxuriance of the rain forests. The forests represent a strange,
untamed, natural force in the world that is forever beyond the
hieratic discipline of Catholicism: '"In long houses/ I raised the
chalice above headdresses/ *In hoc signo*. . . . On that abandoned/
mission compound, my vocation/ is a steam off drenched creepers."'
The country and its climate, we gather, destroyed him in mind and
body. As it turns out, there is about the priest something more than
his polished shoes that is 'unexpectedly secular' beneath his clerical
vestments.

Self-doubt plagues the priest, but the poet is constrained to
acknowledge his value to the community. However, references to
the priest being as 'glossy as a blackbird' and arriving like 'some
kind of holy mascot' once again betray the poet's attitude. He speaks
as an outsider. He cannot resist a note of gentle ridicule. Occasion-
ally the criticism is more pointed, as when he accuses the priest of
giving 'too much relief'. While the poet is sensitive to the people's
need, he is irritated by their sentimental observance.

For Carleton there was still a true, albeit submerged, source of
power which lay in the earth of Irish rural life. The Carleton section
implies the sanctity of this rich, deep, intimately known life that was
available to him and which, under pressure from the outside world,
he could never wholly possess. For the priest, the source has proved
to be an illusion. All that remains to him are the outward forms.
There is nothing lying deep within him or his community to sustain

him – only the knowledge of his people's need, and that he continues to serve without conviction and without faith. What surprises him is that the sceptic poet who, unlike himself, has not been 'unaware', should also be seen to be 'going through the motions' of a pilgrim on Station Island. It must be the poet 'taking a last look', he thinks.

'The last look' is a phrase which, through repetition, accrues weight. The action of the pilgrim-poet following the priest's shade through the mist as he prays round the beds dissolves into the childhood memory of accompanying the priest on his 'circuits', in much the same way as he had imagined attending his ancient progenitor in 'Kinship' (as 'squire of his circuits'). He recalls a visit to a man taking his 'last look' on life, perhaps the Donegal man who, earlier in the book, is the subject of an elegy called 'Last Look'. The 'bare' road, the 'drizzly evening/ when steam rose' and 'knee-deep mists' of Station Island merge with the childhood scene; but also with the exotic conditions in which the priest's health and faith failed him: the poet recognizes the mystifying, demoralizing spirit of the rain forests which is present, though less overwhelmingly, in both the immediate scene and his memory of the past. In the circumstances of death, however, he can also perceive the promise of life and re-birth ('when steam rose like the first breath of spring') – hope which resides, significantly, not in the Christian gospel administered by the priest, but in the instinctive, pagan apprehension of natural cycles. The earlier elegy is a celebratory 'last look' at a man whose life exemplified this kind of mystical intercourse with the ordinary but still miraculous world. So complete is his self-absorption that not even a dazzling vision of Niamh could have distracted his attention and 'drawn him out/ from the covert of his gaze'. In that poem, as in Kavanagh's 'Epic', the parochial gods make their own importance.

Both poet and priest describe the eternal image of the circle. '. . . where a sick man/ had taken his last look one drizzly evening . . .': this is the thin, sickly music of mortality; but it modulates into the sure, broad vowels and deliberate measure of the following solid-sounding lines:

> when steam rose like the first breath of spring,
> a knee-deep mist I waded silently
>
> behind him, on his circuits, visiting.

The last, heavily-accented 'visiting' achieves a special emphasis, while its participial form reinforces notions of recurrence, protraction and denial of finality, thus helping to enact the full meaning of the circuit or circle. 'Visiting', we understand, is as much a part of the artistic vocation as the priestly one. Both priest and poet are 'going through the motions', the priest the motions of his vocation, the poet the 'circuits' of his pilgrimage, but also the motions that carry him back and forth through time and space, the motions of his life, of memory and consciousness. The priest's circle has exemplary significance in that his 'circuit' at all points touches on the community, is, in fact, constituted by it. The force with which the last 'visiting' occurs emphasizes this kind of contact, and it is one to which the poet aspires in the very writing of this poem. The crucial difference between them is that the priest's circle does not include himself: it is a 'convention'; while the circle of the poet's art is created out of a surrender to energies that spring within the centre of his mind. The assured and intimate portrait he gives us of the priest and the people, along with his personal return to a Catholic ethos in the choice of Lough Derg as setting for the whole poem, constitute the poet's 'solidarity with orthodox ways and obedient attitudes'. That is crossed with a 'personal realism' which continually 'probes the validity of his commitment'. Heaney is taking 'the last look' on the personal and cultural implications of his Catholic origins. And the precision of his delineation, the intimacy and sensitivity of his understanding, are proof that while he is 'clear' of all this, as the priest can see, he is clear *about* it too.

In hoc signo: for Heaney this is the poem, with its 'openness to life' (Leavis' phrase) its delicate equilibrium of contending attitudes, its disinterested reconciliation of opposing impulses. The poem as verbal icon. We can appreciate how attractive that project must be to a sceptical, liberal, 'aware' intellectual like Heaney, disoriented by the clash between the communal imperative and the need for personal realism.

In the next section (Section V) Heaney continues to research his origins in a luxuriant, childhood world of morning field smells, the 'sex-cut' of sweetbriar after rain, new-mown meadow hay, birds' nests filled with leaves. Three more 'fosterers' rise from this setting – two schoolmasters and the poet, Patrick Kavanagh, whom the poet follows 'like a man lifting swathes at a mower's heels'. These ghostly masters and mentors seem to be almost a part of the landscape and its vegetation. The master's sibilant whisper is like the sound of scythes in his 'lost meadows', and when he speaks it is to lament the passing of the world he knew. An unmistakeable sense of tentativeness, insubstantiality and loss pervades these childhood recollections, which can only be fixed and kept alive by a kind of incantation. We feel throughout the strain to make a landscape of the past speak, the effort to make whispers intelligible:

> As I stood among their whispers and bare feet
> the mists of all the morning I set out
> for Latin classes with him, face to face,
> refreshed me. *Mensa, mensa, mensam*
> sang in the air like a busy whetstone.

As the poem proceeds the spirit of place gradually crystallizes out of the fragmented obliqueness and nostalgia of the green world of the past. The language of mind 'sings'. It articulates itself in direct speech and straightforward moralizing. The two masters, though they may be distinguished from the communal life of their place by their position and their Latin learning, are nevertheless the bearers and keepers of native tradition.

Kavanagh makes a fleeting appearance as the author of 'Lough Derg', his posthumously published poem written in 1942. Kavanagh is a no-nonsense, brusque, sardonic figure, and speaks with the same oracular authority as the masters. Refusing to take the public life too seriously, his 'parting shot' (' "In my own day/ the odd one came here on the hunt for women" ') demonstrates his much-vaunted attitude of 'not caring',[28] the detached view from above, the anarchic tendency of the imaginative and speculative mind, which, he argued, produces the comic vision of the true poetic spirit. Heaney catches the voice of a sensibility acutely of its time and place, its colloquial vigour affirming an imagination that refreshes itself in the humble and common. This is the Kavanagh who in his own writings proclaimed that the purpose of a poem is 'to explode the atoms of our ordinary experience',[29] to offer 'the small unique thing which is the most the greatest possess',[30] 'to give people an enthusiasm for life, to draw their attention to the wonder of the fields, the weeds'.[31] For Kavanagh the great poet 'turns neither to Dublin, London nor Paris, but to the Eternal. He dreams from his tiny foothold of the Known to the Unknown.'[32] Heaney's Kavanagh jibes at the poet who craves for wider experience than that afforded by fidelity to roots (' "Where else would you go? Iceland, maybe?

Maybe the Dordogne?"'). Such was Louis MacNeice who had turned
to the distant shores of Iceland, who, frustrated by the tangible
world, found a theme in the evocation of Nordic mists. Heaney sees
himself following in Kavanagh's footsteps, the word 'pad' relating
the poetic life to the original drives of animal instinct, and
continuing the poem's opening animal image of the schoolmaster
who swims towards the poet and enters his consciousness as a
species of desperate, primitive energy.

Heaney's poem enacts Kavanagh's 'need to go back', to return to
the past, to roots, to the idyllic world, to the womb, to the Mother
which is 'the thing which gives us a world of our own'.[33] Kavanagh
exemplified for Heaney the poet who, in expressing the 'hard,
buried life'[34] of his community, divested of all picturesque elements,
was the Antaean voice of his people. And the prerequisite of such
endeavour is love. 'Real roots lie in our capacity for love and its
abandon',[35] Kavanagh has said. Heaney's schoolmaster urges the
same virtue: his poem is a demonstration of it. And all the more
pressingly so because the original objects of that love exist now only
as shufflings on the concrete, weakened voices, rustlings, whisper-
ings, withdrawings, figures gone quiet and small, faces that have
gone distant, breath that rushes the air softly.

Section VI of 'Station Island' has the poet retreating from the
external adult world, whose pressures are symbolized by the
summoning bell, and surrendering to the irresistible magic of the
woods. He enters, intimately and passionately, into an alternative,
secret, childhood world in which the human form merges with the
embowering mystery of fern and broom and catkin:

> Freckle-face, fox-head, pod of the broom,
> Catkin-pixie, little fern-swish:
> Where did she arrive from?
> Like a wish wished
> And gone, her I chose at 'secrets'
> And whispered to.

This is a complex mesh of sound and echo, the delicate beauty of the
musical textures almost excessive, though rhythmic strength
balances the soft-edged lyricism. The tone is a blend of tenderness,
love, yearning, frustration and pain. This hidden, whispering
sanctuary with its 'tramped neolithic floor' is a primordial state of
being. Yielding to its seducements brings unease and guilt:

where the bent grass
Whispers on like reeds about Midas's
Secrets, secrets. I shut my ears to the bell.
Head hugged. Eyes shut. Leaf ears. *Don't tell. Don't tell.*

The unease the poet feels about opting for the woods rather than responding to the bell is related to Midas's predicament when he was given a pair of ass's ears for preferring Pan over Apollo in a musical contest. Pan was the personification of deity displayed in creation and pervading all things. He was the god of flocks and herds, of the woods and all material substances. His lower part was that of a goat because of the asperity of the earth; his upper part that of man because ether was the 'hegemonic of the world'. The lustful nature of the god symbolized the spermatic principle, and his libbard's skin the immense variety of created things. The character of 'blameless Pan' represented that wisdom which governs the world. All of these details, glossed from Phornutus (*De Natura Deorum*) are relevant to Heaney's poem. The story goes that when Apollo, contemptuous of Midas's judgement, gave the king a pair of ass's ears, Midas tried to hide them under his cap, until a servant discovered the King's secret and, unable to contain himself, confided his secret to the earth and the sounds of a river bank. The reeds of this river were used for pan-pipes and hautbois, which repeated the secret about Midas's ears that had been whispered to them.

The secret life of Pan embraces the poet's most intimate feelings about the woods, sexuality and language. It is the *id*, the secret self, the free imagination, the buried impulse. The repressive force of Christianity is what inhibits his full and free embracement of this primitive, pagan, secret life, which the shades of Horace and Dante seem to express for him. Dante, as the last line of the poem indicates, is 'translated, given, under the oak tree'; but Heaney, too, is 'translated', as Bottom or Midas was; by the end of the poem he, too, has surrendered, 'given' himself, to the sustaining, transfiguring power of the old tree magic.

In the next section (Section VII), however, Heaney is recalled from his enchantment by the frightening ghost of a friend who had been gunned down in cold blood in his own shop. The elliptical, almost surrealistic style of the last section is replaced by a more solid, documentary, narrative form. The odd, tantalizing whispering of private utterance gives way to a public language of colloquial speech that employs the repetitive structures of tension and anguish, and a swift, unceremonious music which relies on a kind of unremitting, consonantal battering. The classical measures of Dante are exchanged for a flexible, decasyllabic, three-line stanza, animated by the frequent use of idiomatic direct speech and discomfiting half-rhyme. The circumstances of the anonymous death are vividly dramatized in all their pathos and brutality, and the guilty poet, his confidence in himself and his art shaken, pleads for forgiveness:

> 'Forgive that I have lived indifferent –
> forgive my timid circumspect involvement . . .'

It is not simply the directly impinging political horror that leaves him incapable in the face of death. Nor does he worry only about his role as a poet, but about his life as a man in relation with other men. These central sections are wracked by a pervasive sense of guilt and emptiness. Section VIII has the poet on his knees at the 'hard mouth' of St Brigid's Bed, confronting the most troubling memories of all. One of them is of his last visit to a young archaeological friend dying in hospital of a chest disease. Friend and poet though he is, Heaney feels he has failed his friend in not being able to find the words that would confirm the bond between them. He feels he has deserted him in his time of need, his own hard mouth incapable of more than uneasy 'banter':

> as usual,   I had somehow broken
> covenants, and failed an obligation.

The young man is Tom Delaney who was Assistant Keeper of Medieval Antiquities at the Ulster Museum in Belfast until his death in 1979. As a tribute to his memory, his songs were collected, and the book, including an early version of Heaney's poem, formed the basis of the 'Tom Delaney Memorial Concert', which Heaney introduced. In the words of appreciation from friends and colleagues, Delaney was remembered as one who worked to forge cross-border links to help remove the traditional partisan approach to Irish Studies, and as one whose passion for medieval archaelogy had promoted the integration of Irish medieval studies into the mainstream of European archaeology. The sudden deterioration of his health took place when he was excavating at Carrickfergus. Heaney speaks of him digging in 'in that hard place/ in a muck of bigotry under the walls/ picking through shards and Williamite cannon balls'. The dying man's only comfort lay in 'still-faced archaeology'. These are, of course, the tactics and resources which Heaney sought to develop into an aesthetic. In the early version the archaeologist confirms for Heaney 'the fierce need for love', and makes explicit the affinity between them in identifying his archaeology and Heaney's poetry as 'Soft weeds from the slime of history'.[36] Heaney refers to him as a 'woodkerne' (an ancient Irish foot soldier), the same term he applies to himself in 'Exposure'.

Heaney knows the isolation and disappointment the archaeologist must have felt about his quiet, patient quest for understanding of what has made us what we are: it was, after all, the same feeling which haunted Heaney about his own work. The sense of frustration and waste felt by the man dead at thirty-two recalls that of Owen's alter-ego in 'Strange Meeting', and, faced with it, the poet is reduced through guilt and despair to a state of speechless immobility. But then a new movement is inaugurated when the poet, impelled by the same archaeological instinct as his friend, turns to the past and the solid, incontrovertible objects from the past, to possess them imaginatively, as the source of both knowledge and comfort. The failures and injustices of the individual life can only be managed when they are seen in relation to the great timeless continuities of human history that are revealed in archaeology and poetry, the soft weeds rooted in primeval slime. The new momentum, the new direction and confidence, are signalled by the repetition: 'I saw . . . And then I saw . . .'. The first thing he sees is a hoard of polished stone axes – the Malone Axe Hoard in the Ulster Museum – found in 1872 off the Malone Road in Belfast. Commenting on this find, Heaney had this to say: 'Ever since I first saw these stones they have stayed with me. Because of their colour and shape and size, and because they were worked and handled by Stone Age men from this part of the country, they have a tremendous aura. There is a charge of primitive force around them, and a definite touch of menace.'[37] Hence, in the poem they have the smoothness of an enormous black beetle's back, and the shape and colour of a cairn that looks like a bomb; they are 'the eggs of danger'. Only after this disturbing primal energy is acknowledged can it be displaced: what the poet finally seizes on is a kind of expressive antidote to the perennial nameless horror hidden in the stones. The second object he sees is a composed and elegant art-work, a plaster cast of an abbess done by the Gowran master, 'mild-mouthed and cowled, a character of grace', which is the treasured gift his dead friend once had given him, the expression of the sanative, civilizing mind.

As befits a tribute to the dead, this is where the early version ends, but in the final one the tentative affirmation of art promoted by the poet's dead friend is abruptly reversed. Once again Art is challenged by Atrocity. Another ghost, a bleeding, pale-faced boy, rises up to take the archaeologist's place. More frigtening still, this one openly charges the poet with breaking covenants and failing obligations. It is Heaney's cousin, Colum McCartney, whom Heaney had commemmorated in *Field-Work*. The ghost arraigns him for those gentle, 'artistic', unvengeful verses, and demands tribal solidarity:

> 'You confused evasion and artistic tact . . .
> . . . you whitewashed ugliness and drew
> the lovely blinds of the *Purgatorio*
> and saccharined my death with morning dew.'

Section IX is even more tortuous and tortured. Speaking about the sense of guilt which throbs behind the writing of this section, Heaney once detailed at a poetry-reading the circumstances out of which it was composed: his family was at the wake of a neighbour who had died on hunger strike, while he was at an Oxford poetry-reading, staying in Sir Keith Joseph's room at All Souls.[38] The section begins with the voice of the hunger striker recounting his short, desperate life. There is a dream-like quality, a light-headedness, about this section that is created by the continually shifting perspectives, abrupt transitions, the telescoping of past and present, the half-rhyme and the relentlessly pursuant rhythms. This structure expresses the fluid, heightened sensations of the hunger striker's disorientated state of mind, and it is continued into the poet's own introspective probing. The poet 'dreamt and drifted' until he finds himself confronting the nightmare experience of his own guilt. The lines have more than an echo of Kinsella's 'Nightwalker':

> All seemed to run to waste
> As down a swirl of mucky, glittering flood
> Strange polyp floated like a huge corrupt
> Magnolia bloom, surreal as a shed breast,
> My softly awash and blanching self-disgust . . .
> Then, like a pistil growing from the polyp,

> A lighted candle rose and steadied up
> Until the whole bright-masted thing retrieved
> A course and the currents it had gone with
> Were what it rode and showed.

The long, open vowels and slack trailing rhythm emphasize the dark sense of futility and self-disgust. But that pivotal 'Then' initiates an accelerating movement, made purposeful by the plosives and gutturals, prolonged and deepened by the cumulative assonance of 'growing', 'rose', 'whole', 'course', 'rode', 'showed', 'no', 'more', which gives an impression of straining toward effulgent revelation. The lighted candle recalls the archaeologist's gift in the previous poem, the plaster cast of the abbess done by the Gowran master, which the poet says 'will be a candle in our house'. What he perceives is the enlightening and steadying influence of a kind of phallic power that renovates the disoriented feminine principle. It is the confluence of instinctual feminine flow and masculine control that is the guarantee of both revelation and mastery: that twin achievement is rhetorically expressed by the internal rhyme of 'rode and showed'.

These ideas are further developed in the next part where Heaney remembers coming upon an old brass trumpet in a loft. The trumpet is an incongruous image, not in keeping with the ethos of the place. It dazzles and mesmerizes the poet with its enchanting circles. He shies away from the mystery, thinking it beyond him. The trumpet is an image of art, one of the means of symbolically resolving contradictory impulses. Unwilling or unable to assent to it, he is left with only hate and frustration, a loss of dignity. His expression is reduced to 'mouthings', his mirror-image to 'a half-composed face'. He feels like a man standing drunk before a bathroom mirror, 'Lulled and repelled by his own reflection' – an echo of his earlier sickening dream-experience. He longs for totalization, for plenitude and wholeness, for a relationship of correspondence between subject and object: subject reflected in object and object in subject. 'How exquisitely the individual mind/. . . to the external world/ Is fitted', Wordsworth wrote, 'and how exquisitely too,/ The external world is fitted to the mind'. What such a mirror relationship offers is a vision of the self as a unified whole, a comforting sense of the world as 'home'. In this mode of being, the cairnstone does not defy the cairn, the eddy does not reform the pool, the stone can never be ground to a different core. Insofar as art provides an image of this

self-enclosed organic unity, there is a hidden analogy between God
and the artist, and between God's relation to his world and the artist
to his art. Guranteeing the mirroring relationship is Wordsworth's
'Spirit of Being', Heaney's 'life-force': it is the pervasive power
'Whose gracious favour is the primal source/ Of all illumination.'[39]
The culminating image in Heaney's poem is of desire satisfied by the
kind of symbolic resolution about which Jung theorized, and which
is the provenance of art:

> Then I thought of the tribe whose dances never fail
> For they keep dancing till they sight the deer.

Section X develops the ideal of art as an inviolable core than
cannot be ground down to something else. It uses the image of a
cherished mug 'beyond my reach on its high shelf'. The section
begins by describing the hustle-bustle on Station Island as the
pilgrims awaken in the morning and prepare for another day. The
poet's observations are clipped and fragmented, the sounds are
hard and vigorous. It is in this context of noisy, rough activity that
the mug, 'as quiet as a milestone', comes to occupy his thoughts.
The mug which has 'stood for years/ in its patient sheen and
turbulent atoms,/unchallenging, unremembered *lars*', is a reposi-
tory of the past, and at the same time seems to exist outside time.
With its pattern of cornflowers 'blue sprig after sprig/ repeating
round it', it recalls Keats's 'Sylvan historian', the 'still unravish'd
bride of quietness', the 'foster-child of silence and slow time'.[40] That
Heaney uses a mug while Keats an urn to contemplate the nature of
art highlights Heaney's sense of art as something intimate, some-
thing homely and natural, even childlike. Yet it enjoys a miraculous
permanence: Heaney hardly recognizes his mug when it is used by
actors as a stage-prop, but when returned he found that it was as
'miraculously unharmed' as Ronan's psalter which had lain a day
and a night under lough-water until it was retrieved by an otter.
Heaney affirms the capacity of art to survive appropriation,
'estrangement' and 'translation'. It contains 'the dazzle of the
impossible'. It is 'a sun-glare'.

Section XI registers a growing confidence, reinforced by the
memory of a monk who 'spoke again about the need and chance/to
salvage everything, to re-envisage/ the zenith and glimpsed jewels of
any gift/ mistakenly abased'. '"Read poems as prayers"', the monk
tells him. Recovery, replenishment, emergence from darkness into

light are the key-notes. After all the guilt and doubt, the poet discovers a renewed faith in the validity of his life and work. The monk makes him feel there was 'nothing to confess'. Poetry is seen in the context of religious endeavour. The translation of the St John on the Cross poem, with its confident, undulant measures and liturgical language, is a vision of 'that eternal fountain, hidden away', which is the secret source of poetry. Its waters are life-giving and inexhaustible, 'although it is the night'. To tap these resources lying deep within him, the poet must, as the sixteenth century Spanish mystic emphasized, void all allegiances and renounce the world. Through this act of positive sacrifice, the poet prepares himself to produce an art that is sustaining and assuaging, 'a marvellous lightship' that will surface from 'muddied water'.

The sequence of poems culminates with the appearance of James Joyce, brisk, cutting, insistent, under whose influence the poet feels 'free' and 'alone'. Joyce's uncompromising *'non serviam'* is a dismissal of Carleton's wary accommodations with the public world, and an even more pointed repudiation of the priest's conventionalism: '"You lose more of yourself than you redeem/ doing the decent thing"', is Joyce's echoic rebuttal. Seeking to fly the nets of nationality and religion, Joyce refuses both Colum McCartney's political demands and the priest's ideal of service. What Heaney, in Joyce's voice, commands himself to do is strike out for loneliness and joy, to probe along tangents beyond the expected.

In this long central sequence of poems, Heaney responds to the Northern Ireland tragedy, not with rhetoric and commitment (always plentiful commodities), nor with the kind of market-conscious hysteria that is so often taken for insight, but with appropriately modern reactions of doubt, pain and self-distrust. 'Station Island' is a catharsis, and Heaney has not been easy on himself. It works towards a resolution of personal dilemma in artistic terms. Joyce urges him forward to a new confidence: '"Take off from here. And don't be so earnest."' But the poem does not press on to the exultant affirmation of romantic heroism such as we find at the end of *A Portrait of the Artist as a Young Man*, where depreciation, cynicism and cowardice have been indubitably outfaced and irony surpassed. The poet's meeting with Joyce contains the promise of renewal: 'Raindrops blew in my face/ as I came to'; at the end, however, 'the shower broke in a cloudburst, the tarmac/fumed and sizzled', as if by entertaining Joyce's notions of defiant individualism he had incurred the apocalyptic anger of the gods.

His reaction to Stephen's linguistic self-consciousness in *A Portrait* further dramatizes his difficulty in freeing himself from the 'common rite'. Stephen's triumphant affirmation of mastery of an 'acquired speech'[41] which he recorded in his diary entry for 13 April is received in Heaney's poem as 'a revelation' set among his stars, 'a password' in his ears, 'the collect of a new epiphany' – which he dubs 'the Feast of the Holy Tundish'. The deliberate over-writing here, the pompous, high-flown, rhapsodic style with its sacramental associations, while ostensibly celebrating Joycean insight, betrays the speaker's histrionic posturing. Joyce quickly deflates his pretension, asserting as commonplace the Irish writer's mastery and possession of the English language, and going on to criticize Heaney's peasant pilgrimage as an infantile charade. At the end, Joyce 'moved off quickly/ the downpour loosed its screens round his straight walk': the master is sure and steady, but can the poet, immobile and silent, find the resources to maintain a similar confident independence in the face of a hostile world which threatens to engulf him and render him invisible?

In the third part of the volume, 'Sweeney Redivius', Heaney resuscitates the voice of Sweeney to continue his exploration of the conditions under which his own particular kind of composition takes place. Joyce had urged him to strike his own note, to swim out on his own, to conduct his own echo soundings, his own probes and investigations of elver-gleams in the dark. With the 'Sweeney Redivivus' poems, he resumes his inquiry into the heroics of the spirit, the kind of interior freedom advocated by Joyce, which expresses itself in an aesthetic of privacy, insulation, isolation and exile. Despite Joyce's air of brisk certainty, the project is one which is fraught with anguish.

In the title poem of 'Sweeney Redivivus' Sweeney is 'incredible to myself/ among people far too eager to believe me/ and my story, even if it happened to be true'. It is not as a purveyor of practical 'truths' that the poet would wish to recommend himself to his public. Sweeney, stirring wet sand, his head dense with soakage, smelling the bitter river smells, lost amid the old trees which were 'nowhere', is an image of the exposed and susceptible state of mind existing beyond and beneath the level of civilized expectation and decorum where composition occurs, and where the only limits are those defined by what is punningly referred to as the poet's own 'penwork'. Under such conditions it is the struggle which counts, irrespective of whether it leads to 'truth' or whether 'truth' can be found. This notion is enacted in the poem itself – in the intensely subjective, impressionistic rendering of Sweeney's perceptions and sensations. Art has its own justification independent of its social usefulness or paraphraseable meaning. The artist engages the world and the self, not in a spirit of explication or explanation, but as communion with mystery. In venturing into these zones where language finds it difficult to penetrate, the poet must submit to a process of 'unwinding', of learning to unlearn. He must relax into a mood where the inhibitions engendered by a tradition of rationalism and materialism are dispelled, and he can respond with clarity and precision to the casual, negligible invitations and echoes that reach him from 'all the realms of whisper'. In 'Sweeney Redivivus' Sweeney's head is 'like a ball of wet twine', and in the next poem, 'Unwinding', 'the twine unwinds and loosely widens/ backward through areas that forwarded/ understandings of all I would undertake'. The idea is similar to that which concludes the early poem, 'The Plantation', where 'You had to come back/ To learn how to lose yourself,/ To be pilot and stray – witch,/ Hansel and Gretel in one'.

The relationship between the poet and community is the subject of 'In the Beech.' This poem has the poet detached from the human world, hiding in the tree. He feels like a forgotten lookout. His vantage-point is positioned significantly at the junction of the civilized world ('On one side, under me, the concrete road') and the hushed and hidden primitive world that is redolent of grass and water, mud and gland ('On the other the bullocks' covert/ the breath and plaster of a drinking-place/ where the school-leaver discovered peace/ to touch himself in the reek of churned-up mud'). From his position in the tree he can see the steeplejacks, like flies against a mountain, building a factory chimney – a vision of constructive human activity. But the wartime ethos which pervades the poem motivates other observations – observations (drawn from Heaney's memories of military manoeuvres near his home in the 1940s) of a more sinister phallic power in human life. His secret place is not immune from the world's hurt: the tanks' advance seems to originate in the very centre of the vibrating tree. More vulgar signs of their proud power are present in the public world: the poet winces at the tokens of an alien authority stamped on the landsape by the tanks' powered bolt marks. A pilot with his goggles back comes in so low that even his cockpit rivets are visible. These are the incursions of a violent, adult world, the swift, tearing penetration of a dramatic macho presence, into the poet's childhood domain. But as the poem's stately measures and the classical decorum of vocabulary like 'cynosure' and 'imperium' suggest, he has appropriated the official idiom to his original language of instinct and sensation so that he can contemplate the public regime in close-up while holding on to his emotional and intellectual composure.

In describing the tree as both 'a strangeness and a comfort' we recognize the paradox Heaney would lay claim to for his art. Poetry has a sustaining, assuaging force because like the tree it is rooted in the earth, in a specific place, it is a manifestation of the 'life-force'. At the same time the artist cultivates a detached, godlike perspective so that, standing above his material, he is able to control it and transform it into a coherent vision, one that aspires to the status of revelation, and one that is unique to him.

The poem ends with a summarizing, celebratory address to the tree:

> My hidebound boundary tree. My tree of knowledge.
> My thick-tapped, soft-fledged, airy listening post.

'Hidebound' – neatly catching the notion of 'hiding place' and suggesting a primal indivisibility of plant and animal life – is the name given to a tree which has bark so close that it impedes growth. Here, however, constraint is enabling, leading directly to 'knowledge' – of the Biblical kind which is knowledge of good *and* evil. Precise, vigorous, rhythmic language combines with a serene and stable authority. The last line is a series of subtly modulated pulsations: the low back vowels and staccato thump of strongly accented consonants in the first phrase move through the middle register of 'soft-fledged' into the light, sibilant sway of the final phrase, to enforce a sense of the tree which is hard and solid and goes deep, is at the same time soft, flying and airy – an evocative image of that psychic 'space' where opposing qualities and forces can be miraculously reconciled.

'The First Kingdom' affirms illiterate piety as the ground of an individual's sense of place and cultural affiliation, as opposed to the more superficial, literate kind of kinship that depends on the tribe's 'acclamation'. The 'first kingdom', as well as an allusion to Sweeney's original state, is the primeval world of childhood. Heaney pictures it as a largely harmonious estate, a scene of intimacy between man and nature, a place where the nobility are also the workers on the land. But it is no pristine Golden Age, no wholly idealized landscape, no Eden myth. There are mishaps, murders and miscarriages. What gives the community its cohesion and continuity is the way it acts as a repository of lore and superstition wherein the people can find an image of themselves that nourishes their sense of themselves. Hence the poem's emphasis on daily routines, calendar customs, superstitious mythologies and backward rotes. At this atavistic level of inchoate piety, the poem implies, the poet feels his most intimate involvement. His kinship is affirmed in his recognition of the inward spiritual structures of the community to which he belongs. The danger is, however, that the degree of his love and loyalty will be judged by how warmly he assents to opportunistic political pressure or artificial control. Kinship cannot be exacted, and the community is demeaned that tries to do so.

'The First Kingdom' is not a great poem. But when Heaney turns from the binding force of community to rendering the nervous, fugitive experience of independence in the companion poem, 'The First Flight', the verbal performance is much more animated and exciting. Freeing itself from abstraction, from the prosaic and the pedestrian, the poetry soars too. It soars and falters, flutters, stoops, hangs suspendend, soars again. Rhythm is the great enacting agency of Sweeney's timidity and undulant exhilaration. Once 'mired in attachment' and now hotly pressed by his exacting pursuers, he welcomes the freedom of flight:

> so I mastered new rungs of the air
> to survey out of reach
> their bonfires on hills, their hosting
>
> and fasting, the levies from Scotland
> as always, and the people of art
> diverting their rhythmical chants
> to fend off the onslaught of winds
> I would welcome and climb
> at the top of my bent.

'The First Flight' is another version of the man working himself into 'his own proper haunt, somewhere, well out, beyond'.

Sweeney's only consorts now are the birds of the air. 'Drifting Off', the title like *Sweeney Astray* referring to both a mental and a physical state, is about Sweeney's process of discovering his new zone of being through the various birds he encounters. The poem is a kind of medieval Bestiary in which the birds are described in terms of human types. Their variety is vividly observed and exquisitely conveyed in the subtle modulations of sound and rhythm:

> I yearned for the gannet's strike,
> the unbegrudging concentration
> of the heron.
>
> In the camaraderie of rookeries,
> in the spiteful vigilance of colonies
> I was at home.

By the end of the poem Sweeney is stooping, unsure but exhilarated, inspired by goldfinch or kingfisher when it 'rent/ the veil of the usual'. This is the crucial drive behind the poet's own endeavours. 'Go beyond what's reliable', is the advice he gives himself in 'Making Strange', a poem from the first part of the book. In that poem, a kind of parable of the poetic life, he introduces two figures, one the 'travelled intelligence', the other the 'unshorn and bewildered/ in the tubs of his wellingtons' – two sides of the poet's personality that we have already encountered in the guise of Hercules and Antaeus, and then King Sweeney and Mad Sweeney. A 'cunning middle voice' advocates a synthesis of the two. This synthesis is presented as a crucial discovery for the poet and constitutes the climax of the poem. Its value lies in the fact that it makes for an art which, like the beech tree, is both a strangeness and a comfort:

> I found myself driving the stranger
>
> through my own country, adept
> at dialect, reciting my pride
> in all that I knew, that began to make strange
> at that same recitation.

In the structure and beat of these lines we recognize the rhythm of incipient flight. There is a mounting impetuousness and headiness, an intoxication, which is the impulse to make strange or, as the Russian formalists would say, to defamiliarize; an unruly energy which threatens to disrupt the poem's comforting authority.

After 'Drifting Off' there is a group of poems about the circumstances which prompted Sweeney's flight. In 'Alerted' Sweeney's quibbling reason is overwhelmed by the uncompromising, untamed power of the wilderness, which he hears in the 'bark of the vixen in heat', the voice of elemental reality. It marks the limits of 'obedience', of the decorum of reserve and detachment; it is a reminder of the vast darkness that the ideal of scientific rationalism initiated by Copernicus can never hope to explain, a symbol of life's perpetual mystery. However, Sweeney's attitude is ambivalent. He begins by toying with the idea of outstripping 'obedience', and is confirmed in his resolve by the vixen's bark. But this moment comes to him with the disorienting force and suddenness of revelation, immobilizing him; and, so ingrained in him are the civilized values and habits, he is 'disappointed' by the incapability of reason and progress.

Sweeney is further resolved in 'The Cleric', a gloss on the episode in the Sweeney story where the king comes upon Ronan staking out a site for a new church on Sweeney's ground. The poem registers Sweeney's indignation at the insinuating power of the presumptious cleric, who seeks, ultimately, to co-opt Sweeney's pagan earth, 'to get in on the ground'. The poem ends, however, not with resentment, but, like 'The First Flight', with a triumphant flourish, a glorious and exhilarated affirmation of freedom and sense of achievement:

> he opened my path to a kingdom
> of such scope and neuter allegiance
> my emptiness reigns at its whim.

The opposition between Sweeney and Ronan is the opposition between Oisin and St Patrick. On one hand there is the pagan wilderness, on the other cloistered Christian asceticism that sought to contain the natural world within its spiritual principle and religious calling. The conflict extends into 'The Scribes'. They are engaged in the process of exchanging mythology for history and religion, the oral tradition for a learned one. They are disrespectful of the ancient druidical tokens like the holly tree, which now fulfils a strictly utilatarian purpose in being used to make ink. The flowers and trees are no longer hallowed; the wilderness is kept at bay by the intellectual force of the scholar's cell. The scribes set about taming and stylizing nature in their 'penwork'. But Sweeney's 'deconstruc-

tive' reading detects inside their writing a play of sadistic drives
which subverts and contradicts the scribes' Christian authority:

> Under the rumps of lettering
> they herded myopic angers.
> Resentment seeded in the uncurling
> fernheads of their capitals.

The civilized ideal is undercut by human pettiness. The scribes may
be 'excellent', but they are also 'petulant' and 'jaggy'. They scratch
and claw and snarl while inscribing their texts of praise. Divorced
from origins, from the life and lore of the woods, they have
degenerated from a state of natural grace into the confinements of
civilized existence where they have become self-aggrandizing and
jealous: their 'lettering' is the index of the degree to which nature is
corrupted and divided against itself by the false sophistications of
culture. The ideal, as Heaney expressed it in the earlier 'Oracle',
would be to become the lobe and larynx of the mossy places: this
pure, preliterate, unmediated expression would be the healthiest,
most 'natural', most innocent condition of language. But such a
Rousseauesque assumption of a pure metaphysics of presence can
only be a mythology of origins, for none of us – Sweeney no more
than the scribes – can escape the word. The word is the medium of
blindness as of insight, of immorality as of morality. What
Sweeney's discourse shows in its various forms of word-play is a
poetic self-consciousness (as opposed to the scribes' authoritarian
illusion of wholeness), a recognition of the operation of unconscious
desire and ideological repression. There is a linguistic foregrounding
in the poem which exhibits the encounter of *pagus* and scholar: the
native vigour of common speech ('I never warmed to them', 'the old
dry glut', 'they scratched and clawed./ They snarled', 'rumps of
lettering', 'Now and again I started up') weaves in and out of the
remote and weighty elegance of 'scriptorium', 'rendered down',
'myopic angers', 'sloped cursive', 'perfect themselves against me'.
The poet's adeptness at moving back and forth between the
polysyllabic refinement of classical and ecclesiastical speech and the
barbarous plainness of the tribe dramatizes his control of both
worlds. He acknowledges the ideal of refinement, obedience and
composure enshrined in the classical orthodoxy, but challenges it
with the free natural compulsions of all the instinctive, non-
utilitarian elements in the creative life.

Two portraits of exemplary isolation, that of 'The Hermit' and

'The Master', represent further incentives to flight. 'The Hermit' is a harsh, tense image of asceticism, in which the rhythms sustain a sense of quiet, strenuous introspection throughout the poem's single sentence. The master, like the hermit, having cast off all 'affection', lives like a rook in an unroofed tower, constantly prepared for disinterested flight, the experience of which is inscribed in his 'book of withholding'. His achievement is a secret, a mystery that reveals itself only gradually. It was 'nothing arcane', but its setting down has a permanence, a solidity and perfection that are wholly satisfying:

> Like coping stones where you rest
> in the balm of the wellspring.

The poem's capacity to provide 'rest' and 'balm' depends on that process wherein the experience of flight is converted into the solid structures of art. All that is fluttering and faltering is composed, by virtue of the master's courage and watchfulness, into form, which is the poetic realization of the grace and mystery of flight. Descending the master's tower and hearing the 'purpose and venture/ in a wingflap' above him, the poet is assailed by self-doubt; but in the poem's own hard, durable music we have the proof of his own achieved synthesis of purpose and venture, his own mastery.

A more direct treatment of the artist's self-absorption and self-sufficiency is found in 'An Artist.' Heaney admires the artist whose relationship to his material is an uncompromising struggle to wrest from it an image of himself. Fidelity to his vision, regardless of its effect in the public world; the relentless pursuit of whatever as yet lies blank and unconceived – these are the things which count. To describe the artist's lonely and aggressive individualism, Heaney risks a simile of arresting incongruity:

> His forehead like a hurled *boule*
> travelling unpainted space
> behind the apple and behind the mountain.

Sweeney, astray, has entered these unpainted spaces, but there are times when the longing for safety and security overcomes him. In 'Sweeney's Returns' (based on sections 30, 31, 32 and 55 of *Sweeney Astray*) he succumbs to the desire to revisit the world he has left and see his wife, Eorann. It is a moving poem in which the outcast's pain of loss is delicately understated. A man's sensuous delight in his wife is complicated by his awareness that he has chosen to reject her. Sweeney's nervousness and self-consciousness about finding himself in dangerous and forbidden territory give the poem an inner tension, which finally explodes in the culminating, shocking, mirror-looking perception of how wild and irretrievably removed from his original state he has become. The imagery emphasizes how the wilderness has so completely inhabited his imagination that every aspect of the world now seems to give back its reflection: returning to his home, he imagines his wife's 'eyelids'/glister and burgeon', he feels like 'a scout at risk behind lines/ who raises his head in a wheatfield/ to take a first look'; his wife rising is like 'the fleshed hyacinth' which has begun to bud.

The 'Sweeney Redivivus' section ends with another group of poems in which Sweeney affirms his resolution, his faith in the wilderness. 'Holly' proclaims that there is no substitute for direct, intimate experience of the natural world, untrammelled by sentimentality or conventional expectation. The first half of the poem is a sensuous evocation of what it is like to gather holly in the rain. The language is colloquial, energetic, vivid. The poet is disappointed things didn't turn out as anticipated – it rained when it should have snowed, the holly didn't have berries – but his obvious relish in the activity and the startling beauty of the sharp-edged holly that 'gleamed like bottle-glass' confirm the value of the experience. In the second half the poet is in more comfortable, civilized surroundings: but despite warmth and ease and fulfilled desire, something is missing. He longs for sensation, for the brightness and hardness of winter. Sentience is the sign of being. Passionate involvement in the hardships and delights of the natural world assumes the status of revelation. This is suggested by the image of the brand or burning bush:

> I reach for a book like a doubter
> and want it to flare round my hand,
>
> a black-letter bush, a glittering shield-wall
> cutting as holly and ice.

The poem's relaxed manner of speech suddenly tightens up here into impetuous utterance, an effect produced by the emphatic but broken rhythm, and the clustering of both sound (the repeated *b*'s, *t*'s, *l*'s and *s*'s) and sense (the compacting activity of the appositional metaphors and hyphenated compounds). Thus, Heaney enforces a greater muscular effort of articulation and reconstructs the action of impassioned intelligence, of thinking and feeling at the same time, his portentous fantasy of what literature might be finally clarifying itself in terms of the simple, clinching certainty which the ice and holly represent. There is, Heaney realizes, a truth latent in the details so vividly summoned earlier in the poem: it is given to us not as a conclusion deduced from promises but as the process of realization itself. The implications of the holly proliferate, are pushed into the foreground – nothing as crass as 'interpreting' or 'imposing' meanings: instead, the vigour of the poet's sensuous intensity has a quite natural intellectual overflow that becomes an organic and convincing part of the poem's total effect. The holly is an emblem of the Heaney voice, vibrant with irrational magics, mysteries and rituals, yet hard and precise. It is not insignificant that he imagines the holly as an image of a fundamental literature, something deep and unknowable, whose vowelling amplitude is yet contained within and defined by a forceful consonantal authority.

'On the Road', the last poem in the book, has the poet, an itinerant spirit still, driving along in his car. In his tranced and vacant state, he imagines himself becoming the archetypal figure of the man searching for purpose and meaning in his life. He thinks of the words of the rich young man in the Bible. Christ's answer is juxtaposed with an image of a colourful bird wheeling above the poet's head, as if in demonstration of Christ's command to forsake the world. The poet, now stimulated to flight himself, is up and away like a soul that 'plumes from the mouth/ in undulant, tenor/ black-letter Latin'. The language and imagery are unexpected, but not simply a baroque gesture on the surface of the poem. A religious imagery of 'votive granite', 'stone-faced vigil' and 'font of exhaustion' which runs throughout the poem emphasizes the connection between the binding force and strenuous discipline of both the religious and artistic vocations. But there is this difference between the two: the free imagination is neither confined nor sanctioned by any ritual other than its own. The poet's vocation is one which draws his adventurous spirit far beyond the sumptuous elegance of imperial 'black-letter Latin', beyond the chapel gable or the sanctuary of the churchyard wall. He commits himself to an inward journey that will take him into a dark, primitive zone untouched by the light of Christianity or of rationality. It leads back in time, through a cave-mouth and along clay-floored passages, penetrating deep into the earth, till he reaches 'the deepest chamber'. This is another version of the journey the poet makes in poems like 'The Plantation' or 'Summer Home', where, after the exhaustion of tension and discord, he treads the worn, white path back to the heart. It is the movement inwards, the Wordsworthian listening in, in order for the poet to speak himself out. The poet submits to a psychic force that is archaic and only half-apprehended, but one which puts him in contact with the powers of the Celtic otherworld, with the neglected, primal springs of instinct, the petrified nimbus of the wood whose potential energy is waiting to be unleashed. Cut into the rock of the deepest chamber is the image of a drinking deer straining for refreshment at a dried-up source. This is the deer of poetry referred to in an earlier poem ('A Migration') when it 'stood/ in pools of lucent sound/ ready to scare'. The poet in 'On the Road' proclaims:

> I would meditate
> that stone-faced vigil
>
> until the long dumbfounded
> spirit broke cover
> to raise a dust
> in the font of exhaustion.

Such devotion is required if the poet is to give voice to, to bring into the open, to quicken, what lies hidden and forgotten in the depths of consciousness. The 'exhaustion' of both deer and poet becomes a 'font' – the source of energy, the symbol of redemption, an image of a sacramental aesthetic. We can trace this progression in terms of the poem's imagery. The first four stanzas emphasize the poet's disconsolate emptiness, his sterility and defeatism: the steering-wheel in his hands is a worthless trophy, an 'empty round'; but then the ceremonial 'empty round' is metamorphosed first into the pool etched in rock where the deer is drinking and, finally, into the sacramental 'font'. From emptiness to querulous, panicky restlessness, the poem tracks inward to quiet meditation and ends with sudden activity, the whole thing an enactment of the process of turning abstract 'exhaustion' into palpable, religious artifact. What starts as description finishes as a way of defining a psychic quest.

In Heaney's Sweeney poems, the more vivid and imaginative the details are, the more resolutely he turns them inwards. And for this emerging psychic landscape, he devises a syntax which telescopes feelings rather than subduing them to the logic of consecutive statement. In the middle section of 'On the Road' describing the bird's disordered, excited movement before it commits itself to the journey to the deepest chamber, the pivotal line, 'If I came to earth . . .' is followed by a series of programmatic verbs – '. . . it would be by way of . . . I would roost . . . I would migrate . . . I would meditate . . .' – in which the conditionals suggest both speculative fantasy-projection and past experience gained through habitual action: there is a sense of hallucinatory ambivalence about the reality of such moments. This quality pervades the rest of the poem where it is the agitated movement of the bird/poet that is described; it changes with the introduction of the simple present tense towards the end of the poem, when the transcendent image of the deer cut into the rock is foregrounded.

The difficulty of the poem lies in sorting out the relationship of one element to another. And yet this is also the theme. The movement of the imagery is a merging and migration, in which we pursue the poem's fugitive, shifting elements until they relapse into the original womb, the nest of the 'deepest chamber', where they are incubated and finally gathered in the poem's last, passionate, symbolic, concentrated statement. Poetry is a 'book of changes', but what motivates the changes is the quest for ultimacy.

The poetic preoccupations that are conducted into a fiction in the Sweeney poems and organized within the drama of ritual process of Part II of *Station Island*, are developed along the suggestions of disparate images in Part I. The life that is led away from civilized concern and tribal pressure is the subject of one of the first poems in the book, 'Away From It All'. The poem (which is very reminiscent of 'Oysters' in *Field-Work*) begins with a picture of conviviality – the poet and his friends are enjoying a lobster – and a typical Heaney image of excavation – a cold, steel fork probes a water tank to extricate a lobster. The description of the lobster is richly evocative:

> articulated twigs, a rainy stone
> the colour of sunk munitions.

In these depth-charged waters, the act of retrieval gives utterance to the old tree magic, activating the racial memory and penetrating the hoard of superstitious lore. But the poet tries to repress these troubling intuitions at the outback of the mind. The strain in doing so makes the poem taut and uneasy. Enjoyment of the lobster carries with it notions of predatory despoliation and blatant defiance. The diners have withdrawn from the world and, in insouciant disregard of all that is going on around them, attack the lobster-meat with self-absorbed relish. They are oblivious to the ominous signs outside – the wind against the window, the darkening sea. Inside, there is a growing uneasiness, a twitchy nervousness, that cannot be ignored for much longer. The speaker repeats the word 'twilight' over and over in the effort to blot out the impish questions which 'hopped and rooted' in the mind. 'Twilight' comes to refer to his own limbo-state, half-way between the clear light of free mind and the dark outback of social conscience, between the pleasure principle and the reality principle, between the sensuous particularity and intensity of immediate experience and its larger, abstract historical background. The questions spring from thoughts of the danger and hardship endured by the fishermen who made possible this 'glut of privilege'. The guilty feeling intensifies in the yawing, co-ordinate rhythms and whispering sibilance: 'as the sea darkens/ and whitens and darkens/ and quotations start to rise/ like rehearsed alibis'. One of the quotations which rise is from Czeslaw Milosz's *Native Realm*: it turns on the opposition between motionless 'contemplation' and active 'participation'. Heaney responds to this dilemma by re-asserting the condition of 'twilight' as itself the source and subject of his poem:

> '*Actively*? What do you mean?'
> The light at the rim of the sea
> is rendered down to a fine
> graduation, somewhere between
> balance and inanition.

In the first line he questions the meaning and value of 'active participation' in the unstoppable flow of history. The statement which follows, beginning with 'light' and ending with 'inanition', is a version of the space in which the poem occurs, a reference to the 'balance' sought in the twilight before it dissolves in nothingness.

'Active participation', Heaney implies in the abrupt turning away from the conceptual abstraction of that phrase to the simple concreteness of the reference to the light at the rim of the sea, is an ambition of reckless arrogance for the poet whose first and major function is to make the finest kind of discrimination, to wrestle with the most delicate shades and differences of a 'twilight' existence; only this way – via the concrete realization of felt experience – can he aspire to the most abstract and general realization. This dual concern is, in fact, formally reproduced in the stanza just quoted. The difference between the two is clear enough in the contrast between the self-consciously particularized image of the second and third lines and the explicit generalization of the second half of the fourth and the fifth lines. The intimacy of the two is also clear in the way the unique depends on the universal: a statement about one is equally a statement about the other.

Further complicating this creative tension, this double-consciousness, and adding further significance and richness to the poet's 'contemplation', is the secret life of community and tradition which informs his every recognition, and which is imaged in the last stanza by the lobsters in their element on the cobbled floor of their tank. This is an aspect of understanding which, Heaney emphasizes, cannot be disregarded. But there's another kind of double-consciousness involved here. His response does not emerge exclusively from a sense of community or a sense of history: it is also informed by an affinity with the isolated and the alienated, in whom he recognizes the qualities of strength and courage, as well as confusion and lack of direction – 'the hampered one, out of water,/ fortified and bewildered'. All of these elements constitute an exceedingly complex kind of 'contemplation', and Heaney insists on it before conceding the claims of the other life of 'active participation'.[42]

Sweeney's wariness of people and the traps they would lay for him is reflected in other poems which cling to objects and textures because they, unlike people, can be relied on not to denounce you or demand your allegiance, and yet, if you probe them keenly enough and with the right kind of sensitive openness, have the capacity to reveal, as 'the given note' in the early poem had the capacity to reveal, 'the whole thing'. Sloe gin (in the poem of that title) is 'bitter/ and dependable'; a sandstone keepsake (in the poem of that title) is 'reliably dense and bricky'. Sharing this kind of intensity and inviolability is the internal landscape of a writer's 'ghost life' which Heaney describes in 'The Birthplace' as 'unperturbed, reliable'.

In 'Sandstone Keepsake' the poet is 'one of the venerators' of life's casual, everyday things. Heaney is walking along a shingle beach in

Donegal at sunset. Just across the estuary is Magilligan internment camp. Contemplating the things around him – the lights of the camp, the wet red stone, the way his hand dipped in the sea seems to smoke in the frosty air – he does so from his 'free state of image and allusion'. The play of words in 'free state' indicates the complexity of his response: he denies the trammelling influence of nationality and at the same time acknowledges the inevitably nationalistic vantage-point from which the 'autonomous imagination' operates. To the British soldiers with their 'trained binoculars' he is merely an innocuous shadow.

Heaney's response to simple, quotidian things, especially things in nature, springs from a childlike piety. It is in the fish in the rock, the fern in the fissure, the eel-drugged flats and dunes, the brine-maddened grass, the clatter of stones, that 'conscience and healing' may be found. This is the lesson taught by 'the angel of the last chance' in 'An Aisling in the Burren'. As in 'North' and 'Exposure', where the poet is to compose in darkness and expect aurora borealis in the long foray but no cascade of light, the Muse in 'An Aisling in the Burren' arrives 'not from a shell/ but licked with the wet cold fires of St Elmo'. Only by clinging to the precious tokens of durability on the site of catastrophe can disintegration be resisted and the 'startling deer' of poetry be arrested. The imagination refreshes itself, the mind is purified, in the common and humble sights and sounds the poet has tested in his own experience. His language is sensitively attuned to divine these secrets of the natural world and to register this childlike, open-eyed wonder and innocent delight at the small and the familiar. In his essay on early Irish nature poetry, 'The God in the Tree', Heaney writes:

Poetry of any power is always deeper than its declared meaning. The secret between the words, the binding element, is often a psychic force that is elusive, archaic and only half-apprehended by maker and audience. For example, in the context of monasticism, the god of my title would be the Christian deity, the giver of life, sustainer of nature, Creator, Father and redeemer Son. But there was another god in the tree, impalpable perhaps but still indigenous, less doctrinally defined than the god of the monasteries but more intuitively apprehended . . . the deities remained shrouded in the living matrices of stones and trees, immanent in the natural world.[43]

Heaney's poetry shares with early Irish nature poetry this deep, sustaining affiliation to the old mysteries of the grove, the same primeval energy and exhilaration of feeling. His poetic imagination is linked with the mysterious, barbaric natural world, as Sweeney, wood-lover and tree-hugger, picker of herbs and drinker from wells, was entangled with the vegetation and weathers and animals of his countryside.

Life's random objects also tell Heaney about himself. A clutter of keepsakes in the poem-sequence 'Shelf Life' includes a granite chip from Joyce's Martello tower, 'jaggy, salty, primitive/ and exacting', which he recognizes as an opposite to himself. An old smoothing iron evokes a memory of a strenuous, precise expertise that recalls his earlier admiration for the poise and skill of diggers and ploughmen. An old pewter plate, slithery, fogged-up, gives him an image of his own soul:

> Glimmerings are what the soul's composed of.
> Fogged-up challenges, far conscience-glitters
> and hang-dog, half-truth earnests of true love.
> And a whole late-flooding thaw of ancestors.

An iron spike that was part of a North American railway line provokes thoughts of mutability. Such troubling thoughts occur when the beholder is without the reference points of inheritance, for they are the means whereby past and present are endowed with meaning and a man is more than an historical organism, casual and impermanent. A stone from Delphi speaks to him with sybilline authority, warning him to keep himself apart from the toils of bloodshed and to wait until the god is ready to speak through him. Finally, there's a snowshoe, its loops hanging from the wall, 'a hieroglyph for all the realms of whisper'.

Each object in Heaney's thickly textured world contains its past, like a memory, like the bog. 'The Sandpit' takes his grandparents' housing estate and disintegrates it into its constituent sand and gravel to watch it slowly grow again. Part 1 takes us back to 1946, and the first excavation of the sandpit. Part 2 focuses on a demobbed bricklayer resuming his civilian work after the war. Part 3 describes the bricks being made, the river gravel 'bonded and set to register/ whatever beams and throbs into the wall'. The bricks are not only ready to absorb the future but still contain the past: foxgloves and saplings on the worked-out pit floor, anglers by the deepened stream. The poet's contemplation of these ghostly presences is developed in the final part, 'What the Brick Keeps'. Whatever happened around the houses when they were being built – the bricklayer's memories of standing on the tank's gun-turret merging with his 'point of vantage' on the scaffolding from which he views the surrounding countryside, the sound of river water – all of this was tapped like a code into the walls with a chop of the trowel. And what happens afterwards in the house – floors hammered down, the sound of water in the pipes, the flap of phone wires and flags on the gable, a bed creaking, the doors shaking, the ripples that cross the water tank – are all kept in the brick, just as the swollen Moyola in 'Gifts of Rain' bedded the locale and contained the 'antediluvian lore' of 'soft voices of the dead . . . whispering by the shore'. Similarly, a house brick, Heaney tells us, stands at the intersection of a whispering past that refuses to be annihilated and a mysterious future not yet born.

In 'Sheelagh na Gig' the object under contemplation is a gargoyle on the corbel table of the Norman church of St Mary and St David at Kilpeck in Herefordshire. It is one of a series of curious carvings which includes human heads of bewildered horror and hopeless idiocy, some dancers, a lost little figure playing a musical instrument, monsters and animals – dogs, bulls, rabbits, serpents, bears, pigs, hounds and hares – all seen in nightmarish mutations. The sheelagh na gig is the most grotesque and demented of the figures: a woman with huge round eyes, skeletal ribs, legs haunched high and wide and stick-like arms which reach under the thighs to hold open an enormously exaggerated vulva. She is pre-Christian and pre-Celtic, found in only two or three places in Britain but more common in Ireland. It has been suggested that for the masons of the Marches who ornamented Kilpeck church around 1135 she may have represented lust or prostitution, or, in the light of her close resemblance to certain Celtic figures, the Holy Virgin, symbolizing Christ's fleshly origin.[44] According to B. S. Johnson, she is a representation of 'the twin aspects of life: death and procreation'.[45]

It is curious that while the carving draws attention to the vulva, *Sheelagh na gig* literally means 'Sheelagh of the breasts,' the representation of the breasts in the carving being notable for their emaciated and skeletal appearance. *Gig* is an anglicized form of *gcíoc*, the genitive of *cíoc*, meaning breast. In Dineen's Irish Dictionary we find *Síle na gcíoc* – 'a stone fetish representing a woman supposed to give fertility, thought to have been introduced by the Normans.' *Síle* and its anglicized form 'Sheelagh' are from *Celia* or *Caelia*, the feminine of the Roman gentile name *Caelius* which is usually taken to mean 'heavenly'. What these meanings imply is the inseparable conjunction of the sensual and the spiritual – reminiscent of the Yeatsian mystery, 'But Love has pitched his mansion in/ The place of excrement.'[46] The principle behind this (and Johnson's) interpretation is that of the interpenetration of opposites, and as the exemplary embodiment of paradox, the sheelagh na gig has an obvious attraction for the poet who sees poetry as the free play of thought and feeling, in a spirit of passionate detachment, over images of the widest possible relevance.

From the adult Heaney's perceptions of the sheelagh na gig, we are suddenly transported to a barn: the sheelagh na gig holding herself open merges with a sack's 'lapped and supple mouth' from which the boy Heaney watches grain being poured. The adult Heaney's attention moves from the sheelagh na gig to take in other corbels around the church – two birds, the heads of a rabbit and a ram, a mouth devouring heads: this is a repetition of how the young Heaney's concentration on the gaping sack running grain wanders to other things in and around the barn: the 'mouth' of a bird's nest or 'eye' of a rat-hole; the earthy smell and fecund warmth of the place. Moving from the womb-like barn, he thinks of a time when he stood in the rain in the farmyard, his head covered by a sack: in comparing the sack to a caul (a caul being a portion of the amniotic sac which covers the heads of some infants at birth), he continues the train of procreative association initiated by the sheelagh na gig. What he discovers in his own experience has an ancient, collective prototype, rooted in elementary perceptions of human existence. What he sees in the present is coloured and defined by what he once saw. The meaning of experience is the complex product of the relationship which obtains between the present and the past. And it is also a product of the relationship between the primary focus of attention at any given point in time and the contingent registrations surrounding it. Each of the poem's three sections ends with a sentence beginning with 'And . . .' in which the centre of interest which has occupied the section up to that point is displaced, and what follows, we are to understand, is in the nature of a conjunctive but peripheral addition or afterward to the main structure of image and feeling. In each section there is a modulation away from concentrated interest in a specific image toward a looser, more diffuse perceptual field and a more relaxed expression (particularly in the first and third sections where the final sentence takes the form of an extended list of things as they are noted by the poet's roving eye).

This is an austere poetry. Its distinctive features are economy and simplicity. The intensity is of an inner character because it is not merely the product of intelligence but of the poet's negotiations with underlying primary powers of being. Through simplicity we gain access to actual depth. The poem's meditative echoes reverberate from an exceptionally precise, clean style. Colloquial spontaneity is fashioned into a dignified formality. Delicate variations of tone make the words suggestive and reveal their hidden tension. If the verbal texture of the early poems was that of squelching mud, 'Sheelagh na Gig' has the hard, durable quality of sculpted stone. It is a wholly concrete realization of what the sheelagh na gig stands for: openness to life, resistance to fixation, complex seeing. These are the prerequisites for an appreciation of life's mystery – the continuity of past and present, death's inseparability from the life-force, the interpenetration of the sensual and the spiritual. The poem's emphasis on eye and mouth, and the carving's advice, ' "Yes, look at me to your heart's content/ but look at every other thing" ', stress the importance of receptivity and connective suppleness.

The artist is devoted to discovering these relationships and divining the meaning of things. The subject of 'The Birthplace' is the power of art (especially that of Thomas Hardy) to animate and illuminate. Section I introduces the figure of the artist at his table, surrounded by and yet detached from the external world. That world is composed out of a subtly worked imagery reflecting the poem's central tensions: the opposition between the comfortingly familiar and the mysterious, between geometry and jumble, pre-cision and proliferation (the small plain rectangle of the writer's table where new fictive worlds are conjured into being; the single bed which is a 'dream of discipline'; the flagged kitchen barred with 'thick light' containing a 'ghost-life'; the high trees shaken by the breathings of the wind as the 'reluctant heart' might be stirred by the fiddler's air). The prevailing syntactic structure is one of co-ordination rather than subordination, and this, along with the absence of finite verbs, refuse us the satisfactions of direction and hierarchical meaning. Indeed, as the focus widens and we move from the writing table to the rest of the room, to the rest of the house, to outside the house, then to the market and beyond, there is an increasing syntactical convolution and greater and greater element of abstraction: beginning with the centre point, the point of catalysis – the highly specified 'deal table' where the poet conducts his artistic negotiations with the world and the word (his 'deals'), the section ends with the 'reluctant heart' – a return to the intimate but now abstract and affective point of poetic activity. This section, framed by the images of writing table and heart, presents the 'birthplace' of the poem, and introduces the range of contraries which the poem will then proceed to resolve.

Section II takes as its theme the nature of experience: 'unforgettable' but 'speechless' and 'unmentionable' until it is subjected to the ordering structures of art, and thereby given meaning. Experience has a dream-like quality, which can easily become nightmarish; it is presented as a sub-human and sub-literate mode of being where the human participants, once under pressure, are 'like cattle' that have been stampeded. What is needed is the sanctifying discipline of art.

Section III turns to this 'discipline', whereby the sickening, restless confusion of experience is transformed astonishingly. The pair 'come back emptied', seeking renewal in 'the words of coming to rest'. But words in themselves – the magic of incantation – is not enough. Words in themselves are unable to overcome the subjective 'resistance' occasioned by knowledge of the inevitable separation between experience and words. Words need to return to experience, to be 'nourished' by experience: as well as that, random, heavy objects that they are, they need to become elements in an active, energetic and creative verbal system before they can achieve absolute necessity. 'Everywhere being nowhere', it takes the transfiguring power of art to define and illuminate the world. Hardy is an artist with whom Heaney feels a special affinity because the sharp 'reality' of his fictive world has compelling authority. It confirms and even seems to precede the 'reality' of direct experience of life. Heaney remembers first reading *The Return of the Native*:

> The corncrake in the aftergrass
>
> verified himself, and I heard
> roosters and dogs, the very same
> as if he had written them.

In our broken and divided world, this is the kind of confirmation and help which constitutes the virtue of a tradition. Tradition is what supports the individual artist's own solitary resources. For Heaney, Hardy represents a 'birthplace' of his own artistic endeavours. Hardy has exerted a profound effect on his consciousness, nourished the poet's own deep and genuine feeling by providing a language for feeling, and not just the vocabulary but the syntax, not just the names, the elements, but these related in subtle and coherent patterns. Reading *The Return of the Native* has helped to make the poet's dumbness articulate. It has shown him ways to break free from set forms of thought and established modes of feeling, from the routine of the cliché.

Heaney reminds us of the limits of the modern structuralist project. The power of art depends on more than a masculine, architectonic, 'stacking' facility, on more than the facility for verbal organization. It requires delicacy of discrimination, a fine and inclusive sense of reality, a genius for actuality. It depends on the artist's sensitive feeling for the distinction and nuance and mystery of the various world – the 'silence at noon/ in a deep lane that was sexual/ with ferns and butterflies'; on his ability to tap the deep springs of nourishment which are the hiding places of the poet's power, and which Heaney discovers in his 'birthplace', in the return to nature and to childhood and to all that is 'native' to him. It involves passive, feminine listening in to 'all the realms of whisper', training an ear attentive to his deepest feelings, a mind capable of understanding them, a will ready to accept them. It means patience in attending and acuteness in recognizing, so that he can guide us towards new experience and richer meaning.

At times in Heaney's poetry there doesn't seem to be a language for the sinuous and intricate subtlety of the feelings that are yeastily working in him, times when we are all too aware that words are, as Wordsworth said, but the imperfect echo of the unheard melody, times when things seem to have a greater evocative power than words. The third section of 'Station Island' is about a long-dead sister, and centres on a seaside trinket, a grotto of glued shells, that was once her prized possession. After her death it was stowed away in tissue paper, and to take it out and touch it was a surer arousal of her presence, and absence, than words could manage:

> It was like touching birds' eggs, robbing the nest
> of the word *wreath*, as kept and dry and secret
>
> as her name which they hardly ever spoke
> but was a white bird trapped inside me
> beating scared wings . . .

Feeling and object were too closely knit for words to intervene. Words themselves, in Heaney's mind, John Carey says in a review of *Station Island*, 'sink back into things at last'[47] – though, of course, it is precisely because of the elaborate complexity and coherent organization of Heaney's poetic language that Carey can make such a deduction.

In 'The Loaning' the poet's words 'slip back' into the sounds made by ancestral shades. There is a haunting, melancholic quality about the gently flowing, expansive music of the first part. The voices, originating in raftered sheds and turned-up carts, at crossroads and gable ends, are carried in 'the wind shifting in the hedge'; they stream and flutter out of birch-white throats of the dying, are borne in smoky clouds on the summer sky and settle 'in the uvulae of stones' and the 'soft lungs of the hawthorn'; they breathe 'in a shiver of beaded gossamers/ and the spit blood of a last few haws and rose-hips'. The blood image prepares for the contemporary horror, to which Heaney turns at the end of the poem:

> At the click of a cell lock somewhere now
> the interrogator steels his *introibo*,
> the light motes blaze, a blood-red cigarette
> startles the shades, screeching and beseeching.

The poet's poise and control come under mounting pressure, signalled by the tense rhythms and, finally in the headlong, cacophonous rhyming of 'screeching and beseeching'. The continuum Heaney recognizes is not just one of bucolic peacefulness. All is impregnated with a dark foreboding.

The value of the ghostly voices is that, in their various forms, they have the power to steady and sustain in times of exhaustion or crisis: 'When you are tired or terrified/ your voice slips back into its old first place/ and makes the sound your shades make there.' In 'the limbo of lost words', the poet's job is to retrieve the 'lost words' and save them from annihilation. His poetry has them 'on loan' we might say. And being a poet, his creativity ensures against any undue enslavement to the past or collaboration with the quotidian – a refusal which enables him to transform the pattern of experience, to pursue the impromptu, the new and the 'startling' and to give point to the present, without denying his relationship with the past or any of the other 'realms of whisper'. All that is certain good in the end is the poet's own words. Not only do they let the light of intelligibility into experience (the function of words being to quicken the unformed, the fleeting and the insubstantial into significance), but what they point to (breathings, sighings, screechings, beseechings) is also embodied and enacted by them, compelling not just our assent but our consent and involvement.

Not surprisingly, in his writing for his children, Heaney is anxious that they should also be sensitive to the 'ghost life' hidden in everyday things. In 'Changes' he walks with his daughter to a pump in the long grass, knowing 'I heard much that you could not hear' – the bite of the spade that sank the well, the mason mixing his mortar, the women coming with their buckets. The pump contains a further lesson. In it a bird has nested, and Heaney watches his daughter gently remove the cast-iron cap to see the single egg. It will be good to remember this, he tells her, when she has grown away and stands 'at the very centre of the human city'. What has been revealed to her in the 'rusted' citadel of the pump is that no matter how desolate the self and the world may seem, there are always, in the most unexpected places, and in the most unexpected ways, tokens of life and love to be cherished. This lesson is stated indirectly: it is not explained. The poetry does not argue, it makes itself felt. What Heaney recommends for his children is education in things, not in ideas. Through touch, sight, sensation and memory, the personality will mature.

There are lessons in grief as well as hope. Flying a kite with his sons in 'A Kite for Michael and Christopher', he makes them take the string to feel 'the strumming, rooted, long-tailed pull of grief'. This is what they were 'born for'. Like the early poems about Heaney's own father, these later ones addressed to his own children have a robust intimacy which is essentially comforting. The poet figures in his characteristic steadying and supportive role, in an image which recalls that of his own father's tensed and powerful presence in 'Follower': 'Stand in here in front of me/ and take the strain.' The proposed ideal, which has obvious implications for the artist, reasserts the posture described in 'Old Smoothing Iron', one of the poems in the 'Shelf Life' sequence: 'to pull your weight and feel/ exact and equal to it./ Feel dragged upon. And buoyant'. There are echoes here of Kavanagh's desire to become 'airborne', his longing for 'weightlessness'.[48] The poet has to be pilot and stray – witch, Hansel and Gretel in one, has to find the 'space' where all contrarieties can be held and harmonized, composed in momentary poise. This is the source of what we might call Heaney's sober joy. That, also, explains the attraction of such images as his father ploughing in 'Follower', his aunt baking in 'Sunlight', the fisherman fishing in 'Casualty', the hermit in the poem of that title who, in his self-absorption, 'was like a ploughshare/ interred to sustain the whole field/ or force'.

In Heaney's poems the outer world informs and creates the inner, just as the past informs and creates the present, or the childhood experience determines the adult response. Things are both tough and magical, consolingly solid and a stimulus to the imagination. The hazel stick cut for Catherine Ann, in the poem of that name, possesses an imperishable, magical beauty ('is kept salmon-silver'). 'Seasoned and bendy', it both assures you of your existence in the present ('it convinces the hand') and 'points back' to a rural inheritance of cattle and farms. Like a magic wand it conjures up bright points of light in the silent darkness:

> And when I poked open the grass
>
> a tiny brightening den lit the eye
> in the blunt cut end of your stick.

Much in *Station Island* seems worried and sombre, but the poetry, through barer and more sinewy than the early work, is as richly sensuous, as intensely celebratory as ever. Never more so than in the fine poem, 'The Railway Children', where the telegraph wires curve 'like lovely freehand' and the children think that words travel along them 'in the shiny pouches of raindrops/ Each one seeded full with the light/ Of the sky, the gleam of the lines, and ourselves/ So infinitesimally scaled/ We could stream through the eye of a needle'. This childhood apprehension of the world is, of course, an expression of the poet's adult aspiration to a poetic technology in which words are like raindrops. The self, scaled down and merged with nature, finds its proper vehicle in the miraculously fluid, translucent medium of words. Circles within circles (the vault of the sky in the liquid globes, raindrops streaming through the needle's eye) invoke an image of artistic perfection: words are a reflection of the infinite travelling along the lines of communication that exist in time. The poem acts out a fusion of instinctual, childlike, exhilarated perception and intellectual, adult, technical interest. The voice speaking is measured, formally precise, and at the same time natural and easy. The tension between 'intuitive' and 'explicit', masculine and feminine, which lies at the heart of Heaney's poetry, is resolved in a discourse of supple poise, intimate, intricate, lucid, complete.

7
Only Connect

The object of Heaney's poetry is – as Lawrence said the novel's ought to be – no less than 'the whole man alive'.[1] And this is the reason for Heaney's recalcitrance when confronted with the call from critics such as Seamus Deane for a political art.[2] Heaney is more concerned with an art which will embody the whole, living, extending consciousness at once, not just the cerebral, mechanized mind of the 'slightly aggravated young Catholic male'. In seeking to make his poetry the product of the whole imagination, it is neither driven by the force of unenlightened emotion, helpless inchoate piety or an extreme and disorderly individualism on the one hand, nor is it dry and didactic and subject to public pressure on the other. Living in Ulster, the public pressure which for Heaney would have made itself most strongly felt was of two kinds: that of the nationalist machine and that of Conor Cruise O'Brien style liberalism.[3] The values which emerge from Heaney's work, how-ever, elude both of these patterns of belief, for the nationalist and liberal ideals, too, must enter into relationship with each other. As far as the latter is concerned, Heaney is one with those writers whom Lionel Trilling describes in *The Liberal Imagination*, writers who have chosen hard and unpopular paths, who are out of sympathy with the prevailing ethos:

And if we were those writers who by the general consent of the most serious criticism are to be thought of as the monumental figures of our time, we see that to these writers the liberal ideology has been at least a matter of indifference. . . . All have their own love of justice and the good life but in not one of them does it take the form of the ideas and emotions which liberal democracy has declared respectable.[4]

What both sets of voices – the nationalistic and the liberal – have in common is the note of principle, and Heaney is deeply suspicious of principles, faiths and ideals. He is suspicious of them because it is the inveterate tendency of ideals to lose their actuality. They degenerate into the tired clichés and slogans repeatedly struck off 'the anvil brains' of those who 'hate' the poet. In his poetry, Heaney always seeks to ground the generalization in the particular: it is the fruit – the organic metaphor is hard to avoid – of deep and living roots. The reason for living is, after all, life itself. And life consists, as Lawrence says, 'in the achieving a pure relationship between ourselves and the living universe about us'.[5] Heaney's poetry is a precise and personal, a unique expression of these relationships, as he understands them, between himself and his world, in the effort to recover 'the pure relationship'. Lawrence's emphasis on relationships is entirely relevant to Heaney's vision. 'This is how I "save my soul"', Lawrence says, 'by accomplishing a pure relationship between me and another person, me and other people, me and a nation, me and a race of men, me and the animals, me and the trees or flowers, me and the earth, me and the skies and sun and stars, me and the moon: an infinity of pure relations, big and small'.[6] This is a project of peculiar urgency for Heaney: its motivation is clearly evinced in those poems where the pain of loss and the sense of isolation which numbs and petrifies are keenly felt. He sets out to protect himself against emptiness and exposure by rediscovering the nurture which lies in the richness of his manifold relations, past and present, the most particular and the most general. Such concerns guarantee the 'seriousness' of his poetry. What makes his poetry 'serious' is the depth of his apprehension of reality, its organization about a moral impulse and translation into the transcendent terms of art, so that he may offer a complete truth, a complete vision or revelation.

Instead of merely wishing to confirm or reject a political attitude, or surrender to an extraneous, sporadic, meaningless sensationalism, Heaney seeks to help us develop what Lawrence calls 'an instinct for life'.[7] He displays the courage that tackles new propositions and new feelings without resort to abstraction. He wants to tap the deep, neglected springs of life, eschewing sloppiness and sentimentality at one extreme, and dead abstracted unreality at the other. Metaphor and myth, two of the key-stones of his poetic, are means whereby the concrete, visible, and temporal world enters into relationship with the general and the eternal: through the energy of his language he seeks to multiply incessant and intricate relations of influence and reciprocity between the two, and so affirm the pervasive, creative, sustaining life-force. He wants to revitalize wonder, 'the most precious element in life', the 'religious element inherent in all life', the 'natural religious sense', as Lawrence called it, and in connection with which he warned against 'trying to make it all didactic'.[8] Heaney's purpose is to put us religiously in touch with the natural life of the universe, and so we have in his poetry a return to an older vision of life, a rediscovery of the primary and fundamental sources of human vitality, a descent into the strange, dark recesses of self and inheritance, and a reforming of the broken connection with the roots of being.

This is achieved through what Lawrence again called 'the fundamental pathetic faculty for receiving hidden waves that come from the depths of life'.[9] It is the product of Wordsworth's 'wise passiveness', a sensitivity to 'all the realms of whisper'. The phrase alludes to a shadowy, insubstantial influence which haunts the imagination, determining the tone and timbre of Heaney's poetic voice. It stands in opposition to the clamour of the public world, to literate feeling, the 'beautiful prismatic council' of rational humanism and civilized value. It is associated with the past, with childhood, with personal and cultural origins, illiterate feeling, the mind's 'secret stations' and unconscious sources of power. The sinister, lumbering approach of the armoured cars 'warbling along on powerful tyres' in 'The Toome Road' is a memorable image of the brutal, alien power which threatens to engulf the private sensibility that has been nurtured by and takes its colouring from a particular landscape, history and community. But

> It stands here still, stands vibrant as you pass,
> The invisible, untoppled omphalos.[10]

Behind the voice in Heaney's work is a shadow-world from which, in the midst of terror and death and doubt, he summons energy and ancestry.

Heaney's poetry is a process of evoking the unconscious. He takes a commonplace image – a brick, a harvest bow, a mug, a sunflower, falling rain, or, in the case of the poem from which my title comes, a snowshoe – and pursues it imaginatively to see where it will lead. It is a thread into the unconscious; tugged at, it brings other images, and with them an accumulating complexity of feeling, in its train. The method is used to recreate his childhood and the people and things in it, each with its own function, its history, its drama, its mystery. These things come back urgent with life and meaning – because finished, they are endurable and 'perfect'. Things – always more important than ideas – are the repositories of an affection that he was too preoccupied to notice. When the veil is lifted, things have the power to evoke by shape or texture or sound or taste, a time that has been lost. He is able to live again in a new way. This is the 'philosophic mind' Wordsworth spoke of. The senses are the house of memory, sought not for its own sake, but because to remember, as 'Poem' tells us, is to love: time without affection is time lost.

Language, the house of racial memory, is another of 'the realms of whisper'. And landscape. Sensings, glimmerings, mountings reach the poet from the hiding places amongst the whispering leaves of the trees, and the ferns and broom and catkins where he played the game of 'secrets' as a child. Strange voices of the dead, with their antediluvian lore, are heard in the sound of the rain falling and the Moyola in flood. There is a voracious concern with the sensuous textures of things in the natural world as if, by possessing completely the look and feel and sound of things, he will divine their secret sources of power and commune with the creative principle – the life-force – that gives them their being. He seeks to restore a transcendent or sacramental dimension to life. For a while the bog which from childhood had had a 'strange, assuaging effect'[11] on him is the focus for his exploration of 'the realms of whisper'. The bog 'cheeps and lisps', it is 'the vowel of the earth', and it brings him to 'the edge of centuries' where he finds himself 'facing a goddess'.[12] Contemplating this goddess puts the magic back in life, and also meaning.

Adverse judgements have been made on Heaney's morbid devotion to the goddess. He has been accused of treating the denizens of her dark realm as symbols of enduring beauty and magnificence when they are, in fact, the murdered dead of a barbaric society. Critics have resented the way he seems to have turned his back on the everyday world of morality and politics to pursue a luxuriant, 'poetic' daydream. But if (as in 'Requiem for the Croppies' or 'Kinship') Heaney manages to isolate the heroic, he doesn't deny the other facts – only their power to negate the qualities of beauty and heroism. Wonder, endurance, continuance, beauty – these he offers as having something inescapably to do with life, however we may feel its terrible, deadly qualities too – the qualities which we might all too easily be persuaded to think is all there is. This is an effort to salvage a perspective which will render loss and violence less painfully overwhelming. Refusal or inability to worship, we are reminded, might be itself another kind of death.

In Lawrence's terms, Heaney refuses to be the exclusively social being like Galsworthy's characters, and clings to the psychology of the free human individual whose true condition of wonder he is jealous to protect.

There are key-poems (such as 'Punishment') in which the re-creation of the past is a vital strategy for ordering critical reflections on the present. But even if this were not so, it might be argued that poetry need not always evaluate experience anyway. Sometimes its main function is to extend awareness, creating new areas which the writer can assimilate into his own total morality later. The quality of violence which Heaney explores morally in some poems, is presented in others in a manner which makes us more alive to what certain forces in Irish life really are – especially those which go into the making of a political martyr.

What quickly becomes the distinguishing feature of Heaney's poetry is its inwardness. When he writes about eels or the sunflower or the sound of the rain or the unmolested orchid or Sweeney ranging the peaks of Ben Bolcain, his direction is inward; his concern is with 'a prospect of the mind'. This has led to another complaint: that the poetry is self-absorbed, private, difficult.

Poetry, like the novel or a painting, is often cluttered with all kinds of signals flashing and gesturing so that the artist may direct our attention to a particular response in order that his work may be made simpler for him and for us. These signals assure us of the line we have taken, confirm our grasp of the artist's drift. They make us feel safe because they make us feel we are dealing with the world we know. The danger is that these signals can swamp a poem in the banal, the formulated and the predictable. But one of the special merits of Heaney's work is the deep and subtle placing of his signals. His poems are filled with people, places, weather, animals, things, bits of conversation, presented with a concrete particularity that assures us we are here in the world we understand. But he appropriates them in a highly imaginative way, transforming them, 'perfecting' them, in his own creative alembic, as the murdered corpses were transfigured by the bog. These things must be submitted to the 'dark' before they can be 'encoded'.[13] They can only reveal the actual (as opposed to the blatantly 'real') if they become the creatures of the poet's invention, not signals doing something expected or merely 'believable'. He refuses to lead his imagination, but instead allows it its head. This is Heaney's 'sad freedom'. Consequently, his poems are rarely simple reflections of the world as a 'naturalist' might describe it or that the news tells us is true. His primary obligation is not to the 'facts'. His own poetic experiment with the 'facts' in Part 2 of *North* demonstrated the resultant entrapment and thwarting of his creative powers. He seeks to compose, not a pseudo-reality, but those facets of reality that bring what we do not know – or do not want to know – about ourselves to light.

At the same time, if Heaney's poetic world is not photographic reality, it does not lack any of the solidity or texture of that reality. Many of the early poems are, in fact, so densely textured that the relentless, physical impact of the language impedes it from being the sounding rod or conductor that he wants it to be. Because of his devotion to sense-perception of the physical world, he cannot fully encompass the whisperings of other voices from realms of consciousness at the outback of the mind. The very richness and denseness of the language prevent it from achieving the translucent quality that allows the private to pass into the public, the invisible to penetrate the visible, the past to pervade the present, the general the particular, and the eternal the temporal, as a natural, unpremeditated effulgence. The language of mud does not have the capacity to let light pass through it. This is part of the problem with the bog poems, where he tends to rely on a prefabricated myth to alert us to the other dimensions of reality, rather than the music of his verse. The bog poems are still thick and dense (though the artesian quatrain was a stylistic move towards greater penetration and suggestiveness) rooted in the intractable earth. But all the time there is the search for a poetry of flexible, delicate 'soundings', a poetry composed out of a self-engendering, self-delighting musical system that would be the proper expression of the poet's inner freedom. A poem from his most recent collection will suffice to illustrate this kind of development. This is part of 'La Toilette':

> *Our bodies are the temples*
> *of the Holy Ghost*. Remember?
> And the little, fitted, deep-slit drapes
> on and off the holy vessels
>
> regularly? And the chasuble
> so deftly hoisted? But vest yourself
> in the word you taught me
> and the stuff I love: slub silk.[14]

These lines display Heaney's much-praised ability to render experi-
ence directly and sensuously. We are invited to enjoy the sound and
texture of 'slub silk'. We share the sensation of the poet's delight in
the actual phonetic reality of the words. But what distinguishes this
from early work is the co-operation of the poet's auditory imagin-
ation with the unharnessed intelligence: his whole creative being is
involved in the subtle handling of the poem's ecclesiastical and
erotic contexts, reverberating tellingly against each other.

Throughout the process of refining and clarifying his poetic voice,
making it exploratory and tentative, he never allows his signals to
become all – that is, symbols. He does not exploit that crude
response which makes us think we are learning something because
we are 'seeing beneath the surface of things', when we are really
seeing nothing at all. He is careful to make sure his poems work on
a primary, nonsymbolic level. The symbols function secondarily.
The 'realms of whisper' originate in and are inextricably part of the
world we know by our senses. What we have, then, is a language
that is constantly escaping the local historical moment and the
claims of orthodoxy, carrying us away from what is contingent, as it
becomes the voice of the contemplative mind, the larynx of the dark
wood, the vehicle of the purely creative, intimate experimental act
of writing itself.

It is finally, because of the aural allusion and character of my title
phrase, 'All the realms of whisper', that it seems to me such a
felicitous expression to describe the poet's secret sources of crea-
tivity – his essentially 'auditory imagination'. With the grand,
cavernous sound produced by the long vowels and the *l*s and *r*s we
have the womb-like mystery, closed by the resonating *m*; this slides
easily, by way of the plural phoneme, into the hushed and sibilant
crepitation of the last word – the tensely onamatopaeic re-creation of
the mystery finding utterance. This movement is repeated in the
semantic progression from absolute abstraction ('all') to sensuous
particularity, the word 'whisper' – a miniature of Heaney's 'tenta-
tive art' – actually defining and projecting the manner in which the
mystery makes itself accessible. It is Heaney's attentiveness to these
hypnotic, venturesome urgencies that gives his poetry its distinctive
'mouth-music'. Ultimately, they are the great enabling influence out
of which he creates the ideal melody which transcends the world of
sensual music, and delivers what Sir Philip Sidney called 'a golden
world' out of the 'brazen world' of nature.

Notes

CHAPTER 1: THE GIFT AND THE CRAFT

1. John Haffenden, *Viewpoints: Poets in Conversation* (London: Faber, 1981) p. 68.
2. Seamus Heaney, *Preoccupations: Selected Prose 1968–1978* (London: Faber, 1980) p. 33. Page references will hereafter be incorporated into the text, e.g. *P*. p. 145.
3. Quoted by Michael Longley in 'Poetry' in *Causeway: the Arts in Ulster*, ed. Michael Longley (Arts Council of Northern Ireland: Belfast, 1971) pp. 106–7.
4. Patrick Kavanagh, 'Nationalism and Literature' in *Collected Pruse* (London: Martin Brian & O'Keefe, 1973) p. 269.
5. The phrase is from Heaney's poem, 'Shelf Life', in *Station Island* (London: Faber, 1984) p. 24.
6. T. S. Eliot, *The Use of Poetry and the Use of Criticism* (London: Faber, 1933) p. 119.
7. Heaney, in interview with Patrick Garland, 'Poets on Poetry' in *The Listener* (8 Nov. 1973) p. 629.
8. Partick Kavanagh, 'The Parish and the Universe' in *Collected Pruse*, p. 283.
9. Interview with Garland.
10. Seamus Heaney, *Poetry Book Society Bulletin*, 85 (summer 1975) p. 1.
11. W. B. Yeats, 'Samhain: 1905' in *Explorations* (London: Macmillan, 1962) pp. 198–9. See also *Preoccupations*, p. 7.
12. Heaney, in interview with Seamus Deane, 'Unhappy and at Home' in *The Crane Bag*, no. 1 (1977) p. 67.
13. C. Day Lewis, 'Poetry and Politics' in *Twentieth Century Poetry: Critical Essays and Documents*, eds Graham Martin and P. N. Furbank (Milton Keynes: Open University Press, 1975) p. 178.
14. Seamus Heaney, 'Envies and Identifications: Dante and the Modern Poet' in *Irish University Review* (spring 1985) p. 14.
15. Ibid., p. 14.
16. Ibid., p. 18.
17. Ibid., p. 19.
18. Ibid., p. 18.
19. The 'symbolic order' is the term used by French psychoanalyst Jacques Lacan to refer to that stage of development, corresponding to Freud's Oedipus crisis, where the child moves from an 'imaginary' world of presence and fullness – the 'mirror stage' – to construct an identity as a subject out of its perceptions of difference and similarity to the other objects around it. The 'mirror stage' is that in which the child discovers his 'self' by identifying with the image he sees in a mirror. No gap exists between subject and world. What the child

204

knows of the external is dependent upon himself: what the child knows of himself is a matter of making identifications with images in the outside world. In the very act of doing so, he misperceives and misrecognizes himself. Then comes the stage when, finding himself confronted with the father, which Lacan calls the Law, and separated from the now prohibited, precious body of the mother, the child is severed from the 'real', that inaccessible realm beyond signification, and banished to the 'symbolic order' of prescribed linguistic, sexual and social relations in which there is no final meaning, no rest. For discussion see Jacques Lacan, 'Le Stade du miroir comme formateur de la fonction de Je' in *Ecrits* (Paris: Seuil, 1966) pp. 93–100.

20. Heaney, 'Lovers on Aran' in *Death of a Naturalist* (London: Faber, 1966) p. 47.

CHAPTER 2: *DEATH OF A NATURALIST* AND *DOOR INTO THE DARK*

1. Heaney, in interview with Seamus Deane, 'Unhappy and at Home', p. 66.
2. Heaney, 'The Sense of Place' in *Preoccupations*, p. 142.
3. Heaney, 'Feeling into Words' in *Preoccupations*, p. 56.
4. Ibid., p. 56.
5. The phrase is from 'The Seed Cutters' in *North* (London: Faber, 1975) p. 10.
6. The phrase is from 'Funeral Rites' in *North*, p. 16.
7. 'An Interview with Seamus Heaney' (James Randall), in *Ploughshares*, 5, 3 (1979) p. 14.
8. Wordsworth, *The Prelude*, ed. Ernest de Selincourt (London: Oxford University Press, 1966), edn. of 1805, Book 1, 428.
9. Wordsworth, *The Prelude*, Book 1, 420–4.
10. Wordsworth, *The Prelude*, Book 1, 418–20.
11. Wordsworth, letter to Catherine Clarkson (Dec. 1814).
12. See note 19, pp. 204–5.
13. Heaney, 'Feeling into Words' in *Preoccupations*, p. 48.
14. Ibid., p. 48.
15. Heaney, 'The God in the Tree' in *Preoccupations*, p. 189.
16. Ibid., p. 189.
17. Heaney, 'From Monaghan to the Grand Canal' in *Preoccupations*, p. 119.
18. See Blake Morrison, *Seamus Heaney* (London: Methuen, 1982) p. 19.
19. Heaney, 'Feeling into Words' in *Preoccupations*, p. 49.
20. Ibid., p. 47.
21. Quoted in Robert Buttel, *Seamus Heaney* (Lewisburg: Bucknell University Press, 1975) p. 27.
22. Quoted by Heaney in 'Feeling into Words' in *Preoccupations*, p. 46.
23. Heaney, 'Feeling into Words' in *Preoccupations*, p. 41.
24. Ibid., p. 43.
25. Ibid., p. 41.

26.   Ibid., p. 48.
27.   Ibid., p. 53.
28.   *The Letters of John Keats*, ed. Maurice Buxton Forman, 3rd edn. (London, 1947) p. 421.
29.   Wordsworth, *The Prelude*, Book II, 310.

CHAPTER 3: *WINTERING OUT*

1.   Heaney, interview, in Monie Begley, *Rambles in Ireland* (Old Greenwich, Conn.: Devin-Adair, 1977) p. 165.
2.   Christopher Ricks, 'Lasting Things' in *The Listener* (26 June 1969) p. 900.
3.   Heaney, 'Feeling into Words' in *Preoccupations*, p. 56.
4.   Heaney, 'The Trade of an Irish Poet' in *The Guardian* (25 May 1972) p. 17.
5.   Heaney, 'Landlocked' in *The Irish Press* (1 June 1974) (review of P. V. Glob's *The Mound People*).
6.   John Hewitt, 'Conacre' in *Collected Poems 1932–1967* (London: MacGibbon and Kee, 1968).
7.   John Hewitt, 'The Colony' in *Collected Poems 1932–1967*.
8.   Heaney, 'The Sense of Place' in *Preoccupations*, p. 147.
9.   Heaney, interview with Seamus Deane, 'Unhappy and at Home' in *The Crane Bag*, 1, 1 (1977) p. 65.
10.   'An Interview with Seamus Heaney' (James Randall) in *Ploughshares*, 5, 3 (1979) p. 17.
11.   The lines are from 'Exposure', in *North*, p. 73.
12.   These were phrases used by Heaney at a poetry reading, quoted by Robert Buttel, in *Seamus Heaney* (Lewisburg: Bucknell University Press, 1975) p. 71.
13.   Heaney, 'Feeling into Words' in *Preoccupations*, p. 57.
14.   Interview with Randall, p. 18.
15.   Heaney, 'Feeling into Words' in *Preoccupations*, p. 59.
16.   D. H. Lawrence, *Phoenix* (London: Heinemann, 1967) p. 224.
17.   *Selected Writings of Jules Laforgue*, ed. and trans., William Jay Smith (New York: Grove Press, 1956) p. 211.
18.   T. S. Eliot, 'Rhapsody on a Windy Night' in *Collected Poems 1909–1962* (London: Faber, 1963).
19.   Walter Pater, *Appreciations* (New York: Macmillan, 1903) p. 260.
20.   W. B. Yeats, *Essays* (London: Macmillan, 1924) p. 239.

CHAPTER 4: *NORTH*

1.   W. B. Yeats, 'On Being Asked for a War Poem' in *Autobiographies* (London: Macmillan, 1966) p. 58.
2.   '*Negative Capability*, that is, when a man is capable of being in uncertainties, mysteries, doubts, without any irritable reaching after fact and reason'. *The Letters of John Keats*, ed. Maurice Buxton Forman,

3rd edn. (London, 1947) p. 72.

3. Ibid., p. 426.
4. See Terence Brown, *Northern Voices* (Dublin: Gill & Macmillan, 1975) p. 183.
5. Michael Allen, 'Provincialism and Recent Irish Poetry' in *Two Decades of Irish Writing*, ed. Douglas Dunn (Manchester: Carcanet Press, 1975) p. 36.
6. Heaney, 'Belfast' in *Preoccupations*, p. 34.
7. See P. V. Glob, *The Bog People* (London: Faber, 1977) pp. 77–8.
8. Blake Morrison, *Seamus Heaney* (London: Methuen, 1982) p. 62.
9. Heaney, 'Feeling into Words' in *Preoccupations*, p. 57.
10. Heaney, 'Belfast' in *Preoccupations*, p. 34.
11. Ibid., p. 30.
12. John Haffenden, *Viewpoints: Poets in Conversation* (London: Faber, 1981) p. 61.
13. James Joyce, *Portrait of the Artist as a Young Man* (Harmondsworth: Penguin) p. 253.
14. Ibid., p. 253.
15. Heaney, in interview with Seamus Deane, 'Unhappy and at Home' in *The Crane Bag*, 1, 1 (1977) p. 66.
16. John Aubrey, *Brief Lives* (Harmondsworth: Penguin, 1972) p. 418.
17. Ciaran Carson, 'Escaped from the Massacre?' in *The Honest Ulsterman*, no. 50 (winter 1975) p. 184.
18. Edna Longley, '"Inner Emigré" or "Artful Voyeur"?' in *The Art of Seamus Heaney*, ed. Tony Curtis (Bridgend: Poetry Wales Press, 1982) p. 85.
19. Arthur E. McGuinness, 'The Craft of Diction: Revision in Seamus Heaney's Poems', in *Image and Illusion: Anglo-Irish Literature and its Contexts*, ed. Maurice Harmon (Portmarnock, Co. Dublin: Wolfhound Press, 1979) p. 73.
20. Wordsworth, *The Prelude*, Book 1, 590–1.
21. Ibid., p. 631.
22. John Foster, 'Private Worlds: the Stories of Michael McLaverty' in *The Irish Short Story*, eds Patrick Rafroidi and Terence Brown (Gerrards Cross: Colin Smythe, 1979) p. 250.
23. Ibid., p. 250.
24. Ibid., pp. 257–8.

CHAPTER 5: *FIELD-WORK*

1. Heaney, in interview with Seamus Deane, 'Unhappy and at Home' in *The Crane Bag*, 1, 1 (1977) p. 72.
2. 'An Interview with Seamus Heaney' (James Randall), in *Ploughshares*, 5, 3 (1979) p. 21.
3. *The Letters of John Keats*, ed. Maurice Buxton Forman, p. 223.
4. Heaney, 'The Makings of a Music' in *Preoccupations*, p. 65.
5. Heaney, 'Englands of the Mind' in *Preoccupations*, p. 154.
6. Ibid., p. 154.

7.   Patrick Kavanagh, 'From Monaghan to the Grand Canal' in *Collected Pruse*, p. 224.
8.   *The Letters of John Keats*, p. 223.
9.   See Heaney's review of Robert Lowell, 'Full Face' in *Preoccupations*, pp. 21–4.
10.   Ibid., p. 223.
11.   The edited transcript of a series of radio talks given by Sean O'Riada in 1962 was published under the title, *Our Musical Heritage* (Portlaoise: Dolman Press, 1982).
12.   Arthur Miller, 'On Social Plays', Preface to *A View From the Bridge* (London: Cresset Press, 1957) p. 8.
13.   Heaney, in interview with Seamus Deane, 'Unhappy and at Home' in *The Crane Bag*, 1, 1 (1977) p. 68.
14.   Wordsworth, *The Prelude*, Book 1, 64–67.
15.   Heaney, 'The Makings of a Music' in *Preoccupations*, p. 63.
16.   J. M. Synge, Preface to *The Tinker's Wedding* in *J. M. Synge: Plays*, ed. Ann Saddlemyer (Oxford University Press, 1979) p. 33.
17.   J. M. Synge, Preface to *The Playboy of the Western World*, in *J. M. Synge: Plays*, p. 103.

CHAPTER 6: *SWEENEY ASTRAY* AND *STATION ISLAND*

1.   Heaney, 'Introduction' in Sweeney Astray (Derry: Field Day Publications, 1983) p. viii.
2.   Heaney, in interview with Seamus Deane, 'Unhappy and at Home' in *The Crane Bag*, 1, 1 (1977) p. 70.
3.   Heaney, 'Introduction' in *Sweeney Astray*, p. ix.
4.   Ibid., p. viii.
5.   Ibid., p. vii.
6.   Ibid., p. ix.
7.   Heaney, poetry reading at The New University of Ulster, Mar. 1984.
8.   Ciaron Carson, 'Sweeneys Ancient and Modern' in *The Honest Ulsterman*, 76 (autumn 1984) pp. 74–5.
9.   Flann O'Brien, *At-Swim-Two-Birds* (Harmondsworth: Penguin, 1980) p. 66.
10.   J. G. O'Keefe, 'Introduction' in *Buile Suibhne*, ed. and trans. J. G. O'Keefe (Irish Texts Society, 1913) p. xxxvi.
11.   Ibid., p. xxxvi.
12.   Heaney, 'The God in the Tree' in *Preoccupations*, p. 185.
13.   *The Letters of John Keats*, p. 96.
14.   Heaney, 'Introduction' in *Sweeney Astray*, p. vii.
15.   Heaney, 'Envies and Identifications: Dante and the Modern Poet' in *Irish University Review*, 15, 1 (spring 1985) p. 18.
16.   Ibid., p. 18.
17.   Ibid., p. 19.
18.   Heaney, 'Introduction' in *Sweeney Astray*, p. ix.
19.   Thomas Kinsella, 'The Divided Mind' in *Irish Poets in English*, ed., Sean Lucy (Dublin: Mercier Press, 1973) pp. 208–18.

20. Seamus Deane, *A Short History of Irish Literature* (London: Hutchinson, 1986), p.111.

21. Heaney, 'A Tale of Two Islands' in *Irish Studies I*, ed. P. J. Drudy (Cambridge University Press, 1980) p.12.

22. Patrick Kavanagh, *The Autobiography of William Carleton* (London: MacGibbon and Kee, 1968) p.9.

23. Heaney, 'A Tale of Two Islands' in *Irish Studies I*, p.12.

24. Thomas Flanagan, *The Irish Novelists 1800–1850* (New York and London: Columbia University Press, 1958) p.256.

25. These lines echo Carleton's own description in his *Autobiography* of the hanging of Paddy Devaun and his band of twenty-three Ribbonmen in County Louth on 29 Oct. 1816:

    > Thee were in all twenty-four dead bodies swinging from gibbets in different directions throughout the county of Louth. The autumn was an unusually hot one; the flesh of the suspended felons became putrid, and fell down in decomposed masses to the bottom of the sacks; the pitch which covered the sacks was melted by the strong heat of the sun, and the morbid mass which fell to the bottom of the sacks oozed out, and fell . . . in slimy ropes, at the sight of which, I was told, many women fainted.

    The Autobiography of William Carleton, p.157

    About a year before, Devaun and his men had brutally murdered a Catholic farmer and his family, an incident that formed the basis of one of Carleton's best-known and most ferocious stories, 'Wildgoose Lodge'.

26. Thomas Flanagan, *The Irish Novelists: 1800–1850*, p.314.

27. Heaney, 'A Tale of Two Islands' in *Irish Studies I*, p.12.

28. Patrick Kavanagh, 'Self Portrait' in *Collected Pruse*, p.20.

29. Patrick Kavanagh, 'Auden and the Creative Mind' in *Collected Pruse*, p.247.

30. Patrick Kavanagh, 'From Monaghan to the Grand Canal' in *Collected Pruse*, p.230.

31. Patrick Kavanagh, 'Kavanagh's Weekly' in *Collected Pruse*, p.150.

32. Patrick Kavanagh, 'Critics, Actors and Poets' in *Collected Pruse*, p.243.

33. Patrick Kavanagh, 'The Parish and the Universe' in *Collected Pruse*, p.283.

34. Heaney, 'From Monaghan to the Grand Canal' in *Preoccupations*, p.116.

35. Patrick Kavanagh, 'From Monaghan to the Grand Canal' in *Collected Pruse*, p.223.

36. Heaney, 'Encounter on Station Island' in *Home on the Page*, a collection of Tom Delaney's songs compiled by David Hammond (Belfast: published privately, 1979) pp.44–5.

37. Heaney, *A Personal Selection* (Belfast: Ulster Museum Publication, 1982) – no page numbers.

38. Heaney, at a poetry reading in The New University of Ulster, Mar. 1984.

39. Wordsworth, Preface to 'The Excursion.'

40. Keats, 'Ode to a Grecian Urn'.
41. James Joyce, *A Portrait of the Artist as a Young Man*, p. 189.
42. One might compare Heaney's position with that of Walter Pater, whose ideas were essentially those of Wordsworth, of Shelley and of Arnold:

> That the end of life is not for action but contemplation – being as distinct from doing – a certain disposition of the mind: is, in some shape or other, the principle of all the higher morality. In poetry, in art, if you enter into their true spirit at all, you touch this principle, in a measure: these, by their very sterility, are a type of beholding for the mere joy of beholding. To treat life is the spirit of art, is to make life a thing in which means and ends are identified: to encourage such treatment, the true moral significance of art and poetry. . . . Not to teach lessons, or enforce rules, or even to stimulate us to noble ends: but to withdraw the thoughts for a little while from the mere machinery of life, to fix them, with appropriate emotions, on the spectacle of those great facts in man's existence which no machinery affects. . . . To witness this spectacle with appropriate emotions is the aim of all culture.

Walter Pater, *Appreciations* (New York: Macmillan, 1903) pp. 62–3.
43. Heaney, 'The God in the Tree' in *Preoccupations*, p. 186.
44. See *The Kilpeck Anthology*, ed. Glenn Storhaug (Oxford: Five Seasons Press, 1981) pp. 36–7.
45. B. S. Johnson, 'Sheela-na-gig' in *The Kilpeck Anthology*, op. cit., p. 16.
46. Yeats, 'Crazy Jane Talks with the Bishop'.
47. John Carey, 'The Joy of Heaney' in *The Sunday Times* (14 Oct. 1984).
48. Patrick Kavanagh, 'Self Portrait' in *Collected Pruse*, p. 22.

CHAPTER 7: ONLY CONNECT

1. D. H. Lawrence, *Selected Literary Criticism*, ed. Anthony Beale (London: Heinemann, 1955) p. 105.
2. See Heaney's interview with Seamus Deane, 'Unhappy and at Home' in *The Crane Bag*, 1, 1 (1977) pp. 66–72.
3. The ideas of Conor Cruise O'Brien, writer, playwright, historian, diplomat and politician, have absorbed a good deal of Irish intellectual life over the last fifteen years. Opposed to any belief at all in unity as a solution to the Irish problem, he has been an outspoken critic of IRA violence. His views, propounded in newspaper articles, journal essays, public lectures, television appearances and in his book, *States of Ireland* (1972), challenge the cosily and complacently held emotions of republican nationalist orthodoxy. That orthodoxy, he believes, is founded on a false view of history – the romantic, literary myth of an indestructible, historic, predestinate nation, which had been the inspiration of the 1916 Rising and continues to stimulate the current campaign of violence in the North:

> To minds that are possessed by that idea of sacrifice it is irrelevant to prove that a campaign like the current IRA campaign, for

example, cannot possibly accomplish any desirable political objective. That can be demonstrated, it can be quite logically and clearly demonstrated, but it doesn't matter. The objective is to become part of 'history' in the abstract or mythological sense, to achieve immortality by getting oneself killed for Ireland's sake. That the actual people of Ireland, in their overwhelming humdrum majority, want no such sacrifice is also irrelevant, having no other effect than to cause the people in question to disappear from 'Irish history' which in every generation consists of the doings and sayings of the martyrs.

> (Conor Cruise O'Brien, 'Politics and the Poet' in
> *Irish Times*, 21 Aug. 1975, p. 10)

One of O'Brien's central concerns has been to encourage a more realistic attitude to the Northern conflict. Southerners, he argues, have failed to understand the Northern unionist opposition to integration. As Heaney has remarked, O'Brien helped to create in the 1970s:

some kind of clarity in Southerners' thinking about the Protestant community in the North. And it is not enough for people to simply say 'Ah, they're all Irishmen,' when some Northerners actually spit at the word Irishmen. There is in O'Brien a kind of obstinate insistence on facing up to this kind of reality, which I think is his contribution.

> ('Unhappy and at Home', interview with Seamus Deane, in
> *The Crane Bag*, 1, 1 (1977) p. 64)

4. Lionel Trilling, *The Liberal Imagination* (London: Secker & Warburg, 1951) p. 290.
5. D. H. Lawrence, *Selected Literary Criticism*, p. 109.
6. D. H. Lawrence, *Phoenix* (London: Heinemann, 1967) p. 528.
7. D. H. Lawrence, *Selected Literary Criticism*, p. 118.
8. Ibid., p. 8.
9. *The Letters of D. H. Lawrence*, ed. Harry T. Moore (London: Heinemann, 1970) p. 232.
10. Heaney, 'The Toome Road' in *Field-Work*, p. 15.
11. Heaney, 'Feeling into Words' in *Preoccupations*, p. 54.
12. Heaney, 'Kinship' in *North*, pp. 40–5.
13. See Heaney, 'The Peninsula' in *Door into the Dark*, p. 21.
14. Heaney, 'La Toilette' in *Station Island*, p. 14.

Bibliography

WORKS BY SEAMUS HEANEY

Death of a Naturalist (London: Faber, 1966).
Door into the Dark (London: Faber, 1969).
Wintering Out (London: Faber, 1972).
North (London: Faber, 1975).
Field Work (London: Faber, 1979).
Selected Poems 1965–1975 (London: Faber, 1980).
Preoccupations: Selected Prose 1968–1978 (London: Faber, 1980).
Sweeney Astray (Derry: Field Day, 1983, London: Faber, 1984).
Station Island (London: Faber, 1984).
'Envies and Identifications: Dante and the Modern Poet', Uncollected article in *Irish University Review*, vol. 15, no. 1 (Spring 1985) pp. 5–19.

INTERVIEWS

'Le Clivage traditionnel' (anon.), *Les Lettres nouvelles* (Mar. 1973) pp. 87–9.
Interview in Monie Begley, *Rambles in Ireland* (Old Greenwich, Conn.: Devin-Adair, 1977) pp. 159–69.
Interview (Harriet Cooke), *Irish Times* (28 Dec. 1973) p. 8.
'Unhappy and at Home' (Seamus Deane). *The Crane Bag*, 1, no. 1 (1977) pp. 61–7.
'Poets on Poetry' (Patrick Garland), *The Listener* (8 Nov. 1973) p. 629.
Interview in John Haffenden, *Viewpoints: Poets in Conversation* (London: Faber, 1981, pp. 57–75.
Interview (Ian Hamilton), *Bookmark*, BBC 2 (24 Oct. 1984).
'An Interview with Seamus Heaney' (James Randall), *Ploughshares*, 5, no. 3 (1979) pp. 7–22.
'Brooding Images' (John Silverlight), *The Observer* (11 Nov. 1979) p. 37.
'The Saturday Interview' (Caroline Walsh), *Irish Times* (6 Dec. 1975) p. 5.

SELECTED CRITICISM OF SEAMUS HEANEY

Books

Buttel, Robert. *Seamus Heaney* (Lewisburg: Bucknell University Press, 1975).
Curtis, Tony (ed.), *The Art of Seamus Heaney* (Bridgend: Poetry Wales, 1982).
Morrison, Blake, *Seamus Heaney* (London: Methuen, 1982).

Selected Articles

Alvarez, A., 'A Fine Way with Language', *New York Review of Books* (6 Mar. 1980) pp. 16–17.

Anon, 'Fear in a Tinful of Bait', *The Times Literary Supplement* (17 July 1969), p. 770.

Anon, 'Semaphores of Hurt', *The Times Literary Supplement* (15 Dec. 1972) p. 1524.

Bailey, Anthony, 'A Gift for Being in Touch', *Quest* (Jan./Feb 1978) pp. 38–46, 92–3.

Beer, Patricia, 'Seamus Heaney's Third Book of Poems', *The Listener* (7 Dec. 1972) p. 795.

Bloom, Harold, 'The Voice of Kinship', *The Times Literary Supplement* (8 Feb. 1980) pp. 137–8.

Brown, Terence, *Northern Voices: Poets from Ulster* (Dublin: Gill & Macmillan, 1975) pp. 171–213.

Browne, Joseph, 'Violent Prophecies: the Writer and Northern Ireland', *Éire–Ireland*, 10, no. 2 (summer 1975) pp. 109–19.

Carey, John, 'The Joy of Heaney', *The Sunday Times* (14 Oct. 1984).

Carson, Ciaran, 'Escaped from the Massacre?', *The Honest Ulsterman*, 50 (winter 1975) pp. 183–6.

Carson, Ciaran, 'Sweeneys Ancient and Modern', *The Honest Ulsterman*, 76 (autumn 1984) pp. 73–9.

Curtis, Tony, 'Seamus Heaney's *North*', *Critical Quarterly*, vol. 16 (spring 1974) pp. 35–48.

Dunn, Douglas (ed.), *Two Decades of Irish Writing* (Manchester: Carcanet Press, 1975).

Dunn, Douglas, 'Manana is Now', *Encounter* (Nov. 1975) pp. 76–81.

Foster, John Wilson, 'The Poetry of Seamus Heaney', *Critical Quarterly*, vol. 16, 1 (spring 1974) pp. 35–48.

Foster, John Wilson, 'Seamus Heaney's "A Lough Neagh Sequence": Sources and Motifs', *Éire–Ireland*, 12, no. 2 (summer 1977) pp. 138–42.

Grant, Damian, 'Verbal Events', *Critical Quarterly*, vol. 16 (spring 1974) pp. 81–6.

Hederman, Mark Patrick, 'Seamus Heaney: the Reluctant Poet', *The Crane Bag*, 3, no. 2 (1979) pp. 61–70.

Kiely, Benedict, 'A Raid into Dark Corners: the Poems of Seamus Heaney', *The Hollins Critic*, vol. 4 (4 Oct. 1970) pp. 1–12.

Liddy, James, 'Ulster Poets and the Catholic Muse', *Éire–Ireland*, 13, no. 4 (winter 1978) pp. 126–37.

Lloyd, D. 'The Two Voices of Seamus Heaney's *North*, *Ariel*, vol. 10 (Oct. 1979) pp. 5–13.

Longley, Edna, 'Fire and Air', *The Honest Ulsterman*, 50 (winter 1975) pp. 179–83.

Longley, Edna, 'Stars and Horses, Pigs and Trees', *The Crane Bag*, 3, no. 2 (1979) pp. 54–60.

Longley, Edna, 'Heaney: Poet as Critic', *Fortnight* (Dec. 1980) pp. 15–6

Longley, Michael. 'Poetry', in Michael Longley (ed.). *Causeway: the Arts in Ulster* (Belfast: Arst Council of Northern Ireland, 1971) pp. 95–109.

Mahon, Derek, 'Poetry in Northern Ireland', *Twentieth Century Studies* (Nov. 1970) pp. 89–92.

McGuinness, Arthur E., '"Hoarder of the Common Ground": Tradition and Ritual in Seamus Heaney's Poetry', *Éire–Ireland*, 13, no. 2 (summer 1978) pp. 71–82.

McGuiness, Arthur E., 'The Craft of Diction: Revision in Seamus Heaney's Poems' in Maurice Harmon (ed.) *Image and Illusion: Anglo–Irish Literature and its Contexts* (Portmarnock: Wolfhound Press, 1979) pp. 62–91.

Montague, John, 'Order in Donnybrook Farm', *The Times Literary Supplement*, 17 (Nov. 1972) p. 313.

Mullan, Fiona 'Seamus Heaney – the Poetry of Opinion', *Verse*, (1984) pp. 15–21.

O'Brien, Conor Cruise, 'A Slow North-East Wind', *The Listener*, (25 Sept. 1975) pp. 404–5.

Redshaw, Thomas D., '"Ri" as in Regional: Three Ulster Poets', *Éire–Ireland*, 9, no. 2 (summer 1974) pp. 41–64.

Ricks, Christopher, 'Lasting Things', *The Listener* (26 June 1969) pp. 900–1.

Ricks, Christopher, 'The Mouth, the Meal, the Book', *London Review of Books* (8 Nov. 1979) pp. 4–5.

Schirmer, G. A., 'Seamus Heaney: Salvation in Surrender', *Éire–Ireland*, 15, no. 4 (winter 1980) pp. 139–46.

Sharratt, Bernard, 'Memories of Dying: the Poetry of Seamus Heaney', *New Blackfriars*, vol. 57 (July 1976) pp. 313–21, and vol. 57 (Aug. 1976) pp. 364–77.

Silkin, Jon, 'Bedding the Locale', *New Blackfriars*, vol. 54 (Mar. 1973) pp. 130–3.

Thwaite, Anthony, 'Neighbourly Murders', *The Times Literary Supplement* (1 Aug. 1975) p. 866.

Thwaite, Anthony, 'The Hiding Place of Power', *The Times Literary Supplement* (31 Oct. 1980) p. 1222.

Index

215